W9-AHR-784

The Best AMERICAN ESSAYS 2000

GUEST EDITORS OF
THE BEST AMERICAN ESSAYS

1986 ELIZABETH HARDWICK
1987 GAY TALESE
1988 ANNIE DILLARD
1989 GEOFFREY WOLFF
1990 JUSTIN KAPLAN
1991 JOYCE CAROL OATES
1992 SUSAN SONTAG
1993 JOSEPH EPSTEIN
1994 TRACY KIDDER
1995 JAMAICA KINCAID
1996 GEOFFREY C. WARD
1997 IAN FRAZIER
1998 CYNTHIA OZICK
1999 EDWARD HOAGLAND
2000 ALAN LIGHTMAN

The Best AMERICAN ESSAYS 2000

Edited and with an Introduction
by ALAN LIGHTMAN

Robert Atwan, Series Editor

HOUGHTON MIFFLIN COMPANY
BOSTON • NEW YORK 2000

Visit our Web site: www.houghtonmifflinbooks.com.

ISSN 0888-3742
ISBN 0-618-03578-8
ISBN 0-618-03580-x (pbk.)

Printed in the United States of America

QUM 10 9 8 7 6 5 4 3 2 1

Contents

Foreword

A CENTURY AGO, one of our finest essayists wondered what Americans would be like in the year 2000. Henry Adams had devised a theory of history based on his observation that scientific advancement appeared to be "doubling or quadrupling its complexities every ten years." Given this definite "Law of Acceleration," he argued, "every American who lived into the year 2000" would not only "know how to control unlimited power" but would by necessity "think in complexities unimaginable to an earlier mind" and "deal with problems altogether beyond the range of earlier society."

Adams stopped short of making specific technological predictions. He had, much to his discomfort, driven in automobiles. He envisioned no airplanes, though even as he wrote two brothers had begun sailing through the air on a gas-propelled flying machine of their own construction. And a little over a decade earlier, two scientists had measured a new physical constant — the speed of light. Though Adams must have known about these marvelous experiments, he based his futurist calculations exclusively on the exponential increase in "coal power," presciently adding, however, that the "new American" would also be the child of "chemical power, electric power, and radiating energy, as well as of new forces yet undetermined." For Adams, the actual material transformations that lay ahead seemed unimportant compared to the speed at which they would occur and the new forms of consciousness this acceleration would somehow demand.

Some sixty years later, in 1965, Adams's Law of Acceleration found confirmation in another exponential law, one that may appear more technologically applicable as we, like Adams, anxiously enter a new century. Moore's Law, named after Gordon Moore, one of the founders of Intel, maintains that microchip complexity will roughly double every year or two, a principle that describes the staggering development in computer speed and electronic capacities so familiar to us today. Adams would not have been surprised by the exhilarating speed at which the digital revolution is taking place. But what would surely interest him most, were he alive today, is assessing whether the exponential increases in scientific complexity predicted by his or Moore's Law have resulted in any dramatic alteration of human consciousness. Have we acquired the "new social mind" Adams believed would be necessary to understand the complexities of the year 2000?

Put another way, the question we might ask is: does the Law of Acceleration also apply to the human mind and its representations in literature, philosophy, and the arts? Does the exponential speed of complexity mean that a modern tragedy like *Death of a Salesman* is far more complex than the centuries-old *Macbeth* and infinitely more so than the millennia-old *Oedipus Rex*? Can we legitimately say that Duchamp's *Nude Descending a Staircase* is more complex than Titian's *Pastoral Concert*? How would we even begin to measure such levels of complexity? Judging from the students I've taught over the years, contemporary essays are no more challenging in their complexity than Emerson's or Montaigne's, though the latter were products of much "slower" cultures. Then there's the incredibly complex "A Law of Acceleration" itself; given Adams's theory, that essay by now should be the intellectual equivalent of *Chicken Soup for the Soul.*

When informed that the new telegraph system could speed up communication between Maine and Texas, Thoreau wondered what Maine and Texas had to say to each other. Every day we now hear people with state-of-the art cellular phones publicly (and it seems proudly) engage in the most banal conversations. Despite Marshall McLuhan's dictum, the microchip complexity of their media hasn't led to any observable complexity in their messages. Does any reasonable person think that political discourse, with its rigged polarization and sound bites, has grown more nuanced and sophisticated? After several weeks with television sitcoms, a daily newspaper, a few radio talk shows, and an Internet provider, Henry Adams might well decide to reverse his famous law and conclude that as the technological speed of information increases, complexity decreases.

There's no reason to be a Luddite; the digital revolution is here to stay, and one can amply enjoy its products and conveniences. A younger generation may be more comfortable reading electronic books than paper ones, but if they are reading something worth reading, they will more than likely — to borrow the title of Ruben Brower's seminal essay — do their "reading in slow motion." Though retrieving and downloading *Walden* or *Portrait of a Lady* can be done in the blink of an eye, savoring the prose, word by word, sentence by sentence, will always take time. One danger, of course, is that as people become more accustomed to the instantaneous acquisition of texts, they will simultaneously grow so impatient with the time-consuming process of reading them that the activity itself will become as obsolete as Sunday family strolls down Main Street.

For those who enjoy leisurely reading, the essay is still the ideal form, as the selections in this volume amply demonstrate. A ruminative, unhurried style has long been part of the essay's tradition. While Henry Adams was formulating his theory of acceleration, literary critics were in turn predicting that the slow-paced "old-fashioned essay" would soon disappear. It was, as William Dean Howells observed in 1902, being driven out by newsworthy articles with no interest in the "lounging gait" and the "wilding nature" that characterized what Howells called the "right" essay. His concerns about a readership so corrupted and depraved, so bereft of a lyrical sense, that it prefers articles to essays have been echoed through every decade of the century. Yet somehow "right" or true essays still manage to be written, published, and admired. This collection, with its many sinuous selections that wind through time and memory, that blur the distinctions between past and present, that take us intimately into the multilayered processes of thought, also reminds us throughout of the special language of essays. As William H. Gass says here, in his wonderful essay on the pleasures of books, "nothing is more frequently overlooked or more vital to language than its pace and phrasing."

*

The Best American Essays features a selection of the year's outstanding essays, essays of literary achievement that show an awareness of craft and forcefulness of thought. Hundreds of essays are gathered annually from a wide variety of national and regional publications. These essays are then screened, and approximately one hundred are turned over to a distinguished guest editor, who may add a few personal discoveries and who makes the final selections.

To qualify for selection, the essays must be works of respectable literary quality, intended as fully developed, independent essays on subjects of general interest (not specialized scholarship), originally written in English (or translated by the author) for publication in an American periodical during the calendar year. Periodicals that want to be sure their contributors will be considered each year should include the series on their complimentary subscription list (Robert Atwan, Series Editor, *The Best American Essays,* P.O. Box 220, Readville, MA 02137).

For this volume I want to thank Gerard McCauley for his many years of support and encouragement. As always, I appreciate the enormous help I receive from the people at Houghton Mifflin, especially Janet Silver, Sean Lawler, and Liz Duvall. It was deeply rewarding to work this year with such an exceptionally gifted writer as Alan Lightman, whose outstanding essays and fiction consistently display the same remarkable fusion of thought and imagination, of art and intellectuality, that pervades this collection.

R.A.

Introduction

LAST WINTER, at the end of December, my family and friends rented neighboring apartments on an island off Florida and waited together for the new millennium. We came from Massachusetts and Connecticut, Maryland and South Carolina, all of us sensing some cosmic event. For the past twenty-five years, we had been visiting each other at birthdays, naming ceremonies, the deaths of parents, bat mitzvahs, postmortems of love affairs gone bad.

An island off the coast of Florida is an ideal spot to ponder the meaning of one thousand years. First of all, you're cut off from the rest of the world and its day-to-day rumblings. For a millennium-size view, you need distance and space. Second, life moves at a slow pace on an island, and a person has the time and the quiet to think. A half-mile away from the center of town, only a single road meanders through the palm trees and low shrubs at the edge of the sea. Most people get around by cycle or on foot, accompanied by the silent stares of ospreys and crows. The most demanding activity of the day might be embarking on a trip to the small market for milk or shaking the sand from your sandals after a walk on the beach. And the weather is pleasantly warm, adding to the unreality of the place. As you stand on your deck in shorts and T-shirt, gazing at the waves sliding in from infinity, a light-year from e-mail and telephones and faxes, you feel that you might at last be prepared to take stock.

On the eve of the millennium, December 31, 1999, we gather in one of our condos. All in all, there are nineteen or twenty of us, including college-age children born through our years together, a six-month-old baby named Grace, and my mother-in-law, Harriet, perky at age eighty-three. We sit on the screened balcony drinking cold beer and retelling stories until the smooth ocean light starts to fade. Then we begin eating. Sam, a schoolteacher who spent last summer in Zanzibar and received private lessons on the local cooking, serves a Zanzibari feast. In fact, we've been smelling Sam's dinner in preparation all afternoon as aromas wafted from his kitchen window. Rice spiced with cardamom, pepper, cinnamon, and coconut milk; masala and onions, peppers, zucchini, tomatoes, eggplant, seasoned with cumin, garam masala, and Zanzibari red curry; lightly fried pompano caught earlier in the day by David and his two daughters. Sam's cooking for his friends has always been an expression of love.

Sam himself is ablaze in his Hawaiian shirt with yellow blossoms and pink fishtails. "What's your wish for the millennium?" I ask him as he passes around a bowl of kiwi, cantaloupe, and honeydew for dessert.

"That my millennium countdown clock doesn't explode at midnight."

There follows a discussion of the purpose of digital millennium countdown clocks after their final moment. And will they start over on a count to 3000 or freeze in stupefaction at 0:0:0:0?

Mary, often hours or days late for any occasion, arrives from Washington, rumpled, having been driven for the last few hours by an old acquaintance in Tampa. She inquires sheepishly if her friend might sleep here for the night. "She's welcome, no matter what," says Cathy, "but I do have to ask one question. She doesn't snore, does she? It's all right if she does, but I'd like to know in advance." Mary smiles and takes off her trademark floppy straw hat.

Lucile brings me baby Grace to hold. She bends over, and the African necklace that Jean and I gave her twenty years ago dangles from her neck, a large metallic disk made from the bottom of a Masai cooking pot and hung on a strand of dark hemp. Seeing the necklace, I remember the trip to Kenya and our return home after five months of traveling. When Jean and I finally arrived at the airport in Boston, sweaty and dirty and jet-lagged, demolished by a twenty-four-hour vigil in the Charles de Gaulle Airport, dragging our luggage and ourselves across the floor, we passed through customs and heard happy shouts and hollers. Then we saw Sam, Susan, Cathy, and Lucile, holding a huge banner that read KELCOME KOME FROM KENYA, KEAN AND KALAN.

We go to the kitchen for beer. Some of us play cards; others stare at the giant condo television as it jerks back and forth between millennium celebrations in China, Japan, England, and France. For the last week and more, we've been watching the networks summarize past centuries and forecast the next. Fifteen minutes per decade. The printing press, DNA, the steam engine, plastics, computers, Martin Luther, Albert Einstein, Abraham Lincoln. "In twenty years, we'll all be cybers," someone calls from the kitchen. "Our brains will be wired to the Internet." I feel stretched and compressed at the same time. I'm drowning in speed, I feel like a point of nothingness, a blip, my life will be over and done in the ripple of a wave. "Change the channel," I yell in confusion and begin clicking the remote control. One of the enamel fish falls off the wall.

"If you've seen one millennium, you've seen them all," says Lucile. Lucile, who has been asking whether she should color her beautiful silver hair, takes another drink of her single-malt scotch and adds, "Even though I think the millennium is a superficial mark, still, having so many friends with so much history together in one place makes me feel blessed."

"It was supposed to be magic, and it is magic," says Cathy, in vague response. Cathy sometimes pulls up her shirt when she's drinking, so tonight she's wearing a one-piece bathing suit under her clothes to protect the children. At this moment, Cathy, Mary, and Kara sit glaring at each other at the card table, the last three players not yet bankrupt, each intent on winning the forty-two-dollar pot. Kara, my thirteen-year-old daughter, holds her cards close to her chest along with her remaining two dollar bills and says nothing. My other daughter, Elyse, brings out a watercolor sketch she made on the beach this afternoon; people gather around to compliment it.

The TV has been temporarily turned off. A fan hangs on a stem over my head; its arms revolve and beat the air. I listen to voices.

"What are you reading?"

"Not one of the ten best books of the millennium. I'll give it to you when I'm finished."

"Let's see your hat, Celeste. Where'd you get it? That's a great hat on you."

"Half of them come into my classroom with no breakfast. They don't have food at home. How can you teach kids like that? We're giving them breakfast now. It makes a difference."

"My mother doesn't want to live anymore. She mostly stays in her house, wanting to die."

"These roses came to the door and I thought they were for me, but they weren't, they were for my twelve-year-old daughter. Twelve years old, and she's getting flowers from a boy. So I say to Alexis, 'You've peaked. It never gets any better than this.'"

Someone howls. Mary hands me millennium eyeglasses, the frames sparkling with dots of color. I put on the glasses and look toward a candle, where I see the glowing numerals *2000* magically hovering in space.

"What do you see?" asks Jean.

"The millennium," I say.

"I'm so glad our girls are having fun with our friends," Jean says. It's only eleven o'clock, but I am a morning person and already drowsy. I nod and sink into a chair. To wake myself up, I drink some tart apple cider, feel its claws in my throat.

Harriet tries on the millennium glasses and grins and drinks a little beer. "My friends are all too old," she says. We pass around the glasses.

With a last round of shouting, the card game has ended. Cathy, the victor, takes a bow and immediately gives half of her winnings to Kara. We push aside the sliding glass doors and walk to the dark balcony, where we see a navigation buoy blinking on and off near the shore. Farther out, a curved line of lights from the fishing boats glitters like a strand of pearls. Then back to the living room. A few of the women link arms and begin singing. *If you see me walking down the street . . . Walk on by.*

By now, we are all much reduced and sit in the puffy white couches, squeezed against one another, David and his wife, Alice, and their daughters, Celeste and Christine; Christine's boyfriend, Scott; Lucile; Sam; Susan and Flip and their children, Connor and Grace; Harriet; Jean and me and our daughters, Kara and Elyse; Elyse's friend Laura; Mary; Cathy. Bobbi and George and their son, Jake, from Virginia, would have been here, but they were commandeered by a house move.

It's 11:47; thirteen minutes to go. The television, taking an intermission from its distillations and prophecies, has shifted once again to Times Square, to the thousands upon thousands of New Yorkers and others gathered in a sea of heavy coats and scarves, hats and mittens, clouds of steam, the sound of yelling and screaming, the colored floats and the neon signs, the cameras and wires, the newscasters in their elevated booths surveying the scene as if they were Roman emperors. And the huge silver New Year's ball, suspended from heaven. The ball hovers like a galaxy, shimmering, waiting. In all the years I have watched that giant sphere in Times Square, this one seems the biggest, a full moon on the horizon, a bright eye, a world. It vibrates there as we watch, it hums, it absorbs all the air and the light in New York. It seems to promise something, but what? What is happening? Then the final countdown begins. The silver galaxy descends, slowly, slowly. Or perhaps the earth is coasting up to meet it. "Ten, nine, eight, seven, six, five, four, three, two, one." We stand up and we hug and we kiss, and we completely forget to examine Sam's millennium clock.

And it occurs to me now, as I sag half sleeping against a wall, that one thing that matters is genuine human experience — that amid so much superficial and fake in our wired-up nervous digitized modern world, this moment is real, this moment in time with my dear friends around me, the sounds of their voices, the sounds of their breathing, the shapes of their faces.

The qualities I treasure most about these essays are their authenticity and life. In reading an essay, I want to feel that I'm communing with a real person, and a person who cares about what he or she's writing about. The words sound sentimental and trite, but the qualities are rare. For me, the ideal essay is not an assignment, to be dispatched efficiently and intelligently, but an exploration, a questioning, an introspection. I want to see a piece of the essayist. I want to see a mind at work, imagining, spinning, struggling to understand. If the essayist has all the answers, then he isn't struggling to grasp, and I won't either. When you care about something, you continually grapple with it, because it is alive in you. It thrashes and moves, like all living things.

When I'm reading a good essay, I feel that I'm going on a journey. The essayist is searching for something and taking me along. That something could be a particular idea, an unraveling of identity, a meaning in the wallow of observations and facts. The facts are important but never enough. An essay, for me, must go past the facts, an essay must travel and move. Even the facts of the essayist's own history, the personal memoir, are insufficient alone. The facts of personal history provide anchor, but the essayist then swings in a wide arc on his anchor line, testing and pulling hard.

I suppose that in the end, the real subject of an essay is the essayist. Not the bald facts of autobiography, on the one hand, or the bald opinions about issues, on the other, but some kind of union between the inner person and the outer world, a melding of internal and external, the life and mind of the essayist in reaction to the universe. The essayist cannot examine the world without examining herself, and she cannot examine herself without examining the world.

I can make no claim that these twenty-one pieces were the "best essays" of the past year. Despite our combing through dozens of magazines and journals, searching for everything tapped on the keyboards of known essayists, soliciting suggestions from trusted friends, it is inevitable that some essays will have slipped by the editors' notice, perhaps even very good ones. Ultimately, the selection is subjective anyway. What I can say is that I liked all of these essays a great deal, they made me think, they got under my skin, they took me on journeys, they made me feel alive.

ALAN LIGHTMAN

The Best AMERICAN ESSAYS 2000

ANDRÉ ACIMAN

The Last Time I Saw Paris

FROM COMMENTARY

In memory of Eric Breindel, a true friend

MY ROMANCE with Paris begins, as one says of earthquakes, at an epicenter — surrounded by tall, turn-of-the-century buildings, a small empty park, and silent avenues. This is how I always pictured Paris as an adolescent, before ever seeing it. A *marchand de tabacs* who would sell me cigarettes without asking questions; a *papeterie* where I could buy a longed-for Pelikan pen; the smiles of girls outside a vaguely imagined *lycée*; a secret rendezvous at the cinema.

Before I had ever set foot there, France was already my homeland, the place to which I knew I would eventually *return.* But everything stood in my way, starting with the fact that in the early 1960s, roughly the time of which I am speaking, my family was still living in Alexandria, Egypt, decades away from 1960s Paris. There were other inconvenient circumstances as well: many adult members of my family, although educated as French-speakers in the schools of the Alliance Israelite Universelle, had somehow managed to become not French but Italian citizens. Then too, I myself had gone to English schools throughout my childhood and hence knew English better than French — despite the fact that my mother tongue was French, which I spoke with a strange accent. (This was part of my problem all around, seeing that I spoke several languages with a French accent, except French.)

Here I was, a Jewish boy landlocked in Nasser's anti-Semitic Egypt, yearning to be back in a France I had never seen and did not even belong to. As we were losing our fortune and the Egyptian police closed in on us with house inspections, harassing phone calls at night, anonymous letters, secret denunciations, what could be better than to sit at the window in my great-aunt's bedroom at night and imagine myself staring at the Seine — which, she never tired of telling me when she joined me and glued her forehead to the windowpane, flowed ever so close to her old apartment in Paris? "Can you actually see the Seine from your windows?" I would ask. "No, but it's scarcely seven minutes away." And then she would recite the refrain of Guillaume Apollinaire's poem "Le pont Mirabeau":

> Let the night fall and the hours ring
> The days go away, I remain.
> (translation by Richard Wilbur)

It was of those "scarcely seven minutes away" that I kept thinking during my last months in Egypt, as we sold what we could and packed the rest amid daily squabbles between my mother and her mother-in-law and an aunt who could not help taking sides and always picked the wrong one. I learned to understand in the course of those days that there are places on the planet we simply must accept we shall never see again. I thought that place was Egypt. Little did I know that, as happens to men who repeatedly lose women for the same reason, there are families who will lose their homes at least once every generation.

I remember exactly the French authors, old and new, I was reading back then: Molière, François Mauriac, Alain-Fournier, Jean Anouilh, Georges Duhamel, Albert Camus. Like the window in my aunt's bedroom, they looked out onto what seemed the most distantly adjoining spot on earth. All I needed to do was read a sufficient number of pages and I could almost be there, in André Gide's Paris or Marcel Pagnol's Marseilles, the imagined sound of France blending with the perpetual yelling in Arabic that rose up to my room from the street below.

There was another book that appeared from nowhere one day, mixed in among the volumes my father had dumped in a pile in the packing room, a book I assumed he had no need of but later understood he must have left around in the manner of parents who want their sons to know certain things before they find out about them from more direct and less desirable sources. I devoured it, it devoured me. Each sentence opened up a world so vast and so thrilling that at the end of each night's perusal I wished I could forget everything I had just read so as to discover it afresh the next morning.

"You will find," I read on one of the pages, "that, when you're about fourteen or older, should you happen to be walking about at night, certain overdressed women may come up to you and ask you to accompany them. It is better that you do not."

I *was* fourteen. But who were these women, and why had none ever approached me? And why was I not already in France, where overdressed women came up from under the cover of night and asked you to accompany them? I looked out the window at my imagined Seine with its imagined bridges and *quais* that stood seven minutes away from our new home. But this was not Paris; this was still Alexandria.

During our last days in Egypt I learned to my shock that our destination was not to be my imagined Paris but some down-to-earth, working-class neighborhood in Rome. Thus we ended up — my mother, my brother, and I, for my father still remained behind in Egypt — in Italy. We knew no one, barely spoke the language, and did not know where to shop, or how. At night, feeling totally hemmed in by this country we could not love or fathom, we would close the shutters to stave it off. But Italy would not go away: from the buildings surrounding our courtyard there came each evening the echo of an entire society tuned to the same television channel. Sometimes the noise arose from a nearby movie theater, which, on warm summer nights, opened its roof to allow us to hear the roar of laughter or the dubbed voice of Sean Connery. When school started that fall, our twilit street turned sordid, with its grimy groceries, the coffee merchant whose dark quarters looked more like a cave than a shop, the corner bar filling up with workers stopping for wine on the way home from work. How could this be my homeland?

Then came a miracle. My father, who after leaving Egypt had found a temporary job in France, summoned us for a two-week visit during the winter holiday break, *pour voir,* just to see. He made our visit seem a mere stopover, Paris on consignment. More than three decades later, I can remember what we did on each and every one of those fifteen days.

I remember my first visit to the Latin Quarter, where I went with my older girl cousins and their fiancés, all undergraduates and all, apparently, Parisians. On a rainy weekday afternoon we whizzed through narrow streets crowded into two tiny Citroën *deux chevaux* to catch a Humphrey Bogart revival. One of us jumped out to purchase tickets, another to find snacks, while the rest looked for parking places. After the movie we stopped at a café, where everyone ordered tea.

Another day, on our way to buy cigarettes for everyone, my cousin took me into a record shop. She was looking for Bach's double violin concerto. Sitting in a tiny booth, we stole a few minutes to listen to the recording with David Oistrakh as the principal soloist. She found it not to her liking. Did they have Menuhin? They did not. We went across the street, where they had neither Oistrakh nor Menuhin but they did have Heifetz — the best, according to the salesgirl. No, thanks. For the next two weeks, we listened to violinist after violinist. To this day the sound of the double concerto brings to mind those heady first encounters with Paris, when I watched for signs of snow that never came and fell in love with the cool grayness that settled over the city at teatime, presaging evenings when we would crowd into the car and tour Paris-by-night, invariably ending our adventure with crêpes, onion soup, and Vichy candies.

Was it Paris or just the stuffed car and the good fellowship of cousins I had not seen in at least a decade that made me feel I was here to stay? The streets bustling with people my age who spoke my language; the spirited jokes; the movie theaters filled to capacity — this was not just the center of the world, or even the center of my life, it was me. It was my voice, if not when I spoke, then something clearer and deeper, as when I laughed. Perhaps it was not even a voice but a manner of being in the world that made me love that world and, come to think of it, myself as well.

When after about four days we finally visited my great-aunt in the sixteenth arrondissement, it was like walking into our old home in Alexandria — smaller, to be sure, but exactly the same *kind* of home: the same feel, the same smell, the same familial injunctions to be quiet and mind our manners. But this apartment was like a finished version of the rough sketch that had been our home in Alexandria. If Egypt was the base melody, Paris was the full orchestral score, an entire city beaming with the glory of a redeemed *déjà vu*. Like Saint Augustine thinking back to the time when he had not yet known God, only to wonder why he could not have loved him sooner, so I too asked, why wasn't I born here, why can't I live here, when will it happen?

My father had said these two weeks were to be a tryout. But preliminaries were totally unnecessary. I was ready to settle in at a moment's notice. One night, in a tiny park not far from my great-aunt's, my father pointed out two girls in their midteens: "I'll bet you anything they live in the neighborhood; they probably go to Lycée Janson de Sailly." Immediately, I wanted to be in school.

I was too young to know how to seize any opportunities that might have come my way. But presentiments of romance were everywhere. From the way women looked at me, I could tell that this was a language whose syntax I already knew fluently; all I needed was the vocabulary. And then, of course, there were those overdressed women who under cover of night would surely come up and ask me to accompany them. They were the reason I could not wait for the chance to be on my own in Paris — no easy task, since so many relatives were hosting us. But my great-aunt finally gave me my opening. In her refrigerator, she liked to keep bottles of water taken from the Lamartine fountain down the block, an artesian well whose water Jacques Hillairet, in his *Dictionnaire historique des rues de Paris,* had described as having an insipid taste *("un goût fade").* She assigned me the job of keeping them filled.

Never has anyone managed to turn so simple an errand into so time-consuming a task. There were always people at Square Lamartine, including others my age, probably doing the same thing as I for their grandparents or parents. Wedged among them as I waited my turn at the fountain, I became not only a real Parisian but a young Jacob, waiting to meet his Rachel at the well of Beersheba. *Next time,* I thought, as day after day I failed to muster the courage to speak. I went every day, sometimes twice, sitting on a bench and reading when the weather was not too cold, dawdling to watch the sun set and the last girls leave before dragging home the heavy bottles stuffed into two plastic net bags. Over tea one evening, my aunt said she was convinced I was smoking, while my grandmother opined that I was just slow and my mother that I must be losing my place to aggressive housewives. As for my father, he credited me with cunning schemes I let him think were successful.

When, by early January, it became clear that we had to return to

Rome, I felt I would die before I could board the train. It was leaving on a Saturday evening and would arrive in Rome on Sunday afternoon; on Monday we would be back in school. All I could think of on my last day at Lamartine was that Sunday evening in Rome — opening our suitcases, putting everything back in its dull place in an apartment from whose shuttered windows indelible sounds would make it impossible to imagine we were still in Paris, even though our suitcases would still smell of Paris and the sound of Bach would remind me of Paris, as would the cheap pens with the sliding Eiffel Tower I was planning to buy before leaving or the punched *métro* ticket and the residual pack of Vichy candies stuffed inadvertently into my coat pocket and recovered weeks into our humdrum Roman lives. I thought of Square Lamartine and of the fountain that was right in front of me, but already no longer so. What in Egypt had seemed almost a dream had come to life, only to become a dream again.

Perhaps, I thought, in a few days it would help to look back on this very moment and also on the weeks leading up to it, when I was still enjoying myself in Paris and was still unaware of the sorrow that inevitably comes from looking back. Perhaps by rehearsing all this in advance, I might even, in some strange way, dull the pain. The fountain would stay, I would be gone. ("The days go away, I remain.") But at least I had anticipated it; at least I knew.

At the Gare de Lyon, my father boarded the train to say goodbye. He urged me not to be sad: there would be many more chances to visit. I looked out the window. I had no way of knowing that this was only the first time I would think I was seeing Paris for the last time.

For the next three years, following my Christmas, Easter, and summer vacations, I would find myself on the same platform on a Saturday evening, saying goodbye to Paris, worrying lest my father not get off the train in time, trying to convince myself this had indeed been our last visit so as to ward off the hope and the disappointment whenever I would catch myself, later in Rome, wanting to be in Paris with nothing to turn to for consolation but my French books. Each time, in the days leading up to that parting moment at the Gare de Lyon, I would ask very little of Paris — just a replay of my original heady two weeks. Like Stendhal, who would drop a little twig in a spring in Salzburg and return months later to find it covered with speckling crystals, I too would return to Paris to find that the memory of my first visit had been thoroughly crystallized in Square Lamartine.

Not a day went by that I failed to log my impressions there, the better to remember them in Rome, knowing that by cheating Paris of its magic, by numbing the pleasure of the moment with constant reminders of the unavoidable trip back, I was mitigating, if not averting, the shock of departure. It was my way of preempting tomorrow's worries by making tomorrow seem yesterday, of warding off adversity by warding off happiness as well. In the end, I actually learned not to enjoy going to Paris, or even to enjoy being there — because I enjoyed it too much.

It drove my brother insane, this in-a-week-from-now-we'll-be-in-Rome-remembering-everything-we-said-and-did-in-Paris routine of mine. I was like a dying man taking detailed mental notes of sunlight, faces, foods, places, emotions, not only to remember them better when he reaches the hereafter but to give himself the impression of being still rooted in the past and capable of leaving a patch, an afterimage, like one of the shadows imprinted on the bridges of Hiroshima. To this day my brother knows Paris better than I ever will, although I know one tiny corner better than many Parisians. The Paris I cultivated was a Paris one need not stay in too long. It was a Paris made to be yearned for and remembered, a Paris for the mind.

One evening, many years later, on the way to my Paris hotel, I heard a voice behind me and turned to see a girl no older than nineteen come out of the dark and ask the question I would once have given anything to hear a woman say. I shrank back, as one does with a beggar who has come too close and to whom one hands a coin without touching hands. I had long ago learned to prefer the imagined encounter, or the memory of the imagined encounter, to the encounter.

Now, whenever I say goodbye to Paris, I do so without making trouble. At the airport, I do not think this is the last time I'll ever return. I am, I tell myself, happy to be going home. I open a book, talk to my fellow passengers, watch the news. I never, ever look back. Am I aware that the loves we decline to look back upon are those we are not certain we have overcome? In that sense, Lot was far guiltier than his wife: fleeing Sodom and Gomorrah, she just turned her head; he made a point not to.

The final irony is that I eventually learned to love Rome and, later, New York. Not just because they were homes of last resort — as with arranged marriages, these, I am told, make the best homes — but because in them, over the years, I have been able to find the shadow of an imagined and remembered Paris, one that never gels and always hovers, forever transposed and forever unreal.

Thus, I look out from a friend's window on Riverside Drive, catch sight of a Circle Line boat moving up the Hudson, and before I can express a thought, my friend does it for me: "Oh, yes, we know, it's a *bateau-mouche* on the Seine, and you're in Paris thinking of being on Riverside Drive longing to be in Paris."

Last Christmas I called a close friend to let her know my wife and I would be away for a bit — we were going to Paris. In my usual manner, I said I did not like traveling, I never found Paris relaxing, I would much rather stay in New York and imagine having wonderful dinners in Paris. "Yes, of course," she agreed, already annoyed. "Since you're going to Paris, you don't want to go to Paris. But if you were staying in New York, you'd want to be in Paris. But since you're not staying but going, just do me a favor." Exasperation bristled in her voice. "When you're in Paris, think of yourself in New York longing for Paris, and everything will be fine."

And that is precisely what I did. We walked around, went to the stores, visited this or that place. But the one thing I wanted to do — namely, return to the Paris of my adolescence — I kept delaying, because I could not rest until I had done it but did not want to do it too soon. I knew that once I had revisited my sites, Paris would hold no further interest for me.

My wife was hardly unfamiliar with this Paris of mine. I had taken her there ten years earlier, on our honeymoon, and again three years later with our then ten-month-old son. I had wanted to show her the house where my great-aunt lived, and the walks we sometimes took together, and the fountain where I would go with empty bottles to watch the girls.

I still remember how, on the first day of our honeymoon in Paris, walking along the grand avenues of the sixteenth arrondissement, staring at the lit-up buildings with their promise of intimate gatherings, I began to tell my wife about my first sojourn in Paris and of my thwarted love for the city to which I would return so often during my years in Rome, each time summoning up the memory of my prior visit or anticipating my next, leaving almost no room for the visit itself. We walked to the Place de Barcelone, stood and faced Pont de Grenelle, not far from Pont Mirabeau, and I pointed out the small-scale Statue of Liberty that is a reverse imitation of the one in New York, thinking to myself how things get boxed into each other and how cities and bridges and parks, like far-flung cousins, become mirror images of their replicas.

When we reached La Muette, one of my favorite spots, I told my wife about the royal falcon house after which the neighborhood is named — from the verb *muer,* to molt — and of how, centuries ago, this was where the king's birds were brought each year to shed their feathers. As we walked, I began to wonder what the opposite of molting was and why, unlike the body, which sheds everything, the soul cannot let go but compiles and accumulates, growing annual rings around the things it wants and dreams of and remembers. I already knew that in years to come I would turn back to this very evening at La Muette and remember how I had come there with my wife on our honeymoon and how, with her, I had remembered the young man who walked these same sidewalks trying to find a Paris he did not know he had invented.

And now here we are on the same spot, no longer newlyweds, thinking to ourselves how much and how very little things have changed since our last visit. We are having a late lunch, in exactly the same café on the Place du Trocadéro where we lunched a decade ago, and without thinking we have ended up ordering the same meal. I suspect my wife knows where we are headed, though I have not told her yet, nor have I told her that we are to visit not just the old building where my great-aunt lived but the tiny park as well.

The sky as always is a silver gray, and the city is in full ferment as we leave the café down the unavoidable route toward the old apartment. I recognize the silence that descends over that wonderful corner of the sixteenth arrondissement late on a weekday afternoon as children come home from school, bookbags and all, accompanied by a cluster of baby-sitters, who trail behind as their charges scamper quietly ahead. And there — I do it each time — I look up to the fifth floor, where my great-aunt and my grandmother used to live. I can still remember the last time I visited this building with my wife.

Of course, as my wife and I both know, I have already reported that self-same visit in my book *Out of Egypt*. What makes the present situation all the more uncanny is that earlier today, wandering into one of my favorite foreign-language bookshops on the Rue de Rivoli, I had asked for the book — with studied nonchalance, as authors do. I wanted to find out whether they had the British paperback edition, which I had never seen. The salesclerk, who had no idea who I was, turned out to be familiar with the title but reported she could not locate the book on the shelves. I was browsing in another section entirely when suddenly she came rushing up. "*Monsieur,* I've found it!" Damn! Now I had to purchase my own book, or give away the fact that I had been testing the store.

So here I am, two hours later, walking with my own book in my hand in front of a building described in that book, feeling like Don Quixote in the second part of his novel, or like Wordsworth on revisiting Tintern Abbey, or like Saint-Simon holding in his hand the vile character portrait he had penned of the person on whom he was now lavishing compliment after compliment. I feel nothing. My wife, who in my book asks, "Didn't you ever want to go upstairs to visit?" does not speak her lines, and I cannot remember mine and clearly do not want to be caught looking them up now. So we leave the scene quite unsatisfied, knowing we will probably never do *this* again.

I ask my wife if she minds taking a walk around the vest-pocket park stuck in between the grand turn-of-the-century buildings. I feel like a child asking his harried parents to stop at the window of yet another toy store. But I am taking too long, I do not know what I am looking for, we are both jet-lagged and tired, and any moment now it might start raining. And still no epiphany, nothing, just this rushed, desultory prowling around what seems to be a little fountain in a *petit parc* that long ago was named Place Victor-Hugo and then became Square Lamartine. What was I looking for, anyway? Crestfallen, I accompany my wife to the nearest *métro* station.

Four days after our perfunctory visit, on the eve of our departure, I decide to go back alone. I make my rounds again, scouring the scene, trying to squeeze out a droplet of sensation. Nothing. All I remember is coming here four days earlier. It is five o'clock. I could — and the thought races through my mind before I can check it in time — call ahead and then go upstairs for tea.

Last summer I returned yet again to Square Lamartine, this time with my seven-year-old son. I showed him where I had lived when I was barely seven years older than he, took pictures of him in front of my great-aunt's building just as I had done with my wife on our honeymoon, then walked around a bit, snapping the park, him playing in the tiny enclosure by the sandbox, the adjoining buildings, knowing that one day his passage here, like my wife's, my brother's, my father's, my great-aunt's, and mine, would find a place in this concentric planisphere named Square Lamartine.

My son is playing in the park. There is, of course, no way for him to know what I am thinking. But I am standing there the way my father did when he would take me as a child to his father's grave in Alexandria, because there was no one he would rather be with at that moment. Except that in my case, I have accompanied my son not so much to a gravesite as to the resting place of a part of my life that was never even lived, a chapter written in invisible ink. In Lamartine's garden I am still combing the scene, looking for ancient relics and clues, not just memories but generations of memories, deep, artesian memories, the way police inspectors in the movies pick up hair, nails, and lint and drop them with a tweezers into a handkerchief, the way people scour the beaches on summer evenings looking for jewelry that was lost not just that day but many summers before.

As I stare at this tiny park, I think to myself of all I have logged away and why I always feel as though nothing, even when written, remains fixed for too long before it starts to rise from the page, as if it had been but figuratively buried in paper and now aches for life again. I have never learned either to live things or else to let them go.

As if to rescue myself from so disturbing a thought, I suddenly remember a literary character I have not brought to mind since leaving Italy three decades ago. It is a character named Astolph from *Orlando Furioso,* the sixteenth-century epic poem by Ariosto. This Astolph lands on the moon — in the poem, a giant lost-and-found, bric-a-brac landscape containing everything that was ever lost or ever wished for but never granted. Mankind's unrealized artifacts litter the lunar surface, and you must thread your way cautiously through the rubble, for vials containing stolen goods and unhatched schemes crackle underfoot, and wasted years and abandoned hopes are strewn about everywhere.

Like Astolph wandering in search of the flask that contains the sanity misplaced by Ariosto's hero, Orlando, what I knew I would find here in this quiet landscape was my whole Paris: the crowded Citroën with my cousins — it was there — the hunt for Bach's double concerto — it too was there — my love for the *métro,* Apollinaire's poem, the Bogart revival, the smell of cigarettes and damp wool coats, the girls whose gaze was unlike any I had met before, the woman who finally came out of the dark only to be shooed away, the plays, the *brasseries,* the books, down to the late afternoon tea I had conjured the day I came without my wife and thought I was a phone call away from people who had died so long ago, the light drizzle on silver-gray days when Paris is awash in traffic lights, my first walk down by the royal falcon house, the day it finally dawned on me that my life had not even started, or that life, like Paris, was little else than a collection of close calls and near misses and that the objects I loved and would never outgrow and wished to take with me would always litter *this* landscape because they were lost or had never existed, because even the life I had yearned to live when looking out the window with my great-aunt in Alexandria and dreaming of a Seine scarcely seven minutes away was also cast upon this landscape, a past life, a pluperfect life, a conditional life, a life made, like Paris, for the mind. Or for paper.

WENDELL BERRY

In Distrust of Movements

FROM ORION

I HAVE HAD with my friend Wes Jackson a number of useful conversations about the necessity of getting out of movements — even movements that have seemed necessary and dear to us — when they have lapsed into self-righteousness and self-betrayal, as movements seem almost invariably to do. People in movements too readily learn to deny to others the rights and privileges they demand for themselves. They too easily become unable to mean their own language, as when a "peace movement" becomes violent. They often become too specialized, as if finally they cannot help taking refuge in the pinhole vision of the institutional intellectuals. They almost always fail to be radical enough, dealing finally in effects rather than causes. Or they deal with single issues or single solutions, as if to assure themselves that they will not be radical enough.

And so I must declare my dissatisfaction with movements to promote soil conservation or clean water or clean air or wilderness preservation or sustainable agriculture or community health or the welfare of children. Worthy as these and other goals may be, they cannot be achieved alone. I am dissatisfied with such efforts because they are too specialized, they are not comprehensive enough, they are not radical enough, they virtually predict their own failure by implying that we can remedy or control effects while leaving causes in place. Ultimately, I think, they are insincere; they propose that the trouble is caused by *other* people; they would like to change policy but not behavior.

The worst danger may be that a movement will lose its language either to its own confusion about meaning and practice or to preemption by its enemies. I remember, for example, my naive confusion at learning that it was possible for advocates of organic agriculture to look upon the "organic method" as an end in itself. To me, organic farming was attractive both as a way of conserving nature and as a strategy of survival for small farmers. Imagine my surprise in discovering that there could be huge "organic" monocultures. And so I was not too surprised by the recent attempt of the United States Department of Agriculture to appropriate the "organic" label for food irradiation, genetic engineering, and other desecrations of the corporate food economy. Once we allow our language to mean anything that anybody wants it to mean, it becomes impossible to mean what we say. When "homemade" ceases to mean neither more nor less than "made at home," then it means anything, which is to say that it means nothing.

As you see, I have good reasons for declining to name the movement I think I am a part of. I am reconciled to the likelihood that from time to time it will name itself and have slogans, but I am not going to use its slogans or call it by any of its names.

Let us suppose that we have a Nameless Movement for Better Land Use and that we know we must try to keep it active, responsive, and intelligent for a long time. What must we do?

What we must do above all, I think, is try to see the problem in its full size and difficulty. If we are concerned about land abuse, then we must see that this is an economic problem. Every economy is, by definition, a land-using economy. If we are using our land wrong, then something is wrong with our economy. This is difficult. It becomes more difficult when we recognize that in modern times, every one of us is a member of the economy of everybody else.

But if we are concerned about land abuse, we have begun a profound work of economic criticism. Study of the history of land use (and any local history will do) informs us that we have had for a long time an economy that thrives by undermining its own foundations. Industrialism, which is the name of our economy, and which is now virtually the only economy of the world, has been from its beginnings in a state of riot. It is based squarely upon the principle of violence toward everything on which it depends, and it has not mattered whether the form of industrialism was communist or capitalist or whatever; the violence toward nature, human communities, traditional agricultures, local economies has been constant. The bad news is coming in, literally, from all over the world. Can such an economy be fixed without being radically changed? I don't think it can.

The Captains of Industry have always counseled the rest of us "to be realistic." Let us, therefore, be realistic. Is it realistic to assume that the present economy would be just fine if only it would stop poisoning the air and water, or if only it would stop soil erosion, or if only it would stop degrading watersheds and forest ecosystems, or if only it would stop seducing children, or if only it would quit buying politicians, or if only it would give women and favored minorities an equitable share of the loot? Realism, I think, is a very limited program, but it informs us at least that we should not look for bird eggs in a cuckoo clock.

Or we can show the hopelessness of single-issue causes and single-issue movements by following a line of thought such as this: We need a continuous supply of uncontaminated water. Therefore, we need (among other things) soil- and water-conserving ways of agriculture and forestry that are not dependent on monoculture, toxic chemicals, or the indifference and violence that always accompany big-scale industrial enterprises on the land. Therefore, we need diversified, small-scale land economies that are dependent on people. Therefore, we need people with the knowledge, skills, motives, and attitudes required by diversified, small-scale land economies. And all this is clear and comfortable enough, until we recognize the question we have come to: *where are the people?*

Well, all of us who live in the suffering rural landscapes of the United States know that most people are available to those landscapes only recreationally. We see them bicycling or boating or hiking or camping or hunting or fishing or driving along and looking around. They do not, in Mary Austin's phrase, "summer and winter with the land." They are unacquainted with the land's human and natural economies. Though people have not progressed beyond the need to eat food and drink water and wear clothes and live in houses, most people have progressed beyond the domestic arts — the husbandry and wifery of the world — by which those needful things are produced and conserved. In fact, the comparative few who still practice that necessary husbandry and wifery often are inclined to apologize for doing so, having been carefully taught in our education system that those arts are degrading and unworthy of people's talents. Educated minds, in the modern era, are unlikely to know anything about food and drink, clothing and shelter. In merely taking these things for granted, the modern educated mind reveals itself also to be as superstitious a mind as ever has existed in the world. What could be more superstitious than the idea that money brings forth food?

I am not suggesting, of course, that everybody ought to be a farmer or a forester. Heaven forbid! I am suggesting that most people now are living on the far side of a broken connection, and that this is potentially catastrophic. Most people are now fed, clothed, and sheltered from sources toward which they feel no gratitude and exercise no responsibility. There is no significant urban constituency, no formidable consumer lobby, no noticeable political leadership, for good land use practices, for good farming and good forestry, for restoration of abused land, or for halting the destruction of land by so-called development.

We are involved now in a profound failure of imagination. Most of us cannot imagine the wheat beyond the bread, or the farmer beyond the wheat, or the farm beyond the farmer, or the history beyond the farm. Most people cannot imagine the forest and the forest economy that produced their houses and furniture and paper, or the landscapes, the streams, and the weather that fill their pitchers and bathtubs and swimming pools with water. Most people appear to assume that when they have paid their money for these things, they have entirely met their obligations.

Money does not bring forth food. Neither does the technology of the food system. Food comes from nature and from the work of people. If the supply of food is to be continuous for a long time, then people must work in harmony with nature. That means that people must find the right answers to a lot of hard practical questions. The same applies to forestry and the possibility of a continuous supply of timber.

One way we could describe the task ahead of us is by saying that we need to enlarge the consciousness and the conscience of the economy. Our economy needs to know — and care — what it is doing. This is revolutionary, of course, if you have a taste for revolution, but it is also a matter of common sense.

Undoubtedly some people will want to start a movement to bring this about. They probably will call it the Movement to Teach the Economy What It Is Doing — the MTEWIID. Despite my very considerable uneasiness, I will agree to this, but on three conditions.

My first condition is that this movement should begin by giving up all hope and belief in piecemeal, one-shot solutions. The present scientific quest for odorless hog manure should give us sufficient proof that the specialist is no longer with us. Even now, after centuries of reductionist propaganda, the world is still intricate and vast, as dark as it is light, a place of mystery, where we cannot do one thing without doing many things, or put two things together without putting many things together. Water quality, for example, cannot be improved without improving farming and forestry, but farming and forestry cannot be improved without improving the education of consumers — and so on.

The proper business of a human economy is to make one whole thing of ourselves and this world. To make ourselves into a practical wholeness with the land under our feet is maybe not altogether possible — how would *we* know? — but as a goal, it at least carries us beyond hubris, beyond the utterly groundless assumption that we can subdivide our present great failure into a thousand separate problems that can be fixed by a thousand task forces of academic and bureaucratic specialists. That program has been given more than a fair chance to prove itself, and we ought to know by now that it won't work.

My second condition is that the people in this movement (the MTEWIID) should take full responsibility for themselves as members of the economy. If we are going to teach the economy what it is doing, then we need to learn what we are doing. This is going to have to be a private movement as well as a public one. If it is unrealistic to expect wasteful industries to be conservers, then obviously we must lead in part the public life of complainers, petitioners, protesters, advocates, and supporters of stricter regulations and saner policies. But that is not enough. If it is unreasonable to expect a bad economy to try to become a good one, then *we* must go to work to build a good economy. It is appropriate that this duty should fall to us, for good economic behavior is more possible for us than it is for the great corporations with their miseducated managers and their greedy and oblivious stockholders. Because it is possible for us, we must try in every way we can to make good economic sense in our own lives, in our households, and in our communities. We must do more for ourselves and our neighbors. We must learn to spend our money with our friends and not with our enemies. But to do this, it is necessary to renew local economies and revive the domestic arts. In seeking to change our economic use of the world, we are seeking inescapably to change our lives. The outward harmony that we desire between our economy and the world depends finally upon an inward harmony between our own hearts and the originating spirit that is the life of all creatures, a spirit as near us as our flesh and yet forever beyond the measures of this obsessively measuring age. We can grow good wheat and make good bread only if we understand that we do not live by bread alone.

My third condition is that this movement should content itself to be poor. We need to find cheap solutions, solutions within the reach of everybody, and the availability of a lot of money prevents the discovery of cheap solutions. The solutions of modern medicine and modern agriculture are all staggeringly expensive, and this is caused in part, and maybe altogether, because of the availability of huge sums of money for medical and agricultural research.

Too much money, moreover, attracts administrators and experts as sugar attracts ants — look at what is happening in our universities. We should not envy rich movements that are organized and led by an alternative bureaucracy living on the problems it is supposed to solve. We want a movement that is a movement because it is advanced by all its members in their daily lives.

Now, having completed this very formidable list of the problems and difficulties, fears and fearful hopes that lie ahead of us, I am relieved to see that I have been preparing myself all along to end by saying something cheerful. What I have been talking about is the possibility of renewing human respect for this earth and all the good, useful, and beautiful things that come from it. I have made it clear, I hope, that I don't think this respect can be adequately enacted or conveyed by tipping our hats to nature or by representing natural loveliness in art or by prayers of thanksgiving or by preserving tracts of wilderness — although I recommend all those things.

The respect I mean can be given only by using well the world's goods that are given to us. This good use, which renews respect — which is the only currency, so to speak, of respect — also renews our pleasure. The callings and disciplines that I have spoken of as the domestic arts are stationed all along the way from the farm to the prepared dinner, from the forest to the dinner table, from stewardship of the land to hospitality to friends and strangers. These arts are as demanding and gratifying, as instructive and as pleasing, as the so-called fine arts. To learn them is, I believe, the work that is our profoundest calling. Our reward is that they will enrich our lives and make us glad.

IAN BURUMA

The Joys and Perils of Victimhood

FROM THE NEW YORK REVIEW OF BOOKS

IN HIS BOOK *The Seventh Million,* the Israeli journalist Tom Segev describes a visit to Auschwitz and other former death camps in Poland by a group of Israeli high school students. Some students are from secular schools, others from religious ones. All have been extensively prepared for the visit by the Israeli Ministry of Education. They have read books, seen films, and met survivors. Nonetheless, after their arrival in Poland, Segev notes a degree of apprehension among the students: Will they suddenly collapse? Will they reemerge from the experience as "different people"? The fears are not irrational, for the students have been prepared to believe that the trip will have a profound effect on their "identities," as Jews and as Israelis.

These regular school tours to the death camps are part of Israeli civic education. The political message is fairly straightforward: Israel was founded on the ashes of the Holocaust, but if Israel had already existed in 1933, the Holocaust would never have happened. Only in Israel can Jews be secure and free. The Holocaust was proof of that. So the victims of Hitler died as martyrs for the Jewish homeland, indeed as potential Israeli citizens, and the state of Israel is both the symbol and the guarantor of Jewish survival.

This message is given further expression, on those wintry spots where the Jewish people came close to annihilation, by displays of the Israeli flag and singing of the nation anthem. But Segev noticed a peculiarly religious, or pseudo-religious, aspect to the death camp visits as well. The Israeli students in Poland, in his view, were like Christian pilgrims in Jerusalem, oblivious to everything except the sacred places. They marched along the railway tracks in Auschwitz-Birkenau like Christians on the Via Dolorosa. They brought books of prayers, poems, and psalms, which they recited in front of the ruined gas chambers. They played cassette tapes of music composed by a Holocaust survivor named Yehuda Poliker. And at one of the camps, a candle was lit in the crematorium, where the students knelt in prayer.

Some call this a form of secular religion. The historian Saul Friedlander was harsher and called it a union of kitsch and death. I felt the pull of kitsch emotion myself on my only visit to Auschwitz, in 1990. By kitsch I don't mean gaudiness or camp, but rather an expression of emotion that is displaced, focused on the wrong thing, or, to use that ghastly word properly for once, inappropriate. I am not the child of Holocaust survivors. My mother was Jewish, but she lived in England, and no immediate relations were killed by the Nazis. And yet even I couldn't escape a momentary feeling of vicarious virtue, especially when I came across tourists from Germany. They were the villains, I the potential victim. But for the grace of God, I thought, I would have died here too. Or would I? An even more grotesque calculation passed through my mind: how did I fit into the Nuremberg laws? Was I a *Mischling* of the first degree or the second? Was it enough to have two Jewish grandparents, or did you need more to qualify for the grim honor of martyrdom? When would I have been deported? Would I have been deported at all? And so on, until I was woken from these smug and morbid thoughts by the sight of a tall man in American Indian dress, followed by young Japanese, Germans, and others of various nationalities banging on tambourines, yelling something about world peace.

All this seems far away from Primo Levi's fears of oblivion. One of the cruelest curses flung at the Jewish victims by an SS officer at Auschwitz was the promise that even if one Jew survived the camp, no one would believe what had happened to him or her. The SS man was quite wrong, of course. We cannot imagine the victims' torment, but we believe it. And far from forgetting the most recent and horrible chapter in the long book of Jewish suffering, the remembrance of it grows in volume the further the events recede into the past. Holocaust museums and memorials proliferate. Holocaust movies and television soap operas have broken box office records. More and more people visit the camps, whose rotting barracks have to be carefully restored to serve as memorials, and movie sets.

In a curious way, the Jewish Holocaust has been an inspiration for others, for almost every community, be it a nation or a religious or ethnic or sexual minority, has a bone to pick with history. All have suffered wrongs, and to an increasing and in my view alarming extent, all want these wrongs to be recognized, publicly, ritually, and sometimes financially. What I find alarming is not the attention we are asked to pay to the past. Without history, including its most painful episodes, we cannot understand who we are, or indeed who others are. A lack of historical sense means a lack of perspective. Without perspective we flounder in the dark and will believe anything, no matter how vile. So history is good, and it is right that victims who died alone and in misery should be remembered. Also, some minorities are still being victimized — the Tibetans, for example. What is alarming, however, is the extent to which so many minorities have come to define themselves above all as historical victims. What this reveals, in my view, is precisely a lack of historical perspective.

Sometimes it is as if everyone wants to compete with the Jewish tragedy, in what an Israeli friend once called the Olympics of suffering. Am I wrong to detect a hint of envy when I read that Iris Chang, the Chinese-American author of a recent bestseller about the 1937 rape of Nanking, wishes for a Steven Spielberg to do justice to that event? (Her book bears the subtitle *The Forgotten Holocaust of World War II.*) It is, it appears, not enough for Chinese-Americans to be seen as the heirs of a great civilization; they want to be recognized as heirs of their very own Holocaust. In an interview about her celebrity, Chang related how a woman came up to her in tears after a public reading and said that Chang's account of the massacre had made her feel proud to be Chinese-American. It seems a very peculiar source of pride.

Chinese-Americans are not the only ones to be prey to such emotions. The idea of victimhood also haunts Hindu nationalists, Armenians, African-Americans, American Indians, Japanese-Americans, and homosexuals who have adopted AIDS as a badge of identity. Larry Kramer's book on AIDS, for example, is entitled *Reports from the Holocaust.* Even the placid, prosperous Dutch, particularly those now in their teens and twenties, much too young to have experienced any atrocity at all, have narrowed down their historical perspective to the hardship suffered under German occupation in World War II. This is no wonder, since pre-twentieth-century history has been virtually abolished from the curriculum as irrelevant.

The use of Spielberg's name is of course telling, for the preferred way to experience historical suffering is at the movies. Hollywood makes history real. When Oprah Winfrey played a slave in the movie *Beloved,* she told the press, she collapsed on the set, crying and shaking. "I became so hysterical," she said, "that I connected to the raw place. That was the transforming moment. The physicality, the beatings, going to the field, being mistreated every day, was nothing compared to the understanding that you didn't own your life." And remember, this was just a movie.

My intention is not to belittle the suffering of others. The Nanking massacre, during which tens and perhaps hundreds of thousands of Chinese were slaughtered by Japanese troops, was a terrible event. The brutal lives and violent deaths of countless men and women from Africa and China who were traded as slaves must never be forgotten. The mass murder of Armenians in the Ottoman Empire cannot be denied. Many Hindu temples and Hindu lives were destroyed by Muslim invaders. Women and homosexuals have been discriminated against. The recent murder of a gay college student in Laramie, Wyoming, is a brutal reminder of how far we have yet to go. And whether or not they are right to call Columbus a mass murderer on his anniversary day, there is no doubt that the American Indians were decimated. All this is true. But it becomes questionable when a cultural, ethnic, religious, or national community bases its communal identity almost entirely on the sentimental solidarity of remembered victimhood, for that way lies historical myopia and, in extreme circumstances, even vendetta.

Why has it come to this? Why do so many people wish to identify themselves as vicarious victims? There is of course no general answer. Histories are different, and so are their uses. Memories, fictionalized or real, of shared victimhood formed the basis of much nineteenth-century nationalism. But nationalism, though not always absent, does not seem to be the main driving force for vicarious victims today. There is something else at work. First there is the silence of the actual victims: the silence of the dead, but also of the survivors. When the survivors of the Nazi death camps arrived in Israel on rusty, overloaded ships, shame and trauma prevented most of them from talking about their suffering. Victims occupied a precarious place in the new state of Jewish heroes. It was as though victimhood were a stain that had to be erased or overlooked. And so by and large the survivors kept quiet. A similar thing happened in Western Europe, particularly in France. De Gaulle built a roof for all those who had come through the war, former resistants, Vichyistes, *collabos,* Free French, and Jewish survivors: officially all were citizens of eternal France, and all had resisted the German foe. Since the last thing French Jews wanted was to be singled out once again as a separate category, the survivors acquiesced in this fiction and kept quiet.

Even though the suffering of Japanese-Americans, interned by their own government as "Japs," cannot be compared to the destruction of European Jews, their reaction after the war was remarkably similar. Like the French Jews, they were happy to be reintegrated as citizens and to blanket the humiliation they had suffered with silence. The situation in China was more political. Little was made in the People's Republic of the Nanking massacre because there were no Communist heroes in the Nationalist capital in 1937. Indeed, there had been no Communists there at all. Many of those who died in Nanking, or Shanghai, or anywhere in southern China, were soldiers in Chiang Kai-shek's army. Survivors with the wrong class or political backgrounds had enough difficulty surviving Maoist purges to worry too much about what had happened under the Japanese.

It was left up to the next generation, the sons and daughters of the victims, to break the silence. In the case of China, it took a change of politics: Deng Xiaoping's open-door policy toward Japan and the West had to be wrapped in a nationalist cloak; dependency on Japanese capital was compensated for by stabs at the Japanese conscience. It was only after 1982 that the Communist government paid any attention to the Nanking massacre at all. But leaving China aside for the moment, why did the sons and daughters of other survivors decide to speak up in the sixties and seventies? How do we explain the doggedness of a man like Serge Klarsfeld, whose father was killed at Auschwitz and who has done more than any Frenchman to bring the history of French Jews to public notice?

There is a universal piety in remembering our parents. It is a way of honoring them. But remembering our parents, especially if their suffering remained mute and unacknowledged, is also a way of asserting ourselves, of telling the world who we are. It is understandable that French Jews or Japanese-Americans wished to slip quietly into the mainstream by hiding their scars, as though their experiences had been like everyone else's, but to their children and grandchildren this was not good enough. It was as if part of themselves had been amputated by the silence of their parents. Speaking openly about the communal suffering of one's ancestors — as Jews, Japanese-Americans, Chinese, Hindus, etc. — can be a way of "coming out," as it were, of nailing the colors of one's identity to the mast. The only way a new generation can be identified with the suffering of previous generations is for that suffering to be publicly acknowledged, over and over again. This option is especially appealing when few or indeed no other tags of communal identity remain, often precisely because of the survivors' desire to assimilate. When Jewishness is reduced to a taste for Woody Allen movies and bagels, or Chineseness to Amy Tan novels and dim sum on Sundays, the quasi-authenticity of communal suffering will begin to look very attractive.

The Harvard scholar K. Anthony Appiah made this point beautifully in an analysis of identity politics in contemporary America ("The Multicultural Misunderstanding," *New York Review of Books,* Oct. 9, 1997). The languages, religious beliefs, myths, and histories of the old countries tend to fade away as the children of immigrants become Americans. This often leads to defensive claims of Otherness, especially when there is little Otherness left to defend. As Appiah said about hyphenated Americans, including African-Americans, "Their middle-class descendants, whose domestic lives are conducted in English and extend eclectically from *Seinfeld* to Chinese takeout, are discomfited by a sense that their identities are shallow by comparison with those of their grandparents; and some of them fear that unless the rest of us acknowledge the importance of their difference, there soon won't be anything worth acknowledging." He goes on to say that "the new talk of 'identity' offers the promise of forms of recognition and of solidarity that could make up for the loss of the rich, old kitchen comforts of ethnicity." Alas, however, those forms too often resemble the combination of kitsch and death described by Saul Friedlander. Identity more and more rests on the pseudo-religion of victimhood. What Appiah says about ethnic minorities might even be applied to women: the more emancipated women become, the more some extreme feminists begin to define themselves as helpless victims of men.

But surely nationalities are not the same as ethnic minorities in America, let alone women. Indeed, they are not. By and large, people of different nations still speak different languages, have different tastes in food, and share distinct histories and myths. These distinctions, however, are becoming fuzzier all the time. To a certain extent, especially in the richer countries, we are all becoming minorities in an Americanized world, where we watch *Seinfeld* while eating Chinese takeout. Few nations are defined by religion anymore, even though some, such as Iran and Afghanistan, are busy reviving that definition. And national histories, celebrating national heroes, are abolished in favor of social studies, which have replaced national propaganda based on historical continuity with celebrations of contemporary multiculturalism. Literary canons, though perhaps less under siege in Europe than they are in the United States, are also becoming increasingly obsolete. Combined with a great deal of immigration to such countries as Britain, Germany, France, and Holland, these developments have eroded what kitchen comforts of ethnicity remained in European nation-states.

Perhaps the strongest, most liberating, and most lethal glue that has bound national communities together is the way we choose or are forced to be governed. Some nations have been defined mainly by their political systems. The United States is such a place. Sometimes politics and religion are combined in monarchies. Nowhere is politics entirely devoid of irrational elements: customs, religion, and historical quirks all leave their marks. It was an extreme conceit born of the Enlightenment and the French Revolution that political utopias could be based on pure reason. Nationalism, in the sense of worshipping the nation-state as an expression of the popular will, was part of this. Politics was destined to replace the bonds of religion, or region, or race. This did some good. It also did a great deal of harm. The twin catastrophes of communism and fascism showed how dangerous it is to see the nation-state as a pure expression of the people's will. In any event, the ideological split between left and right, which was spawned by the division in the French National Assembly in 1789 and was eventually hardened by the cold war, effectively collapsed with the end of the Soviet Union. And the effects of global capitalism and multinational political arrangements, especially in Europe, have to some extent undermined the perception that nations are defined by the way they are governed. It doesn't seem to matter anymore how they are governed: decisions always appear to be made somewhere else. The current English obsession with the culture of Englishness has come just at the time of increasing integration into European institutions.

So where do we go in this disenchanted world of broken-down ideologies, religions, and national and cultural borderlines? From a secular, internationalist, cosmopolitan point of view, it may not seem such a bad world. That is, of course, if one is living in the wealthy, liberal West. It is surely good that nationalistic historical narratives have been discarded, that homosexuals can come out and join the mainstream, that women can take jobs hitherto reserved for men, that immigrants from all over the world enrich our cultures, and that we are no longer terrorized by religious or political dogma. A half-century of secular, democratic, progressive change has surely been a huge success. We have finally been liberated from irrational ethnic comforts. And yet, after all that, a growing number of people seek to return to precisely such comforts, and the form they often take is the pseudo-religion of kitsch and death. Tom Segev argues that the modern Israeli tendency to turn the Holocaust into a civic religion is a reaction against secular Zionism. The "new man" — socialist, heroic, pioneering — turned out to be inadequate. More and more, people want to rediscover their historical roots. To be serious about religion is demanding, however. As Segev says, "Emotional and historical awareness of the Holocaust provides a much easier way back into the mainstream of Jewish history, without necessarily imposing any real personal moral obligation. The 'heritage of the Holocaust' is thus largely a way for secular Israelis to express their connection to Jewish heritage."

The same is true for many of us, whether Jewish, Chinese-American, or whatnot. The resurgence of Hindu nationalism in India, for instance, is especially strong among middle-class Hindus, who are reacting against the Nehruvian vision of a socialist, secular India. Since many urban, middle-class Hindus have only a superficial knowledge of Hinduism, aggressive resentment of Muslims is an easier option. And so we have the peculiar situation in India of a majority feeling set upon by a poorer, much less powerful minority. But there is a larger context too, particularly in the West. Just as the Romantic idealism and culture worship of Herder and Fichte followed the secular rationalism of the French *philosophes,* our attraction to kitsch and death heralds a new Romantic age, which is antirational, sentimental, and communitarian. We see it in the politics of Clinton and Blair, which have replaced socialist ideology with appeals to the community of feeling, where we all share one another's pain. We saw it in the extraordinary scenes surrounding the death of Princess Diana, when the world, so TV reporters informed us, united in mourning. Princess Diana was in fact the perfect embodiment of our obsession with victimhood. Not only did she identify with victims, often in commendable ways, hugging AIDS patients here and homeless people there, but she was seen as a suffering victim herself: of male chauvinism, royal snobbery, the media, British society, and so on. Everyone who felt victimized in any way identified with her, especially women and members of ethnic minorities. And it says something about the state of Britain, changed profoundly by immigration, Americanization, and Europeanization yet unsure of its status in Europe, that so many people felt united as a nation only when the princess of grief had died.

This sharing of pain has found its way into the way we look at history, too. Historiography is less and less a matter of finding out how things really were or trying to explain how things happened, for not only is historical truth irrelevant, but it has become a common assumption that there is no such thing. Everything is subjective, or a sociopolitical construct. And if the civic lessons we learn at school teach us anything, it is to respect the truths constructed by others, or, as it is more usually phrased, the Other. So we study memory, that is to say, history as it is felt, especially by its victims. By sharing the pain of others, we learn to understand their feelings and get in touch with our own.

Vera Schwarcz, a professor of East Asian studies at Wesleyan University, recently wrote a book entitled *Bridge Across Broken Time,* in which she links her own memories as the child of Jewish Holocaust survivors with those of Chinese victims of the Nanking massacre and the violent crackdown in 1989 in Tiananmen Square. With images of 1989 fresh in her mind, Schwarcz visits Yad Vashem, the Holocaust memorial outside Jerusalem. There she realizes

> the immensity both of the suffering that could not be commemorated in China after 1989 and of the Nanking Massacre of 1937 with its countless dead that had yet to become imprinted upon communal memory in Japan and the United States. I also sensed the magnitude of my own loss that could not be assuaged by the light of a candle, even if it was reflected one million times.

Now, I don't doubt the nobility of Professor Schwarcz's sentiments, but I do wonder whether this sort of thing — even Maya Angelou's poetry makes a cameo appearance in her book — is enlightening in any historical sense. In fact it is ahistorical, because the actual experiences of historical victims get blended in a kind of soup of pain. Although it is undoubtedly true that Chinese, Jews, gays, and others have suffered, it is not so that they all suffered in the same way. The distinctions tend to get lost. It is all too typical of our neo-Romantic age that a well-known Dutch ballet dancer and novelist named Rudi van Dantzig should announce in a pamphlet issued by the Resistance Museum in Amsterdam that homosexuals and other minorities in the Netherlands should take anti-Nazi resisters as models for their struggle against social discrimination.

But enlightenment is probably not the issue here. Instead there is authenticity. When all truth is subjective, only feelings are authentic, and only the subject can know whether his or her feelings are true or false. One of the most remarkable statements along these lines was written by the novelist Edmund White. In an article about AIDS literature (*The Nation,* May 12, 1997), he argues that literary expressions of the disease cannot be judged by critical standards. As he puts it, a trifle histrionically, "I can scarcely defend my feelings beyond saying that it strikes me as indecent to hand out grades to men and women on the edge of the grave." He then stretches AIDS literature to encompass multiculturalism in general, and states not only that multiculturalism is incompatible with a literary canon but that "I'd go even further and say multiculturalism is incompatible with the whole business of handing out critical high and low marks." In other words, our critical faculties cannot be applied to novels, poems, essays, or plays expressing the pain of Others. As White says about the AIDS genre, "We will not permit our readers to evaluate us; we want them to toss and turn with us, drenched in our night sweats."

What makes us authentic, then, as Jews, homosexuals, Hindus, or Chinese, is our sense of trauma, and thus our status as victims, which cannot be questioned. The vulgar Freudianism of the view is remarkable in an age of debunking Freud. In fact, Freud's endeavors were themselves a brilliant product of late-nineteenth-century identity politics. To secular, bourgeois, assimilated German and Austrian Jews, psychoanalysis was a logical route to self-discovery. What Freud did for his Viennese patients is in a way what Edmund White and other identity politicians are now doing for their various "communities," and real politicians are borrowing their language.

Apart from the sentimentality that this injects into public life, the new religions of kitsch and death are disturbing for other reasons. Vera Schwarcz's talk of building bridges between mourning communities notwithstanding, I think the tendency to identify authenticity in communal suffering actually impedes understanding among people, for feelings can only be expressed, not discussed or argued about. This cannot result in mutual understanding, but only in mute acceptance of whatever people wish to say about themselves, or in violent confrontation. The same is true of political discourse. Ideology has caused a great deal of suffering, to be sure, particularly in political systems where ideologies were imposed by force. But without any ideology, political debate becomes incoherent, and politicians appeal to sentiments instead of ideas. And this can easily result in authoritarianism, for again, you cannot argue with feelings. Those who try are denounced not for being wrong but for being unfeeling, uncaring, and thus bad people who don't deserve to be heard.

*

The answer to these problems is not to tell people to go back to their traditional places of worship, in an attempt to supplant pseudo-religions with established ones. I am not opposed to organized religion on principle, but as a secular person myself it is not my place to promote it. Nor am I against building memorials for victims of wars or persecution. The decision by the German government (subject to parliamentary approval) to build a Holocaust museum in Berlin is laudable, because it will also contain a library and document center. Without such a center, it would just be a colossal monument. In the new plan, memory will go together with education. Literature, of fact and fiction, about individual and communal suffering should have its place. History is important. Indeed, there should be more of it. And it would be perverse to take issue with the aim of fostering tolerance and understanding of other cultures and communities. But the steady substitution of political argument in public life with the soothing rhetoric of healing is disturbing.*

So how do we deal with this? We can make a start toward resolving the problem by drawing distinctions where few are made now. Politics is not the same as religion or psychiatry, even though it may be influenced by both. Memory is not the same as history, and memorializing is different from writing history. Sharing a cultural heritage is more than "negotiating an identity." It is perhaps time for those of us who have lost religious, linguistic, or cultural ties with our ancestors to admit to that and let go. Finally, and I think this goes to the heart of the matter, we should recognize that truth is not just a point of view. There are facts that are not made up but real. And to pretend there is no difference between fact and fiction, or that all writing is fiction, is to paralyze our capacity to distinguish truth from falsehood. And that is the worst betrayal of Primo Levi and all those who suffered in the past. For Levi's fear was not that future generations would fail to share his pain, but that they would fail to recognize the truth.

*But it is hard to see which ideologies will bring some clarity back to politics. The prevailing ideology in the United States is market liberalism. Free trade in an unstable global market is breeding discontents. But its opponents, on the right and the left, have yet to come up with a coherent alternative.

FRED D'AGUIAR

A Son in Shadow

FROM HARPER'S MAGAZINE

I KNOW NOTHING about how they meet. She is a schoolgirl. He is at work, probably a government clerk in a building near her school. At the hour when school and office are out for lunch their lives intersect at sandwich counters, soft-drink stands, traffic lights, market squares. Their eyes meet or their bodies collide at one of these food queues. He says something suggestive, complimentary. She suppresses a smile or traps one beneath her hands. He takes this as encouragement (as if any reaction of hers would have been read as anything else) and keeps on talking and following her and probably misses lunch that day. All the while she walks and eats and drinks and soaks up his praise, his sweet body-talk, his erotic chatter and sexy pitter-patter, his idle boasts and ample toasts to his life, his dreams about their future, the world their oyster together.

Am I going too fast on my father's behalf? Should there have been an immediate and cutting rebuttal from her and several days before another meeting? Does he leave work early to catch her at the end of the schoolday and follow her home just to see where she lives and to extend the boundaries of their courtship? Throwing it from day to night, from school to home, from childhood play to serious adult intent? Georgetown's two-lane streets with trenches on either side mean a mostly single-file walk, she in front probably looking over her shoulder when he says something worthy of a glance, or a cut-eye look if his suggestions about her body or what he will do with it if given half a chance exceed the decorum of the day — which is what, in mid-fifties Guyana? From my grandmother it's "Don't talk to a man unless you think you're a big woman. Man will bring you trouble. Man want just one thing from you. Don't listen to he. Don't get ruined for he. A young lady must cork her ears and keep her eye straight in front of she when these men start to flock around. The gentleman among them will find his way to her front door. The gentleman will make contact with the parents first. Woo them first before muttering one thing to the young lady. Man who go directly to young ladies only want to ruin them. Don't want to make them into respectable young women — just whores. Mark my words." My grandfather simply thinks that his little girl is not ready for the attentions of any man, that none of them is good enough for his little girl, and so the man who comes to his front door had better have a good pretext for disturbing his reverie. He had better know something about merchant seamen and the character of the sea, and about silence — how to keep it so that it signifies authority and dignity, so when you speak you are heard and your words, every one of them, are rivets. That man would have to be a genius to get past my grandfather, a genius or a gentleman. And since my father is neither, it's out of the question that he'll even use the front door of worship. His route will have to be the yard and the street of ruination.

So he stands in full view of her house at dusk. It takes a few nights before her parents realize he is there for their daughter. Then one day her father comes out and tells him to take his dog behavior to someone else's front door, and the young man quickly turns on his heel and walks away. Another time her mother opens the upstairs window and curses him, and he laughs and saunters off as if her words were a broom gently ushering him out of her yard. But he returns the next night and the next, and the daughter can't believe his determination. She is embarrassed that her body has been a magnet for trouble, that she is the cause of the uproar, then angry with him for his keen regard of her at the expense of her dignity, not to mention his. Neighbors tease her about him. They take pity on the boy, offer him drinks, some ice-cold mauby, a bite to eat, a dhal-pouri, all of which he declines at first, then dutifully accepts. One neighbor even offers him a chair, and on one night of pestilential showers an umbrella, since he does not budge from his spot while all around him people dash for shelter, abandoning a night of liming (loitering) and gaffing (talking) to the persistence and chatter of the rain. Not my father. He stands his ground, with only the back of his right hand up to his brow to shelter his eyes zeroed in on her house. She steals a glance at him after days of seeming to ignore the idea of him, though his presence burns brightly inside her heart. She can't believe his vigilance is for her. She stops to stare in the mirror and for the first time sees her full lips, long straight nose, shoulder-length brunette hair, and dark green eyes with their slight oval shape. Her high cheekbones. Her ears close to her skull. She runs her fingers lightly over these places as if to touch is to believe. Her lips tingle. Her hair shines. Her eyes smile. And she knows from this young man's perseverance that she is beautiful, desirable. She abandons herself to chores, and suppresses a smile and a song. She walks past windows as much as possible to feed the young man's hungry eyes with a morsel of that which he has venerated to the point of indignity. She rewards his eyes by doing unnecessary half-turns at the upstairs window. A flash of clavicle, a hand slowly putting her hair off her face and setting it down behind her ears, and then a smile, a demure glance, her head inclined a little, her eyes raised, her eyelids batted a few times — she performs for him, though she feels silly and self-conscious. What else is there for a girl to do? Things befitting a lady that she picked up from the cinema. Not the sauciness of a tramp.

Her mother pulls her by one of those beautiful close-skulled ears from the window and curses her, as if she were a ten-cent whore, then throws open the window and hurtles a long list of insults at this tall, silent, rude, good-for-nothing streak of impertinence darkening her street. The father folds his paper and gets up, but by the time he gets to the window the young man is gone.

My mother cries into the basin of dishes. She rubs a saucer so hard that it comes apart in her hands. She is lucky not to cut herself. She will have to answer to her mother for that breakage. In the past it meant at least a few slaps and many minutes of curses for bringing only trouble into her mother's house. Tonight her mother is even angrier. Her father has turned his fury against her for rearing a daughter who is a fool for men. Her mother finds her in the kitchen holding the two pieces of the saucer together and then apart — as if her dread and sheer desire for reparation would magically weld them whole. Her tears fall like drops of solder on that divided saucer. Her mother grabs her hands and strikes her and curses her into her face so that my mother might as well be standing over a steaming, spluttering pot on the stove. She drops the two pieces of saucer and they become six pieces. Her mother looks down and strides over the mess with threats about what will happen if her feet find a splinter. She cries but finds every piece, and to be sure to get the splinters too she runs her palms along the floor, this way and that, and with her nails she prizes out whatever her hand picks up. She cries herself to sleep.

The next night he is back at his station, and her mother and father, their voices, their words, their blows, sound a little farther off, fall a little lighter. His presence, the barefaced courage of it, becomes a suit of armor for her to don against her mother's and father's attacks. She flies through her chores. She manages under her mother's watchful eye to show both sides of her clavicle, even a little of the definition down the middle of her chest — that small trench her inflated chest digs, which catches the light and takes the breath away, that line drawn from the throat to the uppermost rib exuding warmth and tension, drawing the eyes twenty-five yards away with its radiance in the half-light of dusk, promising more than it can possibly contain, than the eye can hold, and triggering a normal heart into palpitations, a normal breath into shallowness and rapidity.

"Miss Isiah, howdy! How come you house so clean on the west side and not so clean on the east? It lopsided! Dirt have a preference in your house? Or is that saga boy hanging around the west side of your house a dirt repellent?" The gossip must have been rampant in the surrounding yards, yards seemingly designed deliberately so people could see into one another's homes and catch anything spilling out of them — quarrels, courtships, cooking pots, music — and sometimes a clash of houses, a reaction against the claustrophobia of the yard, but not enough yards, not enough room to procure a necessary privacy in order to maintain a badly sought-after dignity — clean, well dressed, head high in the air on Sundays — impossible if the night before there is a fight and everyone hears you beg not to be hit anymore, or else such a stream of obscenities gushes from your mouth that the sealed red lips of Sunday morning just don't cut it.

My father maintains his vigil. Granny threatens to save the contents of her chamber pot from the night before and empty it on his head. Could she have thrown it from her living room window to his shaded spot by the street? Luckily, she never tries. She may well be telling him that he doesn't deserve even that amount of attention. If there is any creature lower than a gutter rat — one too low to merit even her worst display of disdain — then he is it. How does my father take that? As a qualification he can do without? How much of that kind of water is he able to let run off his back? Poor man. He has to be in love. He has to be wearing his own suit of armor. Lashed to his mast like Odysseus, he hears the most taunting, terrible things, but what saves him, what restores him, is the ropes, the armor of his love for my mother. Others without this charm would have withered away, but my father smiles and shrugs at the barrage of looks, insults, gestures, silence, loneliness.

Watch his body there under that breadfruit or sapodilla tree; the shine of his status as sentry and his conviction are twin headlights that blind her parents. They redouble their efforts to get rid of his particular glare, then are divided by the sense of his inevitability in their daughter's life. My grandmother stops shouting at him while my grandfather still raises his cane and causes the young man to walk away briskly. My grandmother then opens the windows on the west side, ostensibly to let in the sea breeze but really to exhibit in all those window frames a new and friendly demeanor. My grandfather shouts at her that he can smell the rank intent of that black boy, rotten as a fish market, blowing into his living room and spoiling his thoughts.

But the windows stay open. And my mother at them. With the love Morse of her clavicles and her cleavage as she grows bolder. Smiling, then waving. And no hand in sight to box her or grip her by the ear and draw her away from there. Until one night she boldly leaves the house and goes to him and they talk for five minutes rapidly, as if words are about to run out in the Southern Hemisphere.

My father's parents wonder what has become of their Gordon.

"The boy only intend to visit town."

"Town swallow him up."

"No, one woman turn he head, stick it in a butter churn and swill it."

"He lost to us now."

"True."

They say this to each other but hardly speak to him except to make pronouncements on the size of foreign lands.

"Guyana small?"

"What's the boy talking about?"

"Why, England and Scotland combined are the size of Guyana."

"How much room does a man need?"

"That woman take he common sense in a mortar and pound it with a pestle."

The two voices are one voice.

Opportunity is here now. The English are letting go of the reins, a whole new land is about to be fashioned. And he is planning to leave! What kind of woman has done this to our boy? The boy is lost. Talking to him is like harnessing a stubborn donkey. This isn't love but voodoo, obeah, juju, some concoction in a drink, some spell thrown in his locus. A little salt over the shoulder, an iodine shower, a rabbit foot on a string, a duck's bill or snake head dried and deposited into the left trouser pocket, a precious stone, lapis lazuli, amethyst, or anything on the middle finger, a good old reliable crucifix around the neck, made of silver, not gold, and at least one ounce in weight and two inches in diameter. A psalm in papyrus folded in a shirt pocket next to the heart. A blessing from a priest, a breathing of nothing but incense with a towel over the head. A bout of fasting, one night without sleep, a dreamless night, and a dreamless, sleepless, youngest son restored to them. He wants to stay around the house, he shows them why he loves his mummy and poppy and the bounteous land. There is no plan to flee. There is no city woman with his heart in her hand. And his brain is not ablaze in his pants. His head is not an empty, airless room.

They have one cardboard suitcase each, apart from her purse and his envelope tied with a string that contains their passports and tickets, birth certificates, and, for him, a document that he is indeed a clerk with X amount of experience at such-and-such a government office, signed "supervisor" — a worthless piece of shit, of course, in the eyes of any British employer. But for the time being, these little things are emblematic of the towering, staggering optimism that propels them out of Georgetown, Guyana, over the sea to London, England.

So what do they do? My mother is a shy woman. My father, in the two photos I've seen of him, is equally reserved. Not liable to experimentation. The big risk has been taken — that of leaving everything they know for all that is alien to them. My mother knows next to nothing about sex, except perhaps a bit about kissing. My father may have experimented a little, as boys tend to do, but he too, when faced with the female body, confronts unfamiliar territory. Each burns for the other, enough to pull up roots and take off into the unknown. Yet I want to believe that they improvise around the idea of her purity and respect it until their marriage night. That they keep intact some of the moral system they come from even as they dismantle and ignore every other stricture placed on them by Guyanese society: honor your father and mother; fear a just and loving God; pledge allegiance to the flag; lust is the devil's oxygen. All that circles in their veins.

Over the twelve days at sea they examine what they have left and what they are heading toward. At sea they are in between lives: one life is over but the other has not yet begun. The talking they do on that ship, without any duties to perform at all! My mother tells how her father, despite his routine as a merchant seaman, finds time to memorize whole poems by the Victorians: Tennyson, Longfellow, Browning, Jean Ingelow, Arnold, and Hopkins. The sea is his workplace, yet he makes time to do this marvelous thing. She tells how when he comes back to land he gathers them all in the living room and performs "The Charge of the Light Brigade" or "Maud" or "My Last Duchess" or "Fra Lippo Lippi" or "The High Tide on the Coast of Lincolnshire" or "Dover Beach" or "The Kingfisher" or "The Wreck of the *Deutschland*." He recites these poems to his creole-thinking children, who sit there and marvel at the English they are hearing, not that of the policeman or the teacher or the priest, but even more difficult to decipher, full of twists and impossible turns that throw you off the bicycle of your creole reasoning into the sand. If any of them interrupts my grandfather, he stops in midflow, tells them off in creole, and resumes his poem where he left off. When particularly miffed by the disturbance, he starts the poem from the beginning again. Does my grandfather recite these verses before or after he gets drunk, swears at the top of his voice, and chases my grandmother around the house with his broad leather belt?

*

But when my parents are out at sea, they have only the King James Bible in their possession. What they plan and rehearse is every aspect of their new life.

"Children. I want children."

"Me too. Plenty of them."

"I can work between births."

"Yes, both of us. Until we have enough money for a house. Then you can stay home with the kids."

"A nanny. Someone to watch the kids while we work. What kind of house?"

"Three bedrooms. A garden at the front, small, and back, large. A car — a Morris Minor. With all that room in the back for the children and real indicators and a wood finish." Neither has a notebook or dreamed of keeping one. They do not write their thoughts, they utter them. If something is committed to memory, there has to be a quotidian reason for it, apart from bits of the Bible and a few calypsos. My grandfather's labor of love, his settling down with a copy of Palgrave's *Golden Treasury* and memorizing lines that bear no practical relationship to his life, must seem bizarre to his children. Yet by doing so he demonstrates his love of words, their music, the sense of their sound, their approximation to the heartbeat and breath, their holding out of an alternative world to the one surrounding him, their confirmation of a past and another's life and thoughts, their luxury of composition, deliberation, their balancing and rebalancing of a skewered life. I imagine my mother benefits from this exposure in some oblique way — that the Victorians stick to her mental makeup whether she cares for them or not, that a little of them comes off on me in the wash of my gestation in her.

There is an old black-and-white photo (isn't there always?) and fragments of stories about his comings and goings, his carryings-on, as the West Indian speak goes, his mischief. "Look pan that smooth face, them two big, dark eye them, don't they win trust quick-time? Is hard to tie the man with them eye in him head to any woman and she pickney them. He face clean-shaven like he never shave. He curly black hair, dougla-look, but trim neat-neat. The man got topside." His hair, thick and wavy because of the "dougla" mix of East Indian and black, exaggerates an already high forehead. Automatically we credit such an appearance, in the Caribbean and elsewhere, with intelligence — "topside." And a European nose, not broad, with a high bridge (good breeding, though the nostrils flare a bit — sign of a quick temper!). And lips that invite kisses. "They full-full and pout like a kiss with the sound of a kiss way behind, long after that kiss come and gone." He is six feet tall and thin but not skinny, that brand of thin that women refer to as elegant, since the result is long fingers and economic gestures. Notice I say economic and not cheap. A man of few words. A watcher. "But when he relax in company he know and trust, then he the center of wit and idle philosophizing. He shoot back a few rums, neat no chaser, with anyone, and hold his own with men more inclined to gin and tonic. He know when to mind he p's and q's and when to gaff in the most lewd Georgetown rumshop talk with the boys. What chance a sixteen-year-old closeted lady got against such a man, I ask you?"

But most of the puzzle is missing. So I start to draw links from one fragment to the next. He begins to belong — fleetingly, at first — in my life. As a man in poor light seen crossing a road mercifully free of traffic, its tarmacadam steamy with a recent downpour. As a tall, lank body glimpsed ducking under the awning of a shopfront and disappearing inside and never emerging, no matter how long I wait across the street, watching the door with its reflecting plate glass and listening for the little jingle of the bell that announces the arrival and departure of customers.

Or I cross Blackheath Hill entranced by the urgent belief that my father is in one of the cars speeding up and down it. Blackheath Hill curves a little with a steep gradient — less than one in six in places. It's more of a ski slope than a hill. Cars and trucks, motorbikes and cyclists all come down the road as if in a race for a finish line. Going up it is no different. Vehicles race to the top as if with the fear that their engines might cut off and they will slide back down. I want to be seen by my father. I have to be close to his car so that he does not miss me. I measure the traffic and watch myself get halfway, then, after a pause to allow a couple of cars to pass on their way up, a brisk walk, if I time it right, to allow the rest of the traffic to catch up with me, to see the kid who seems to be in no particular hurry to get out of their way looking at them. I step onto the sidewalk and cherish the breeze of the nearest vehicle at my back — Father, this is your son you have just missed. Isn't he big? Pull over and call his name. Take him in your arms. Admonish him. Remind him that cars can kill and his little body would not survive a hit at these high speeds. Tell him to look for his father under less dangerous circumstances.

I am searching the only way I know how, by rumination, contemplation, conjecture, supposition. I try to fill the gaps, try to piece together the father I never knew. I imagine everything where there is little or nothing to go on. And yet, in going back, in raking up bits and pieces of a shattered and erased existence, I know that I am courting rejection from a source hitherto silent and beyond me. I am conjuring up a father safely out of reach and taking the risk that the lips I help to move, the lungs I force to breathe, will simply say "No." No to everything I ask of them, even the merest crumb of recognition.

"Father." The noun rings hollowly when I say it, my head is empty of any meaning the word might have. I shout it in a dark cave, but none of the expected bats come flapping out. Just weaker and weaker divisions of my call. "Father." It is my incantation to bring him back from the grave to the responsibility of his name. But how, when I only know his wife, my mother, and her sudden, moody silence whenever he crops up in conversation?

You ever have anyone sweet-talk you? Fill your ears with their kind of wax, rub that wax with their tongue all over your body with more promises than the promised land itself contains, fill your head with their sweet drone, their buzz that shuts out your parents, friends, your own mind from its own house? That's your father, the bumblebee, paying attention to me.

My sixteenth birthday was a month behind. He was nearly twenty. A big man in my eyes. What did he want with me? A smooth tongue in my ears. Mostly, though, he watched me, my house, my backside when he followed me home from school. His eyes gleamed in the early evening, the whites of his eyes. He stood so still by the side of the road outside my house that he might have been a lamppost, planted there, shining just for me.

My father cursed him, my mother joined in, my sisters laughed at his silence, his stillness. They all said he had to be the most stupid man in Georgetown, a dunce, a bat in need of a perch, out in the sun too long, sun fry his brain, cat take his tongue, his head empty like a calabash, his tongue cut out, he look like a beggar. They felt sorry for him standing there like a paling, his face a yard long, his tongue a slab of useless plywood in his mouth. "Look what Ingrid gone and bring to the house, shame, dumbness, blackness follow she here to we house to paint shame all over it and us. Go away, black boy, take your dumb misery somewhere else, crawl back to your pen in the country, leave we sister alone, she got more beauty than sense to listen to a fool like you, to let you follow her, to encourage you by not cursing the day you was born and the two people who got together to born you and your people and the whole sorry village you crawl out of to come and plant yourself here in front of we house on William Street, a decent street, in Kitty, in we capital."

I should have thanked my sisters; instead I begged them to leave him alone. Ignore him and he'll go away. My father left the house to get hold of the boy by the scruff of his neck and boot his backside out of Kitty, but he ran off when my father appeared in the door frame. With the light of the house behind him and casting a long, dark shadow, he must have looked twice his size and in no mood to bargain. Your father sprinted away, melting into the darkness. I watched for his return by checking that the windows I'd bolted earlier really were bolted, convincing myself that I had overlooked one of them, using my hands to feel the latch as I searched the street for him. But he was gone for the night. My knight. Shining eyes for armor.

My mother cursed him from the living room window, flung it open and pointed at him and with her tongue reduced him to a pile of rubble and scattered that rubble over a wide area, then picked her way through the strewn wreckage to make sure her destruction was complete: "Country boy, what you want with my daughter? What make you think you man enough for her? What you got between your legs that give you the right to plant yourself in front of my house? What kind of blight you is? You fungus!"

As she cursed him and he retreated from the house sheepishly, she watched her husband for approval. These were mild curses for her, dutiful curses, a warm-up. When she really got going, her face reddened and her left arm carved up the air in front of her as if it were the meat of her opponent being dissected into bite-size bits. That's how I knew she was searching for a way to help me but hadn't yet found it. Not as long as my father was at home. Soon he would be at sea, away for weeks, and things would be different.

That is, if my onlooker, my remote watcher, my far-off admirer wasn't scared off forever. And what if he was? Then he didn't deserve me in the first place. If he couldn't take a few curses, he wasn't good for anything. If I wasn't worth taking a few curses for . . . well, I didn't want a man who didn't think I was worth taking a few curses for! I loved him for coming back night after night when all he got from me was a glance at the window. Sometimes less than a glance. Just me passing across the window frame as I dashed from chore to chore under four baleful eyes.

It seemed like he was saving all his breath and words for when he could be alone with me. Then he turned on the bumblebee of himself and I was the hapless flower of his attentions. He told me about my skin that it was silk, that all the colors of the rainbow put together still didn't come close to my beautiful skin. That my face, my eyes, my mouth, my nose, the tip of my nose, my ears, my fingertips, each was a precious jewel, precious stone. He likened the rest of me to things I had read about but had never seen, had dreamed about but had never dreamed I would see: dandelions, apples, snow, spring in England's shires, the white cliffs of Dover. In his eyes my body, me, was everything I dreamed of becoming.

That was your father before any of you were a twinkle in his eye. More accurately, that was my lover and then my husband. Your father was a different man altogether. Suddenly a stranger occupied my bed. His tongue now turned to wood. All the laughter of my sisters, the halfhearted curses of my mother, my father's promise of blue misery, all came true in this strange man, this father, this latter-day husband and lover.

I saw the change in him. My hands were full with you children. He went out of reach. He cradled you as if he didn't know which side was up, which down. He held you at arm's length to avoid the tar and feathers of you babies. Soon I earned the same treatment, but if you children were tar and feathers, I was refuse. His face creased when he came near me. What had become of my silk skin? My precious features disappeared into my face, earning neither praise nor blame — just his silence, his wooden tongue, and that bad-smell look of his. I kept quiet for as long as I could. I watched him retreat from all of us, hoping he'd reel himself back in, since the line between us was strong and I thought unbreakable; but no. I had to shout to get him to hear me. I shouted like my mother standing at the upstairs window to some rude stranger in the street twenty-five yards away. I sounded like my father filling the door frame. My jeering sisters insinuated their way into my voice. And your father simply kept walking away.

Believe me, I pulled my hair and beat the ground with my hands and feet to get at him in my head and in the ground he walked on that I worshipped. Hadn't he delivered England to me and all the seasons of England, all England's shires and the fog he'd left out of his serenades, no doubt just to keep some surprise in store for me? The first morning I opened the door that autumn and shouted "Fire!" when I saw all that smoke, thinking the whole street on fire, all the streets, London burning, and slammed the door and ran into his arms and his laughter, and he took me out into it in my nightdress, he in his pajamas, and all the time I followed him, not ashamed to be seen outside in my thin, flimsy nylon (if anyone could see through that blanket) because he was in his pajamas, the blue striped ones, and his voice, his sweet drone, told me it was fine, this smoke without fire was fine, "This is fog."

He walked away and everything started to be erased by that fog. That smoke without fire crossed the ocean into my past and obliterated Kitty, Georgetown, the house on William Street, everything he had touched, every place I had known him in. I swallowed that fog. It poured into my ears, nose, eyes, mouth. He was gone. I got a chest pain and breathlessness that made me panic. There wasn't just me. There were you children. I had to breathe for you children. The pain in my chest that was your father had to be plucked out, otherwise I too would be lost to you all, and to myself.

The first time I see him is the last time I see him. I can't wait to get to the front of the queue to have him all to myself. When I get there, my eyes travel up and down his body. From those few gray hairs that decorate his temples and his forehead and his nose to the cuffs at his ankles and sparkling black shoes. He wears a black suit, a double-breasted number with three brass buttons on the cuff of each sleeve. He lies on his back with his hands clasped over his flat stomach. There is too much powder on his face. Let's get out of this mournful place, Dad. We have a lot of catching up to do. He has the rare look — of holding his breath, of not breathing, in between inhaling and exhaling — that exquisitely beautiful corpses capture. For a moment after I invite him to leave with me, I expect his chest to inflate, his lids to open, and those clasped hands to unfold and pull him upright into a sitting position, as if he really were just napping because he has dressed way too early for the ball.

There are myths about this sort of thing. Father enslaves son. Son hates father, bides his time, waits for the strong father to weaken. Son pounces one day, pounces hard and definite, and the father is overwhelmed, broken, destroyed with hardly any resistance, except that of surprise and then resignation. Son washes his hands but finds he is washing hands that are not bloodstained, not marked or blemished in any way. He is simply scrubbing hands that no longer belong to him — they are his father's hands, attached to his arms, his shoulders, his body. He has removed a shadow all the more to see unencumbered the father in himself. There is the widow he has made of his mother. He cannot love her as his father might. While his father lived, he thought he could. The moment his father expired, he knew his mother would remain unloved.

I alight too soon from a number 53 bus on Blackheath Hill, disembark while the bus is moving, and stumble, trip from two legs onto all fours, hands like feet, transforming, sprouting more limbs, becoming a spider and breaking my fall. That same fall is now a tumble, a dozen somersaults that end with me standing upright and quite still on two legs with the other limbs dangling. Onlookers, who fully expected disaster, applaud. I walk back up the hill to the block of council flats as a man might, upright, on two legs. My other limbs dangle, swing as if they are two hands. Some days I will be out of breath, I will gasp and exhale, and the cloud before me will be not my winter's breath but the silken strands of a web or, worse, fire. Other days I might look at a bed of geraniums planted on the council estate and turn all their numberless petals into stone. A diamond held between my thumb and index finger crumbles in this mood, in this light, like the powdery wings of a butterfly.

I stare out of an apartment on the twenty-fourth floor of a tower block overlooking the nut-brown Thames. That wasp on the windowpane nibbling up and down the glass for a pore to exit through, back into the air and heat, tries to sting what it can feel but cannot see. My father is the window. I am the wasp. Sometimes a helping hand comes along and lifts the window, and the wasp slides out. Other times a shadow descends, there is a displacement of air, and it is the last thing the wasp knows. Which of those times is this? I want to know. I don't want to know. I am not nibbling nor trying to sting. I am kissing, repeatedly, rapidly, the featureless face of my father. It feels like summer light. It reflects a garden. Whose is that interfering hand? Why that interrupting shadow? My child's hand. My child's shadow. My son or my father? My son and my father. Two sons, two fathers. Yet three people. We walk behind a father's name, shoulder a father's memory. Wear another's walk, another's gait. Wait for what has happened to their bodies, the same scars, maladies, aches, to surface in ours.

I want to shed my skin. Walk away from my shadow. Leave my name in a place I cannot return to. To be nameless, bodiless. To swim to Wallace Stevens's Key West, which is shoreless, horizonless. Blackheath Hill becomes Auden's Bristol Street, an occasion for wonder and lament. Blackheath at 5:45 on a foggy winter morning becomes Peckham Rye. There are no trees on Blackheath, but angels hang in the air, if only Blake were there to see them. On the twenty-fourth floor towering above the Thames, water, not land, surrounds me. Everything seems to rise out of that water. Look up at ambling clouds and the tower betrays its drift out to sea.

EDWIDGE DANTICAT

Westbury Court

FROM NEW LETTERS

WHEN I WAS fourteen years old, we lived in a six-story brick building in a cul-de-sac off of Flatbush Avenue, in Brooklyn, called Westbury Court. Beneath the building ran a subway station through which rattled the D, M, and Q trains every fifteen minutes or so. Though there was graffiti on most of the walls of Westbury Court, and hills of trash piled up outside, and though the elevator wasn't always there when we opened the door to step inside and the heat and hot water weren't always on, I never dreamed of leaving Westbury Court until the year of the fire.

I was watching television one afternoon when the fire began. I loved television then, especially the afternoon soap operas, my favorite of which was *General Hospital.* I would bolt out of my last high school class every day, pick up my youngest brother, Karl, from day care, and watch *General Hospital* with him on my lap while doing my homework during the commercials. My other two brothers, André and Kelly, would later join us in the apartment, but they preferred to watch cartoons in the back bedroom.

One afternoon while *General Hospital* and afternoon cartoons were on, a fire started in apartment 6E, across the hall. There in that apartment lived our new neighbors, an African-American mother and her two boys. We didn't know the name of the mother, or the names and ages of her boys, but I venture to guess that they were around five and ten years old.

I didn't know a fire had started until two masked, burly firemen came knocking on our door. My brothers and I rushed out into the hallway filled with smoke and were quickly escorted down to the first floor by some other firemen already on our floor. While we ran by, the door to apartment 6E had already been knocked over by the fire squad and inside was filled with bright flames and murky smoke.

All of the tenants of the building who were home at that time were crowded on the sidewalk outside. My brothers and I, it seemed, were the last to be evacuated. Clutching my brothers' hands, I wondered if I had remembered to lock our apartment door. Was there anything valuable we could have taken?

An ambulance screeched to a stop in front of the building, and the two firemen who had knocked on our door came out carrying the pliant and lifeless bodies of the two children from across the hall. Their mother jumped out of the crowd and ran toward them, screaming, "My babies — not my babies," as the children were lowered into the back of the ambulance and transferred into the arms of the emergency medical personnel. The fire was started by the two boys, after their mother had stepped out to pick up some groceries at the supermarket down the street. They had been playing with matches.

(Later my mother would tell us, "See, this is what happens to children who play with matches. Sometimes it is too late to say, 'I shouldn't have.'" My brother Kelly, who was fascinated with fire and liked to hold up a match to the middle of his palm until the light fizzled out, gave up this party trick after the fire.)

We were quiet that afternoon when both our parents came home. We were the closest to the fire in the building, and the most religious of our parents' friends saw it as a miracle that we had escaped safe and sound. When my mother asked how come I, the oldest one, hadn't heard the children scream or hadn't smelled the smoke coming from across the hall, I confessed that I had been watching *General Hospital* and was too consumed in the intricate plot.

(After the fire, my mother had us stay with a family on the second floor for a few months, after school. I felt better not having to be wholly responsible for myself and my brothers, in case something like that fire should ever happen again.)

The apartment across the hall stayed empty for a long time, and whenever I walked past it, a piece of its inner skeleton would squeak, and occasionally burnt wood that might have been hanging by a fragile singed thread would crash down and cause a domino effect of further ruptures, unleashed like those children's last cries, which I had not heard because I had been so wrapped up in the made-up drama of a world where, even though the adults' lives were often in turmoil, the children came home to the welcoming arms of waiting mommies and nannies who served them freshly baked cookies on porcelain plates and helped them to remove their mud-soaked boots, if it was raining, lest they soil the lily-white carpets. But should their boots accidentally sully the carpet, or should their bright yellow raincoats inadvertently drip on the sparkling linoleum, there would be a remedy for that as well. And if their house should ever catch fire, a smart dog or a good neighbor would rescue them just in time, and the fire trucks would come right quick because some attentive neighbor would call them.

Through the trail of voices that came up to comfort us, I heard that the children's mother would be prosecuted for negligence and child abandonment. I couldn't help but wonder, would our parents have suffered the same fate had it been my brothers and me who were killed in the fire?

When they began to repair the apartment across the hall, I would occasionally sneak out to watch the workmen. They were shelling the inside of the apartment and replacing everything from the bedroom closets to the kitchen floors. I never saw the mother of the dead boys again and never heard anything of her fate.

A year later, after the apartment was well polished and painted, two blind Haitian brothers and their sister moved in. They were all musicians and were part of a group called les Frères Parent, the Parent Brothers. Once my parents allowed my brothers and me to come home from school to our apartment, I would always listen carefully for our new tenants, so I'd be the first to know if anything went awry.

What I heard coming from the apartment soon after they moved in was music, "engagé" music, which the brothers were composing to protest against the dictatorship in Haiti, from which they had fled. The Parent Brothers and their sister, Lydie, did nothing but rehearse a cappella most days when they were not receiving religious and political leaders from Haiti and from the Haitian community in New York.

The same year after the fire, a cabdriver who lived down the hall in 6J was killed on a night shift in Manhattan; a good friend of my father's, a man who gave great Sunday afternoon parties in 6F, died of cirrhosis of the liver. One day while my brothers and I were at school and my parents were at work, someone came into our apartment through our fire escape and stole my father's expensive camera. That same year a Nigerian immigrant was shot and killed in front of the building across the street. To appease us, my mother said, "Nothing like that ever happens out of the blue. He was in a fight with someone." It was too troublesome for her to acknowledge that people could die randomly, senselessly, at Westbury Court or anywhere else.

Every day on my way back from school, I hurried past the flowers and candles piled in front of the spot where the Nigerian, whose name I didn't know, had been murdered. Still I never thought I was living in a violent place. It was an elevated castle above a clattering train tunnel, a blind alley where children from our building and the building across the street had erected a common basketball court for hot summer afternoon games, an urban yellow brick road where hopscotch squares dotted the sidewalk next to burned-out, abandoned cars. It was home.

My family and I moved out of Westbury Court three years after the fire. Every once in a while, though, the place came up in conversation, linked to either a joyous or a painful memory. One of the girls who had scalded her legs while boiling a pot of water for her bath during one of those no-heat days got married last year. After the burglar had broken into the house and taken my father's camera, my father — an amateur photography buff — never took another picture.

My family and I often reminisce about the Parent Brothers when we see them in Haitian newspapers or on television; we brag that we knew them when, before one of the brothers became a senator in Haiti and the sister, Lydie, became mayor of one of the better-off Haitian suburbs, Pétion-Ville. We never talk about the lost children.

Even now, I question what I remember about the children. Did they really die? Or did their mother simply move away with them after the fire? Maybe they were not even boys at all. Maybe they were two girls. Or one boy and one girl. Or maybe I am struggling to phase them out of my memory altogether. Not just them, but the fear that their destiny could have so easily been mine and my brothers'.

A few months ago, I asked my mother, "Do you remember the children and the fire at Westbury Court?"

Without missing a flutter of my breath, my mother replied, "Oh those children, those poor children, their poor mother. Sometimes it is too late to say, 'I shouldn't have.'"

WILLIAM H. GASS

In Defense of the Book

FROM HARPER'S MAGAZINE

WHEN BEN JONSON was a small boy, his tutor, William Camden, persuaded him of the virtue of keeping a commonplace book: pages where an ardent reader might copy down passages that especially pleased him, preserving sentences that seemed particularly apt or wise or rightly formed and that would, because they were written afresh in a new place, and in a context of favor, be better remembered, as if they were being set down at the same time in the memory of the mind. Here were more than turns of phrase that could brighten an otherwise gloomy page. Here were statements that seemed so directly truthful they might straighten a warped soul on seeing them again, inscribed, as they were, in a child's wide round trusting hand, to be read and reread like the propositions of a primer, they were so bottomed and basic.

Jonson translated or rewrote the quotes and connected them with fresh reflections until their substance seemed his own, and seamlessly woven together, too, which is how the work reads today, even though it is but a collection of loose pages taken, after his death, from the defenseless drawers of his desk. The title, extended in the manner of the period into an explanation, reads, *Timber: or, Discoveries; Made upon Men and Matter: as they have flow'd out of his daily Readings; or had their refluxe to his peculiar Notion of the Times;* and it is followed by an epigraph taken from Persius' *Satires:* "To your own breast in quest of worth repair, and blush to find how poor a stock is there." With a flourish whose elegance is lost on our illiterate era, Jonson fills his succeeding page, headed *Sylva,* with a justification of his title in learned Latin, which can be translated as follows:

(here are) the raw material of facts and thoughts, wood, as it were, so called from the multiplicity and variety of the matter contained therein. For just as we are commonly wont to call a vast number of trees growing indiscriminately "a wood," so also did the ancients call those of their books, in which were collected at random articles upon various and diverse topics, a wood, or timber trees.

My copy of *Discoveries* has its own history. It came from the library of Edwin Nungezer (Catalogue #297), whose habit it was to write his name and the date of his acquisition on the title page (2/22/26), and his name, date, and place, again, at the end of the text, when he had finished reading it (Edwin Nungezer, Ithaca, New York, October 17, 1926). He underlined and annotated the book as a professor might (mostly, with a kind of serene confidence, in ink), translating the Latin as if he knew boobs like me would follow his lead and appreciate his helpful glosses. I have already quoted one of his interlineations. My marginalia, in a more cautious pencil, are there now too, so that Ben Jonson's text, itself a pastiche drawn from the writings of others, has leaped, by the serendipitous assistance of the Bodley Head's reprint, across the years between 1641 to 1923, not surely in a single bound but by means of a few big hops nevertheless, into the professor's pasture a few years after, and then into mine in 1950, upon the sale of his estate, whereupon my name, with stiff and self-conscious formality, was also placed on its title page: William H. Gass, Cornell, '50. Even so, the book belongs to its scholarly first owner; I have only come into its possession. I hold it in my hand now, in 1999.

Another book, which is also a library but in a different way, George Saintsbury's *A History of English Prose Rhythm*, provides testimony concerning what happens when the guest is taken to a hostelry of transformatory power such as Ben Jonson's inn is:

. . . the selection, coadaptation, and application of the borrowed phrases to express Ben's views constitute a work more really original than most utterances that are guiltless of literature.

In setting down the provenance of my copy of *Discoveries* I have also done the same for the following sentence, which I put a faint marginal line beside while researching opinions about metaphor for my dissertation (now, thank God, a distant memory); it is a sentence that (having served in several capacities since) I know quite by heart, and treasure, inasmuch as it is as personal and particular to me now as its book is, having absorbed so much of myself, like the paper wrapped around fish and chips.

> What a deale of cold busines doth a man mis-spend the better part of life in! in scattering *complements,* tendring *visits,* gathering and venting *newes,* following *Feasts* and *Playes,* making a little winter-love in a darke corner.

We shall not understand what a book is, and why a book has the value many persons have, and is even less replaceable than a person, if we forget how important to it is its body, the building that has been built to hold its lines of language safely together through many adventures and a long time. Words on a screen have visual qualities, to be sure, and these darkly limn their shape, but they have no materiality, they are only shadows, and when the light shifts they'll be gone. Off the screen they do not exist as words. They do not wait to be reseen, reread; they only wait to be remade, relit. I cannot carry them beneath a tree or onto a side porch; I cannot argue in *their* margins; I cannot enjoy the memory of my dismay when, perhaps after years, I return to my treasured copy of *Treasure Island* to find the jam I inadvertently smeared there still spotting a page precisely at the place where Billy Bones chases Black Dog out of the Admiral Benbow with a volley of oaths and where his cutlass misses its mark to notch the inn's wide sign instead.

My copy, which I still possess, was of the cheapest. Published by M. A. Donohue & Co. of Chicago, it bears no date, and its coarse pages are jaundiced and brittle, yet they've outlived their manufacturer; they will outlive their reader — always comforting yet a bit sad. The pages, in fact, smell their age, their decrepitude, and the jam smear is like an ancient bruise; but as well as Marcel did by means of his madeleine, like a scar recalling its accident, I remember the pounding in my chest when the black spot was pressed into Billy Bones's palm and Blind Pew appeared on the road in a passage that I knew even then was a piece of exemplary prose.

That book and I loved each other, and I don't mean just its text: that book, which then was new, its cover slick and shiny, its paper agleam with the tossing sea and armed, as Long John Silver was, for a fight, its binding tight as the elastic of new underwear, not slack as it is now, after so many openings and closings, so many dry years; that book would be borne off to my room, where it lived through my high school miseries in a dime-store bookcase, and it would accompany me to college too, and be packed in the duffel bag I carried as a sailor. Its body may have been cheaply made by machine, and there may have been many copies of this edition printed, but the entire press run has by this time been dispersed, destroyed, the book's function reduced to its role as my old school chum, whom I see at an occasional reunion, along with editions of Malory and Mann, Nietzsche and Schopenhauer, Hardy and Spengler, gloomy friends of my gloomy youth. Each copy went forth into bookstores to seek a purchaser it would make fortunate, and each has had its history of success or failure since, years of standing among rarity and leather, say, when suddenly, after a week of weeping that floods the library, it finds itself in some secondhand ghetto, dumped for a pittance by customarily callous heirs into a crowd of those said, like cars, to have been "previously owned."

We all love the "previously owned." We rescue them like orphans from their Dickensian dismay. I first hold the volume upside down and give its fanned-out pages a good ruffle, as if I were shaking fruit from a tree: out will fall toothpicks and hairpins, calling cards and bits of scrap paper, the well-pressed envelope for a stick of Doublemint gum, a carefully folded obituary of the book's author, the newsprint having acidulously shadowed its containing pages, or, now and then, a message, interred in the text, as I had flutter from a volume once owned by Arthur Holly Compton (and sold to me by the library of his own university). It was the rough draft of a telegram to the U.S. high commissioner in charge of our occupation troops in Germany requesting the immediate dispatch of Werner Heisenberg to the United States.

Should we put these feelings for the object and its vicissitudes down to simple sentimental nostalgia? To our commonly assumed resistance to change? I think not; but even as a stimulus for reminiscence, a treasured book is more important than a dance card, or the photo that freezes you in midteeter at the edge of the Grand Canyon, because such a book can be a significant event in the history of your reading, and your reading (provided *you* are significant) should be an essential segment of your character and your life. Unlike the love we've made or meals we've eaten, books congregate to form a record around us of what they've fed our stomachs or our brains. These are not a hunter's trophies but the living animals themselves.

In the ideal logotopia, every person would possess his own library and add at least weekly if not daily to it. The walls of each home would seem made of books; wherever one looked one would only see spines; because every real book (as opposed to dictionaries, almanacs, and other compilations) is a mind, an imagination, a consciousness. Together they compose a civilization, or even several. Utopias, however, have the bad habit of hiding in their hearts those schemes for success, those requirements of power, rules concerning conduct, which someone will one day have to carry forward, employ and enforce, in order to achieve them, and afterward, to maintain the continued purity of their Being. Books have taught me what true dominion, what right rule, is: it is like the freely given assent and labor of the reader who will dream the dreams of the deserving page and expect no more fee than the reward of its words.

A few of us are fortunate enough to live in Logotopia, to own our own library, but for many this is not possible, and for them we need a free and open public institution with a balanced collection of books that it cares for and loans, with stacks where a visitor may wander, browse, and make discoveries; such an institution empowers its public as few do. In fact, it has no rival, for the books in the public library are the books that may take temporary residence in yours or mine. We share their wealth the way we share the space of a public park. And the benefits include the education of the body politic, an education upon which the success of democracy depends, and one that is largely missing from the thrill-seeking, gossip-mongering, and mindless masses who have been content to place their governing, as well as their values, faiths, and future plans, in the hands of the crudest commercial interests. The myths that moved us to worship in ways preferred and planned by the Church, or to feel about things in a manner that served the interests of the State, have less power over our souls now than the latest sale of shoes, which promise, through the glory of their names, the pleasures of sex and health and social rank, and give new meaning to the old expression "leap of faith."

My high school had no library worthy of the name "book," so I would walk about a mile downtown to the public one to borrow, in almost every case, a new world. That's what a library does for its patrons. It extends the self. It is pure empowerment. I would gather my three or four choices, after deliberations governed by ignorant conjecture, and then, before leaving, I would sit at one of the long wide tables we associate with the institution now and read a page or two farther than I had while standing in the stacks. I scorned the books deemed appropriate for my age and selected only those I wouldn't understand. Reading what I didn't understand was, for one blissful period of my life, the source of a profound if perverse pleasure. I also liked to look at the card pasted in the back of the book to record previous borrowings — a card that is, like so much other information, there no longer or discreetly incomplete. It gave me a good deal of satisfaction to be taking home some rarely read, symbolically dusty, arcane tome. I checked out both my books and my pride at the same desk. See, O world, what I am reading and be amazed: Joyce, Wells, Carlyle. Well, Wells I could understand. That, I would realize later, was what was the matter with him.

And the Saturday that *Ulysses* was denied me because my ears were too young to hear its honesty was a large red-letter day, burned upon my symbolic bosom wherever it was then kept, for on that day I learned what righteous indignation was; I realized what libraries were really for, just in the moment that my own was failing its function.

Public libraries have succumbed to the same pressures that have overwhelmed the basic cultural functions of museums and universities, aims that should remain what they were, not because the old ways are always better but because in this case they were the right ones: the sustaining of standards, the preservation of quality, the conservation of literacy's history, the education of the heart, eye, and mind. Now libraries devote far too much of their restricted space, and their limited budget, to public amusement. It is a fact of philistine life that amusement is where the money is.

Universities attract students by promising them, on behalf of their parents, a happy present and a comfortable future, and these intentions are passed along through the system like salmonella until budgets are cut, research requirements are skimped, and the fundamental formula for academic excellence is ignored if not forgotten. That formula is: a great library will attract a great faculty, and a great faculty will lure good students to its log; good students will go forth and win renown, endowments will increase, and so will the quality of the football team, until original aims are lost sight of, academic efforts slacken, the library stands neglected, the finer faculty slip away, good students no longer seek such an environment, and the team gets even better.

The sciences, it is alleged, no longer use books; neither do the professions, since what everyone needs is data, data day and night, because data, like drugs, soothe the senses and encourage us to think we are, when at the peak of their heap, on top of the world. Of course, libraries contain books, and books contain information, but information has always been of minor importance, except to minor minds. What matters is how the information is arranged, how it is understood, and to what uses it is put. In short, what matters is the book the data're in. I just employed the expression "It is a fact of philistine life . . ." That is exactly what the philistine would like the library to retrieve for it. Just the facts, ma'am. Because facts can be drawn from the jaws of some system like teeth; because facts are goods like shoes and shirts and, well, books. This week the library is having a closeout sale on facts about deserts. Get yours now. Gobi will be gone soon, the Sahara to follow.

Frequently, one comes across comparisons of the electronic revolution with that of writing and printing, and these are usually accompanied by warnings to those suspicious of technology that objections to these forward marches are both fuddy-duddy and futile. But Plato's worries that writing would not reveal the writer the way the soul of a speaker was exposed; that spontaneity would be compromised; that words would be stolen (as Phaedrus is about to steal them in that profound, beautifully written dialogue), and words would be put in other mouths than those of their authors; that writing does not hear its reader's response; that lying, hypocrisy, false borrowing, ghostwriting, would increase so that the hollow heads of state would echo with hired words; and that, oddly, the advantages and powers of the book would give power and advantage to the rich, who would learn to read and would have the funds to acquire and keep such precious volumes safe: these fears were overwhelmingly realized.

The advent of printing was opposed (as writing was) for a number of mean and self-serving reasons, but the fear that it would lead to the making of a million half-baked brains, and cause the illicit turning of a multitude of untrained heads, as a consequence of the unhindered spread of nonsense was a fear that was also well founded. The boast that the placement of books in many hands would finally overthrow superstition was not entirely a hollow hope, however. The gift gave a million minds a chance at independence.

It was the invention of photography, I remember, that was supposed to run painters out of business. What it did, of course, was make artists out of them, not grandiose or sentimental describers. And the pixelation of pictures has rendered their always dubious veracity as unbelievable as any other shill for a system. If blessings are mixed, so are calamities. I note also that although the horse-drawn coach or wagon nowadays carries rubes in a circle around Central Park, there are more horses alive and well in the world than there ever were.

So will there be books. And if readers shut their minds down the better to stare at pictures that rarely explain themselves; and if readers abandon reading to swivel-hip their way through the inter-bunk, picking up scraps of juicy data here and there and rambling on the e-mail in that new fashion of grammatical decay, the result will be to make real readers, then chief among the last who are left with an ability to reason, rulers. Books made the rich richer. Books will make the smart smarter.

The elevator at first seemed merely helpful, and the high-rise splendid against the night sky — what you could see of it. Recordings allow us to hear a few elevating strains from the "Ode to Joy" several times a day, the genius long ago beaten out of it. And those miracles of modern electronics that have allowed us to communicate quickly, easily, cheaply, gracelessly with every part of the world permit us to do so in private and in every remove from face to face. Air travel is comfortable, affordable, and swift (right?) and enables us to ignore geography, just as we ignore climate, because we have HVAC and, in addition, can purchase terrible tomatoes any season of the year from stores that are open all night.

Books in libraries, however awful some of them assuredly are, have been screened by editors who have a stake in their quality and their success. Once on shelves, they may receive from readers the neglect they deserve. But at the end of all those digital delivery channels thrives a multitude of pips whose continuous squeaking has created static both loud and distressing. Amid the sound of a million popoffs, how shall we hear and identify a good thought when it pops *out*?

The library is meant to satisfy the curiosity of the curious, offer to stuff students with facts, provide a place for the lonely where they may enjoy the companionship and warmth of the word. It is supposed to supply handbooks for the handy, novels for insomniacs, scholarship for the scholarly, and make available works of literature to those individuals they will eventually haunt so successfully; these readers, in self-defense, will bring them finally to life.

More important than any of these traditional things, I think, is the environment of books the library puts its visitors in and the opportunity for discovery that open stacks make possible. When I wish to look up a word — "golliwogg," which I've encountered spelled with two *g*'s — or when I wish to plenish my mind with some information, say, about the ill-fated library at Alexandria, why don't I simply hit the right keys on my machine, where both a dictionary and an encyclopedia are imprisoned? Well, I might, if the spelling of "golliwog" were all I wished to know, if researches, however large or small, were not great pleasures in themselves, full of serendipity; for I have rarely paged through one of my dictionaries (a decent household will have a dozen) without my eye lighting, along the way, on words more beautiful than a found fall leaf, on definitions odder than any uncle, on grotesques such as "gonadotropin-releasing hormone" or, barely above it — what? — "gombeen," which turns out to be Irish for "usury." I wonder if Ezra Pound knew that.

Similarly, when I walk through the library stacks in search of a number I have copied from the card catalogue, my eyes are not watching my feet or aimlessly airing themselves; they are intently shelf-shopping, running along all those intriguing spines, all those lovely shapes and colors and sizes. That is how one day I stopped before a thick yellow-backed book that gave its name in pale blue letters: *The Sot-Weed Factor.* Although published by Doubleday, so there was probably nothing of value in it, I still pulled the book from its place. What did the title mean? I read the first page, as is my habit. Page 1 and page 99 are my test spots. Then I bore it home, neglecting to retrieve the book for which I had begun my search. Instead, for two days, in a trance of delight and admiration, I read John Barth's novel. That is why I stroll through the encyclopedia, why I browse the shelves.

One does not go to a library once, look around, and leave as if having seen it. Libraries are not monuments or sights or notable piles: churches by Wren, villas by Palladio. Libraries, which acquire the books we cannot afford, retain the many of which we are ignorant, the spate of the new and the detritus of ancient life; libraries, which preserve what we prize and would adore, which harbor the neglected until their time to set forth again is marked, restoring the worn and ignoring fashion and repulsing prejudice. Libraries are for life, centers to which we are recycled, as recursive as reading itself.

If I am speaking to you on the phone, watching your tinted shadows cross the screen, downloading your message from my machine, I am in indirect inspection, in converse, with you; but when I read the book you've written, you are as absent as last year, distant as Caesar's reign. Before my eyes, asking for my comprehension, where I stand in the stacks or sit in the reading room, are your thoughts and feelings, hopes and fears, set down in sentences and paragraphs and pages . . . but in words not yours, meanings not mine, rather words and meanings that are the world's.

Yes, we call it recursive, the act of reading, of looping the loop, of continually returning to an earlier group of words, behaving like Penelope by moving our mind back and forth, forth and back, reweaving what's unwoven, undoing what's been done; and language, which regularly returns us to its origin, which starts us off again on the same journey, older, altered, Columbus one more time but better prepared each later voyage, knowing a bit more, ready for more, equal to a greater range of tasks, calmer, confident. After all, we've come this way before, have habits that help and a favoring wind; language like that is the language that takes us inside, inside the sentence — inside — inside the mind — inside — inside where meanings meet and are modified, reviewed, and revised, where no perception, no need, no feeling or thought, need be scanted or shunted aside.

*

I read around in this reprinted book I've rescued until I stumble on — I discover — my sentence, my marvel, my new found land.

> What a deale of cold busines doth a man mis-spend the better part of life in! in scattering *complements,* tendring *visits,* gathering and venting *newes,* following *Feasts* and *Playes,* making a little winter-love in a darke corner.

This sentence is a unit of human consciousness. It disposes its elements like the bits and pieces of a collage, and even if a number of artists were given the same materials: say, a length of ribbon, empty manila folder, cellophane wrapping, sheet of blue paper, postage stamp, shocking-pink crayon; or a number of writers were allowed a few identical words and asked to form a phrase — with "was," for instance, out of "that," or "fair," or "then," and "all" — they'd not arrange them in the same way, make the same object, or invariably ask, in some wonder, "then was all that fair?" as if a point were being made in a debate. Among them, only James Joyce would write of paradise, in *Finnegans Wake,* "then all that was, was fair."

In this process of constituting a unit of human perception, thought, and feeling, which will pass like every other phase of consciousness into others — one hopes — still more integrated and interesting, nothing is more frequently overlooked or more vital to language than its pace and phrasing: factors, if this were ballet, we would never neglect, because we are well aware how the body of the dancer comes to a periodic point of poise before beginning another figure; and how the central movement of the torso is graced and amplified by the comportment of the arms, the tilt of the head and smile of the eyes; and how the diagram of one gesture is made to flow into another; and how the dancer must land from a leap, however wide or high, as if a winged seed; and how the energy of movement is controlled by the ease of its execution within the beat and mood and color of the music until we see one unified flow of expression. So too must the language keep its feet and move with grace, disclosing one face first before allowing another, reserving certain signals until the end, when they will reverberate through the sentence like a shout down a street, and the vowels will open and close like held hands, and the consonants will moan like maybe someone experiencing pleasure, and the reader will speed along a climbing clause, or sigh into a periodic stop full of satisfaction at this ultimate release of meaning: a little winter-love in a dark corner.

Every day, from the library, books are borrowed and taken away like tubs of chicken to be consumed, though many are also devoured on the premises, in the reading room, where traditionally the librarian, wearing her clichés, shushes an already silent multitude and glares at the offending air. Yet there, or in someone's rented room, or even by a sunny pool — who can predict the places where the encounter will occur? — the discovery will be made. And a finger will find the place and mark it before the book's covers come closed; or its reader will rise and bear her prize out of the library into the kitchen, back to her dorm room, or, along with flowers and candy, to a bedside, in a tote bag onto the beach; or perhaps a homeless scruffy, who has been huddling near a radiator, will leave the volume behind him when he finally goes, as if what his book said had no hold on his heart, because he cannot afford a card. Yet, like Columbus first espying land, each will have discovered what he or she cares about, will know at last what it is to love — a commonplace occurrence — for in the library, such epiphanies, such enrichments of mind and changes of heart, are the stuff of every day.

MARY GORDON

Rome: The Visible City

FROM SALMAGUNDI

My first vision of Rome was an image of St. Peter's seen through the lens of something called a View-Master, which looked a bit like a camera, a bit like binoculars, a bit like a diving mask. It was brown plastic with two cloudy plastic lenses in the front and a slit in the top into which was put a disk with pie-shaped slices of film separated from one another by white cardboard. You looked into the back of the View-Master and saw an image in three dimensions. Then you flicked a lever on the side and the image changed. I owned four series of disks. One was called "California, Land of Sunshine." One was called simply "Disneyland." The other two, befitting my family's religious seriousness, were "The Passion Plays of Oberammergau" and "The Vatican."

Frozen, utterly complete in their unnaturalness, the images I saw seemed more possessed of information than what the eye could take in or the mind contain. Since the vision was entirely private, what was conveyed had the crucial significance of a whispered conversation, the life-or-death quality of an encoded message from a spymaster to a spy. The images seemed embedded in an unbreakable eternal silence; no movement would stir the air. It wasn't clear to me whether the figures I beheld were alive or dead, had ever been alive, or were made of wax. Jesus carrying his cross, crowned with thorns, kneeling in agony in the Garden of Olives, the pope in his tiered, elaborate biretta, raising his hand in blessing, the orange growers on the ladders in their groves — were these actors, or dolls, or the humans they claimed to be?

With the contraption held against my eyes, I was plunged into an atmosphere of equivocal artificiality. Why did I love it so? Did I feel, looking at their false dimensionality, their vividness which could not have come from life, that I was entering into ultimate danger, where I too could be rendered unalive or static, or ultimate safety, where all the dangers of the world could be, at the flick of a lever, neutralized into paralysis, the joke potency of dream?

I loved the silence of those images, their freedom, not only from noise but from the harsh demands of time. Because nothing was alive, nothing would change. Having partaken so entirely of death, they were entirely free of death's surprises. But I wasn't, of course, thinking of death when I put the mask up to my eyes. If you asked me what I liked, I would have said, "The colors."

When I inserted the disk called "The Vatican," the pale face of the pope emerged from a matte background of rose red. His hive-shaped papal hat, embroidered gold and white, dwarfed his refined skull. His ring seemed, in the same way, too big for his fingers. His gaze met nothing, the blessing indicated by his raised hand could fall on no living head. In the next frame, St. Peter's, looking thousands of times more important than the Capitol, pressed itself, gray and essential, against a silver sky where no birds flew. On the ground, ant-sized priests in birettas walked, holding breviaries. There must have been a picture of the Sistine Chapel, but I don't remember it. Only the white face of the pope, his rimless spectacles, the gray dome of St. Peter's, the gray expanse of the square where priests in black read their black books.

And they would never change. Rules would come from these men, from the huge dome, from the gold throne on which the pope sat with his permanently upraised finger. Words would be spoken that were a part of universal truth. *Ex cathedra.* Words removed from the possibility of emendation and of argument. Words rising up from silence, which I, in my privileged position as a Catholic, had only to obey.

I did not imagine that the pope, the cardinals, or the priests spoke to each other, or if they ever spoke, it was in anything but Latin. Not for them the colorful, playful, songlike, or outraged Italian of my downstairs neighbors, from whose apartment the smell of strong coffee, roasting nuts, simmering sauces would waft through our floors. When I thought of Rome, I did not think of Italy, nor did I think of it as a place where anyone like myself might go. My being there was of no importance to my thoughts about the place. I did not contemplate a contemporary city resembling New York, any more than I had images of empire. Rome was the Church, the Vatican. The Vatican had nothing to do with a living people, a living city. Like the images I looked through, it was frozen. The Eternal City. But I knew it was its own country, a state unto itself, outside of ordinary law. At the center of the Vatican, clothed in white, entirely self-contained, his rimless glasses glinting, his cultivated hands raised in blessing, was the pope. Pius XII.

I believed that beneath the place where the pope's throne was fixed lay the bodies of the early Christian martyrs in their catacombs. So, soon after the word "Rome" came to my mind, it was followed by the name of the pope, and then the names of the Christian martyrs: Agnes, Cecilia, Anastasia, Perpetua, Agatha, Lucy.

I was quite afraid of being martyred. Or rather, I was afraid of being given the test (I would have said then the privilege) of martyrdom and failing. In the years I speak of — 1953–59, the years between my first memories and the death of Pius XII — martyrs were on our minds again because we believed a new crop of them was being, as we spoke, raised up. These were martyrs to communism, and I feared a Russian soldier holding a gun to my throat as I imagined the virgin martyrs feared the Roman soldiers with their helmets and sinewy naked legs and swords. Would I have the strength, as they had, to withstand?

Many of the Roman martyrs whom I fixed on were women. And often, in their case, though not in the case of the males, the word "martyr" was preceded by the word "virgin." It would be many years before I would understand the literal meaning of the word "virgin," so innocent was I of the details of sex. For a long time, I thought the word was a synonym for "unmarried."

Each day at mass we said their names. Each met her death in Rome: a sword through her breast, beheaded, her eyes plucked out, devoured by lions. I saw, without knowing it, the imperial light of Rome in them; for they were wealthy Roman women, many of them, and when I imagined them, they stood in high rooms, empty of furniture except for one chair and a couch for their reclining. The young women raised their hands in supplication or in blessing. Or they stood, hands at their sides, and let the lions rush at them. If they were rushed at by lions, they must have been in the Coliseum, but I didn't see the Coliseum walls, only the open ground where women stood, surrounded by invisible cheering crowds. They shed their blood under a cloudless sky, so bright after their underground life, the life of the catacombs, the same light where the Jewish children hid during the war, the same light in which I lived in terror of being forced to hide.

The virgin martyrs wore sandals, they walked on marble floors, they ate olives and flat bread. They suffered torments and violations. They stood in silver light or were suffused in darkness. They gave everything. I saw their pictures in *The Lives of the Saints* or on the holy cards I was given as rewards or prizes. They carried their symbols, a palm, a lamb, a plate holding eyes. They both terrified me and caused me shame, because my shallow spirit prayed to be spared their fate and I was told I ought to be praying for the opposite.

From the ground drenched by their shed blood sprang up the dome of St. Peter's, different from any building on the surface of the earth.

My first hint that there was a city that existed at the same time as my own life came to me from the very first film I was taken to see: *Three Coins in the Fountain.* Why my parents chose this as my first film, rather than some wholesome children's picture, something by Disney, something about animals or fairy-tale creatures, is a question I can't answer.

Three Coins in the Fountain was not an entirely appropriate film to take a five-year-old to see. It was about three American women — now we would say women, but it is more faithful to the spirit of the film to say it was about three American girls. The youngest is a typical midwestern naif. The middle one is voluptuous and good-natured and down-to-earth. She's going home, telling her employers, for no reason that makes any possible narrative sense, that she's about to be married. She's really going home because she believes it's impossible for an American girl to find a husband in Rome.

The third, older and wiser. At the beginning of the film she has been, for fifteen years, the indispensable secretary of a famous American writer, played by Clifton Webb. She is secretly in love with him, as the voluptuous one is secretly in love with an Italian colleague, who is secretly in love with *her.* But neither of them can reveal their love because of the company rule against employee dating. Maggie McNamara is secretly in love with an Italian prince, played by that famous Italian, Louis Jourdan.

All three girls end up in the arms of the men they love at the fountain of Trevi. What did I take away from this film, one of the first in Technicolor? Images of great buildings, of fountains and flowers, of people singing, of women in beautiful dresses with tight waists and full skirts, wearing high heels and small hats, or straw hats and sandals laced halfway up the calf. Never mind: it was style and good fortune that I understood, and the idea that love came to the ardent, the audacious, and the patient, to make everyone's happiness come about, against a background of delightfully splashing water wetting the marble skins of indolent, reclining gods.

Against the same background, but more elegant and more heartbreaking, stood Audrey Hepburn in *Roman Holiday.* I never saw it in a theater, but I watched it at least once a year on *The Late Show,* weeping with my mother or one of my girlfriends. From this film, I learn that Rome is the place that allows you a respite from good behavior, a day off from duty, that you can get your hair cut and eat a *gelato* and ride on a Vespa and drink champagne at an outdoor café which I do not know is on Piazza del Popolo, only that it seems like a place where I can be happy, with a carefreeness open to me nowhere else. Watching Audrey Hepburn and Gregory Peck, I believe that you can kiss and be kissed, offering everything, but only temporarily. Watching this movie, I become a princess, a pretty girl, a girl who gives up love for responsibility, but not yet. It is the *not yet* that Rome offers me; the *not yet* that I dream of traveling to.

But there is another side of Rome, a darker side that my friends and I discovered in 1965, when we sneaked into the city and found the Thalia (a theater on 96th and Broadway that showed old movies), to see a film we had been expressly forbidden to see, a film that had been on the Legion of Decency's "condemned" list for at least five years. This was the Rome of sin and decadence. *La Dolce Vita,* opening, even, with a joke against the Church, the pope. A statue of Jesus hangs from a helicopter like Fay Wray from King Kong's hand. The bathing beauties on the roof ask, in their bikinis, where Jesus is going. Pantomiming from a helicopter, Marcello Mastroianni tells them he is going to the pope.

So it is possible to make fun of the Church, the pope, and not be struck down. Only placed on the "condemned" list, which by 1965 even some priests are ignoring. They are writing articles, for which other priests attack them, talking about the theme of redemption in *La Dolce Vita.* But my friends and I do not see redemption: we see elegance, and sophistication. We are trying to imagine ourselves looking like Anouk Aimée in a little black dress. We are wondering how she can drive at night in sunglasses. We are afraid of what we would say to Marcello Mastroianni; we wonder if, with us, he would no longer be bored. We imagine ourselves talking about how bored we are over drinks at cafés on the Via Veneto, but we cannot imagine how anyone could be bored in such a place. With a terrible inadequacy, which we imagine can be cured only by European travel, we contemplate replacing an ideal of goodness with one of knowingness, a dream of being beloved with a dream of sophistication. We yearn for the possibility of never being surprised, therefore, never being made to look foolish. We think this might happen to us if we ride in Alfa Romeo convertibles and have so much sex that it no longer seems extraordinary. And then, perhaps, like the world-weary partygoers, we will be truly and dependably wise.

The first time I traveled to Europe, I didn't visit Rome. It was 1971. I was twenty-two: I had a knapsack on my back. It had taken me two years to save the five hundred dollars that would allow me to stay in Europe for ten weeks. I went to Florence, where I fell in love with a vacuum cleaner salesman named Giuseppe, whom I met on the Piazza Michelangelo. *Ay-lay-tro-loo* was the way he pronounced the product that he sold, the famous Electrolux. "Electrolux," I would say, trying to coach him in the single bed of his *pensione,* in the double bed of his brother's house, where we would go on Sundays while they picnicked in the country. But he couldn't pronounce that final *x,* any more than I could remember to make the number of my Italian verbs agree with my Italian subjects. I lived with him for a month instead of going to Rome.

So I went to Rome for the first time five years later, with my mother and my first husband, miserably married. The trip had nothing to do with anything I had seen in the movies; it had much more to do with martyrdom. My mother and my husband didn't like each other, and it was her first time in a non–English-speaking country. I was the only one with any Italian. My mother only wanted to see the pope; my husband, naturally, wanted to see the ancient sites and eat in restaurants. I was always on the verge of tears.

Because of my mother, I learned the Italian word for wheelchair, *sedia a rotelle,* and, heart in my mouth, contemplated pushing her across the pathological Roman streets. But she didn't like being on the street. She was panicked by the traffic, by the foreign words buzzing around her, uttered by the quick-moving pedestrians. She wouldn't leave her room in the *pensione* found for her by a priest she knew in New York. Or no, that's not precisely true; we left twice. Once, to visit a priest who was a friend of the priest who had found her her *pensione* in his monastery off the Appian Way. We sat with this priest, a quiet man of Pittsburgh, and drank tea. We left after half an hour. The next day we went to a papal mass at St. Peter's, and because she was in a wheelchair, my mother was shown to a spot near the altar. The pope blessed her as he walked out. All she could say afterward, over and over, like a trauma victim, or one who has seen the face of God and lived, was "He smelled like raisins. He smelled just like raisins."

I spent my days playing cards with my mother on the bed in her room in the *pensione.* The ceilings were ornamented and extravagant, like the ceilings in the Vatican; I had a view of the Roman roofs. But these were my only sights. Because my mother was crippled, the owners and the chambermaids of the *pensione* were indulgent and understanding and kind. They allowed her to take all her meals in her room. I left her only to buy rolls, cheese, and tomatoes; at night, my husband and I, in the room next to hers, fought in dry, tight whispers. After he fell asleep, I wept.

The first time I went to Rome by myself it was to interview Natalia Ginzburg, an Italian writer whom I much admired and who

I believed was underappreciated by American audiences. I came to Ginzburg not through the sacred images of my childhood or the overlarge ones of films but through reading. I was entirely grown up by the time that I read about Rome, before I realized that Rome had had a bad nineteenth century and, more important, a Second World War, which I had thought of as happening only in Germany and France.

It must have been the example of Henry James and his characters that led me to pursue Ginzburg in the way I did. I approached Ginzburg via Moravia and Pavese, but in my thoughts about her there was a touch of appetite for the complicated unhappiness of *La Dolce Vita.* Like any Jamesian innocent, I came reverent, in awe of the distinguished older woman who had lost her husband in a Fascist prison, who had lived underground with her children, who had been the only woman not married to a successful man among the band of postwar Italian writers, who had lost another husband and had a brain-damaged child. I was visiting European suffering; I would arrive, a pilgrim, on my knees.

Months ahead of time, I had written to make an appointment to interview her. She had written back to confirm the date. When I arrived, jet-lagged but full of excitement, having flown across the ocean precisely to see her, she said she was too busy. She was a member of Parliament and that day she was "in camera." I was terribly disappointed. I called the friend of an English friend, a woman who had known Ginzburg for years. I didn't know that this is the only way things are done in Italy: through some kind of private familial or quasi-familial arrangement, at least an inside connection. And so the friend of my friend spoke to Ginzburg, who agreed to see me in four days. I was in Rome, alone, with nothing to do but explore the city.

It was one of those periods of borderless nourishing solitude. I had no expectations. I had only one plan: to stay away from the Vatican. The dome of St. Peter's seemed to me a bully presence, and the overornamented huge interior was a monument not to the spirit but to the pomp and force of the Church of Rome — the part of Catholicism I kept trying to forget. I did the simplest thing I could think of, something unlike myself. I permitted myself to wander the streets, allowing my eyes to fall and rest on whatever pleased them. I could only allow myself to do this alone, because Rome is a very easy city to get lost in, and when I am lost with other people, most particularly a man, I feel simultaneously enraged that they have been so irresponsible as to get us lost and ashamed with a shame that is literally paralyzing. I stand still in the middle of a street and cannot move, because no place seems as if it wouldn't be tainted by the presence of a person who has allowed herself (and others with her) to get lost.

But when I'm alone, I really don't mind getting lost, because there's no one to be ashamed in front of. I can find my own debility amusing, even interesting, leading to some hidden good fortune I could not have planned, or, if nothing else, to some future funny stories. And at first I didn't get lost; I was very proud of myself for being able, with no wrong turnings, to get from Campo dei Fiori to Piazza Navona.

It was January, but the sun blazed and it was warm enough to eat outdoors. The piazza was still tarted up for Christmas. The shops and restaurants were festooned with tinsel. It was the day before the Feast of the Kings, and everyone was out for the *passeggiata.* Someone was playing "I Get Ideas" on an accordion. An antique carousel, set up for children to ride on, spun, empty, in the center of the square. Its pastel horses with floral bridles brought to mind Nellie Melba, Jenny Lind. Chinese lanterns that ought to have looked cheap but didn't swung in the breeze. Six men dressed as medieval peasants did some sort of traditional dance, playing wooden pipes, wearing shoes made of straw that laced up their calves, like the girls in *Three Coins in the Fountain.* A beggar woman carried a sign around her neck reading "I am a poor grandmother." How had this happened in Italy, this failure of family? Even in its failure, though, it was the family that was invoked. The Bernini statues gestured to a sky with a few thick clouds through which the sun shot down in slanted rays: the source of the Baroque.

I allowed myself simply to enjoy everything I saw and smelled and heard and tasted, allowed myself to make mistakes in grammar, to apologize and to go on. Why not? There was, on the Roman streets, not one suggestion of punishment or shame. If there were shadows, my eyes did not fall on them; the narrow streets held no dangers for me, only curiosities — an old dish in a shop window, a bakery, a shoemaker. The sun warmed the white or yellow stones, enlivened the water in the fountains. The blare of the horns was absorbed in sunlight, the shouts on the streets would lead to no recriminations. If this city had been the home of persecutions, that was long ago, and those people had been replaced by a new race that was devoted not to the conquest of empire but to "la bella figura": the ideal that things should look good, that things should be seen and therefore be pleasing to the eye. This was not a people of helmets and swords, constructors of aqueducts and systems of law; allowances would be made on these streets by the people who lived on them. That meant allowances would be made for me.

My humility about my own weak sense of direction returned to me when I tried to find the Church of Santa Maria in Trastevere. I kept asking directions, but I am bad at following directions, particularly in Italian, and once across the Tiber, wherever I turned, I seemed to be walking toward St. Peter's Square.

Finally I gave in and walked into the square. It was comparatively empty, except for a huge crowd of Asian nuns in short gray coats and white veils. A Swiss Guard looked silly in glasses. Silly, too, perched high up on a platform at the top of the staircase was a Christmas tree, which I reckoned must be bigger than the one in Rockefeller Center. But whereas the New York tree gave me a sense that all was right with the world, this one looked apologetic, a false gesture made inexpertly — a bow toward the domestic — and the domestic and the inexpert are exactly what it is the greatness of St. Peter's not to touch.

I entered the basilica thinking of Ezra Pound's idea of the perfect image — "that the child should walk at peace in the Basilica, the light there almost solid." But nothing merely narrative could be set here, except perhaps the impersonal narrative of unquestioned power. And a child, if we are not brutes, must be seen as always narrative and always personal. So Pound's image, in seeming impossible, grew newly intriguing to me. Standing in the Basilica where what he spoke of would not have happened, the image became something else I could not believe in. I passed by the *Pietà*, which like the *Mona Lisa* can no longer properly be looked at. It reminds me only of copies of itself, and of the 1964 World's Fair, where I went with my girlfriends and tried to meet boys.

I passed statues of popes who looked like ancient Romans and saints who looked like the Statue of Liberty. I was moved by Bernini's *Holy Spirit,* but not nearly so much as I was by his *Saint Theresa,* which says something to me about the life of the spirit, which this place does not, any more than the Teddy Roosevelt Rotunda in the Museum of Natural History says something to me about nature. Both were about mastery; both created in me a desire for hopeless rebellion, in which I knew I'd be crushed.

Only downstairs in St. Peter's by the tombs of the popes, particularly the one of Pope John XXIII, did I find the spirit of devotion missing for me in the grand basilica. There was a bouquet of fresh flowers in front of Pope John's tomb, and I knelt there, feeling quieter than I had since I got to Rome. Perhaps it was that quiet, or the flexible spirit of Pope John, that allowed me to find my way to the Church of Santa Cecilia. She was one of the martyrs of my childhood, but this church erased the terror of her fate.

Although it commemorated the vicious beheading of an innocent and musical matron, it did not call to mind blood or hacking swords: the memorial was not accomplished by mimesis. In the courtyard there was a Roman urn filled with dark pink roses, a fountain, a place to sit, to rest, to look at the eighteenth-century facade, the twelfth-century portico, the Roman columns. Here in front of me was all of history, and nothing was dangerous. There was no compulsion. Sit, rest, listen to the splash of water, let your eye fall on the color of the roses. Inside the church, the statue of Saint Cecilia recalled not her beheading but her body having been found intact hundreds of years later, a beautiful woman in a golden gown. The reclining statue of her, by the seventeenth-century sculptor Maderno, reminded me of the statue on 106th Street and Broadway. A memorial to those who went down with the *Titanic.*

Cecilia is a prosperous, slumbering matron, overtaken — but gracefully rather than brutally — by a tragic fate. Her face is invisible; it is turned down on the marble slab on which she rests, but her body is slanted toward us. The veil, or turban, that wraps her head spreads out languorously from her body, which we cannot believe dead, only sleeping. In death, she is not only peaceful but fashionable. There is nothing to be feared.

And if that night, when I walked alone behind the Pantheon, in the Piazza Farnese, on the Via Giulia, with its churches whose facades sport embedded stone skulls, I could imagine the crushing hoof of imperial or ecclesiastical power, I knew there would be nothing personal in the force that might destroy whatever came in its path. It would annihilate; but it would not humiliate. The terror would be only physical, not moral, not spiritual. There would be no shame.

In the morning, the streets would be cleaned; water would splash, and a block from the Piazza Farnese, the Via Giulia, in the Campo dei Fiori, fruits and cheese would be once again beautifully for sale. Light, color, movement, would once more do their work. The city, I discovered, was nothing like what I had seen in the View-Master. The death that was invoked in this city was a drama, like Caravaggio's crucifixion of Saint Peter or execution of Saint Matthew. It was not the terrifying end of emotion; not an eternal freeze frame. The death that Rome insists we not forget is simply an afterthought, the last chapter of a story which is, after all, called life. The life of Bernini's figures, whose dramatic gestures are from the same lexicon as Caravaggio's: the lexicon of endless movement, endless change. This is not a lesson that I learned as a child, when I imagined Rome, alone in my room, with my solitary visions; it was a lesson I knew I would have to relearn each time I came back (and I vowed that I would come back again and again), and could relearn, as long as I kept my back turned on the Vatican.

After four days of wandering and musing, it was time to meet with Natalia Ginzburg. She was not warm, she was *stretta,* severe, leaning toward dry, as the word *stretta* suggests; she was impressed by my devotion, but she was impatient with my questions about her as a woman writer. She wanted to talk about politics, Italian politics, which I knew nothing about. Occasionally I could hear a terrible guttural cry from upstairs, and then a nurse would run upstairs and the cries were silenced. Ginzburg said nothing about this and I pretended not to notice, understanding that it was the damaged daughter.

She agreed, at my Italian friend's invitation, to have dinner with me the next evening. We had a moment of communication when we both recalled being teenage girls reading the Russian novelists and feeling that we had finally learned the truth and that because of this, the world would open before us. I began dreaming: I would come back again and again. She would ask me to stay in her huge apartment in Vecchia Roma. She would say, "You are my heir, my daughter." She would say, "I didn't expect so much from an American."

None of this happened. Instead, like a Jamesian character, I was made to do something I didn't want to do, something against my values, something I knew was wrong. She asked that I show her what I was going to write before I published it. This was entirely unprofessional and I should have answered coolly, *"Mi dispiace, ma non è possibile."*

But how could I? She was the real thing, the real European writer who had suffered in the war. Suffered as no American, no one of my generation had. How could I say no to my literary mother? I'd had a hard enough time saying no to my real mother. Fifteen years earlier, I hadn't even been able to get her out of her *pensione* for a meal. I had to bring her cheese and rolls and eat with her on the bed while my husband toured the streets of Rome alone.

Ginzburg hated what I wrote. I never could find out why, so my failure was a mystery, a source only of baffled self-loathing. She claimed never to have said what she said, although I had it on tape. I published a thin, incomplete article. We had no more communication.

But at least I had learned something: the great world of European intellectuals and artists, whose imprimatur I dreamed of as my final burnishing, the last, most trustworthy proof of my worth, would not be opened to me. It might no longer exist, or be on the verge of not existing, and I imagined a time when I might think of it without a sense of having missed out, or having been kept out. One day perhaps I would think of it as a vanished world, like the world of the holy pictures and Henry James and Mastroianni: one more world whose pressures and anxieties no longer had their force. An idea that was a perverse invocation of the phrase I associated with *Roman Holiday:* not yet.

There is no one now in Rome whom I visit. I was too embarrassed by my experience of Ginzburg, I felt too much of a failure, to keep up a correspondence with the friend of my English friend. I don't know the real Rome, the Rome of the poor. I don't know anything about it well enough. I know that everything works badly and by corruption. It doesn't matter. I'm not a person who makes money here, who lives by the mind or the moral faculty. When I am here I am a person who lives by the eye.

Each time I come I vow to do more so that I'll be more ready next time. I say I will read more, particularly about the nineteenth-century Romantic travelers in Rome. I will read about the Risorgimento. I will learn how to look at the Baroque. I will study more Italian. I will do it regularly, every day. I will buy an Italian grammar book.

But I never do. Is it that I like myself inexpert? The sense of chance? I think I must want to know Rome only a little, as a stranger, a dumb cluck of a tourist, a naive and starstruck lover. One of the girls in *Three Coins in the Fountain.* The youngest, the silliest.

It is October and I am back in Rome, by myself, here for a few days to wander and to write, on my way to a friend's house in Tuscany. I am in some ways a regular, or at least a returning visitor. I know my way to a workman's café that makes the perfect pasta arrabiata. The place is without ornament, the dishes prepared simply. I am in love with the waitress with the large nose and the single braid. I think I have had too much wine, because after my meal, walking into the square, the sight of a yellow wall covered with ivy and late roses makes me burst into tears. I take myself to a place I have found, another place for quiet in this city of display, a cloister belonging to the Confraternity of Saint John. Whoever they are. I have learned, though, that to gain admittance you don't ring the bell for the cloister or the confraternity, but another one that says "Sposini." I learned this from a workman fixing the road after I made three unsuccessful attempts at entrance.

I sit by myself, looking at the spiky rose trees, the last remnants of the summer's wisteria. Over the walls, I can hear cars and music and chatter, but for a moment this place is mine. I am alone and hidden. The stucco walls are light blue. The caretaker wants me gone.

But I don't leave, not for a while, and he disappears into his office. After half an hour, I give him five thousand lire and I walk the twisted streets of Trastevere, past artisans repairing furniture or making wooden boxes. I make my way back to my hotel near the Campo dei Fiori. I am beginning to get sick. My throat hurts and I am having trouble breathing. Sick in Rome. It seems all wrong, and I have heard that Italian doctors go through their entire medical training never looking at a cadaver. So how can I trust them?

That evening I stay in my bed and eat only oranges. I'd planned to go to the catacombs the next morning to get real images of the martyrs who so obsessed my early life. But in the morning, it is raining. I have my breakfast at 7:30, but I decide it's all simply too hard. Despair at the idea of navigating multiple buses in the Roman rain, then standing in line at the catacombs under my inadequate umbrella, bought off the street here from a Somali man, defeats me. I close the shutters and I go back to sleep, falling into one of those filthy sleeps where dreams are perverse and murderous and you wake cleansed and healed.

It is eleven o'clock and the sun is shining. I am well. I will not go to the catacombs. I decide to walk to the Villa Borghese.

How has this happened? I am no longer sick, it is October, warm, the light is golden on the turning leaves, it warms the white stone of the palazzo. The sky, torrentially gray-black three hours ago, is cobalt blue. The pure blue light casts shadows behind the statue of a Roman matron. I sit in the beautiful part, empty and formal. Even the trees look as if they have happily conformed to a design: the cypresses like folded umbrellas, the skinny pines with their tufted tops like ladies waving ostrich fans. I have my roll, my cheese, my tomato, bought this morning by the Campo dei Fiori, near the statue of Giordano Bruno, burned by the Church as a freethinker. Another kind of martyr, standing eternally in the midst of the fruit sellers, the flower sellers. The air is chilly. I am glad to be wearing the green coat I bought (thinking of Mastroianni) on the Via Veneto, light green, a wool perfect for early (but not deep) winter.

How has this happened to *me*? I am sitting in the golden light in the park among lovers, dogs, and babies. The birds sing, the fountains splash. There is no place I need to be. No one expects me. Nothing is required. How has it happened to me in Rome, that this is who I am, not kneeling to a man in a black robe, or a red robe, or even a white one? On my own, with enough money for a good lunch and a green coat purchased on the Via Veneto. How has it happened to me? How has it come about that I have, to this point, escaped my fate, that I am here in the sun under the blue sky, not a martyr? How has it happened that I have become someone who, as a child, I would never even have thought of? Someone I would not have seen on holy cards or in movies? Someone I might not even have read about?

EDWARD HOAGLAND

Earth's Eye

FROM SIERRA

WATER IS our birthplace. We need and love it. In a bathtub, or by a lake or at the sea, we go to it for rest, refreshment, and solace. "I'm going to the water," people say when August comes and they crave a break. The sea is a democracy, so big it's free of access, often a bus or subway ride away, a meritocracy, sink or swim, and yet a swallower of grief because of its boundless scale — beyond the horizon, the home of icebergs, islands, whales. Tears alone are a mysterious, magisterial solvent that bring a smile, a softening of hard thoughts, lend us a merciful and inexpensive respite, almost like half an hour at the beach. In any landscape, in fact, a pond or creek catches and centers our attention as magnetically as if it were, in Thoreau's phrase, "earth's eye."

Lying on your back in deep meadow grass facing a bottomless sky is less focusing, but worth a drive of many hours, as weekend traffic will attest. Yet the very dimensions of the sky, which are unfathomable after the early surge of pleasure that they carry, cause most of us to mitigate their power with preoccupations such as golf or sunbathing as soon as we get outdoors. That sense of first principles can be unnerving, whereas the ground against our backs — if we lie gazing up into the starry night or a piebald day — is seething with groping roots and sprouting seeds and feels like home, as the friendliest dappled clouds can't be. Beyond the prettiest azure blue is black, as nightfall will remind us, and when the day ends, cold is the temperature of black.

A pond, though, is a gentle spot (unless you are Ophelia). Amber- or pewter-colored, it's a drinking fountain for scurrying raccoons and mincing deer, a waterbugs' and minnows' arena for hunting insect larvae, a holding pen for rain that may coalesce into ocean waves next year. Mine flows into the St. Lawrence River. I live in Vermont and spent a hundred dollars once to bulldoze a tadpole pond next to my little stretch of stream. A silent great blue heron, as tall as a Christmas tree, and a castanet-rattling kingfisher, a faster flier and brighter blue, showed up to forage for amphibians the next year. Garter snakes also benefited from the occasional meal of a frog, and a red-tailed hawk, cruising by, might grab a snake or frog. More exciting, a bull moose began using it as a hot-weather wallow, soaking for half an hour, mouthing algae, munching sedges, and browsing the willows that lean from the bank. A beaver cut down some poplar saplings to gnaw and stitch into a dam for creating a proper flow, but the depth remained insufficient to withstand a New England winter, so he retreated downstream to a wetland in my woods.

I bought this land for eighty-five dollars an acre in 1969, and today a comparable hideaway would probably still cost no more than about the price of a good car. We're not talking luxury: as with so much of life, your priorities are what count, and what you wish to protect and pay attention to. I've been a sinner in other ways, but not in this respect.

Remoteness bestows the amenity of uninterrupted sleep. No telephone or electric line runs by, and the hikers and pickups are gone by sunset. When the season of extravagant daylight shortens so I can't simply sleep from dusk to dawn, I light candles or kerosene, but in balmy weather I can nap with equal ease at any hour in the meadow too, or watch the swallows and dragonflies hawk after midges, as the breezes finger me and a yellowthroat hops in the bushes to eat a daddy long-legs. At dark the bats hawk for bugs instead, or an owl hunts, all wings, slow and mothlike, till it sees a rodent. The trees hang over a swimming hole nearby, with a dovish or a moonlit sky showing beyond the leaves like a kind of vastly enlarged swimming hole, until I feel I was born floating in both the water and the air. It's a hammock all the more beguiling because if you relax too much while swimming and let yourself sink, you might conceivably drown. Similarly, in the meadow, if you lazed too late into the fall, woolgathering, snow could fill your mouth.

Nature is not sentimental. The scenery that recruits our spirits in temperate weather may turn unforgiving in the winter. It doesn't care whether we love it and pay the property taxes to save it from development, having walked over it yard by yard in clement conditions. When the birds flee south and other creatures, from bears to beetles, have crawled underground to wait out the cold, we that remain have got to either fish or cut bait: burn some energy in those summer-lazy muscles cutting wood, or take some money out of the bank.

A mountain can be like that all at once. Summer at the bottom, winter at the top; and you climb through all the climates of the year as you scramble up. In the past half-century I've climbed Mount Jefferson in Oregon (a cousin died there in a fall soon afterward) and Mount Washington in New Hampshire, Mount Katahdin in Maine and Mount Etna in Sicily. I've clambered a bit in Wyoming's Wind Rivers and in the Absaroka Range; also in British Columbia and North Yemen; in the Western Ghats in southern India and the Alpes Maritimes in the south of France; and have scrambled modestly in the High Sierras, Alaska's Brooks Range, and on the lower slopes of Mount Kinyeti in the Imatong Massif in southern Sudan. More particularly, I climbed all of Vermont's firetower mountains, back when Vermont still used towers to locate fires, instead of planes.

This feast of variety is part of a writer's life, the coin of the realm you inhabit if you sacrifice the security Americans used to think they'd have if they weren't freelance in their working lives. In reality, everybody winds up being freelance, but mountains telescope the experience. During a weekend you climb from flowery summer glades to the tundra above treeline, slipping on patches of ice, trudging through snowdrifts; the rain turns to sleet. The view is rarefied until a bellying, bruise-colored sky turns formidable, not pretty. Like climbing combers in a strong surf, there's no indemnity if you come to grief. You labor upward not for money but for joy, or to have *been somewhere,* closer to the mysteries, during your life. Finding a hidden alpine col, a bowl of fragile grassy beauty, you aren't just gleeful; you are linked differently.

Leaving aside specific dangers like riptides, vertigo, or terrific cold, I found I was comfortable on mountainsides or in seawater or in caves or wilderness swatches. In other words, I was fearful of danger but not of nature. I didn't harbor notions of any special dispensation, only that I too was part of it. I'd fought forest fires in the Santa Ana Mountains of southern California when I was twenty and had discovered that moderate hardship energized yet tempered me, as it does many people, just like the natural sorties for which one puts on hiking shoes and ventures where barefoot peoples used to go. In central Africa I've walked a little with tribesmen like the Acholi and the Didinga, who still tend to be comfortable when nearly naked, and have seen that the gap between us seems not of temperament or of intuitions but only acculturation.

As virtual reality captures our time and obsessive attention, some of the pressures that are killing nature may begin to relent. Not the primary one of overpopulation, which is strangling the tropics; but as people peer more and more into computer screens and at television, the outdoors, in affluent countries, may be left in relative peace. This won't stop the wholesale extinction of species, the mauling of the ocean, or other tragedies, but close to home may give a respite to what's left of nature.

Where I live alone each summer, four families lived year-round eighty years ago. The other new landowners don't choose to occupy their holdings even in warm weather because of the absence of electricity. An unusual case, yet I think indicative, and supported by the recent return of numbers of adaptive sorts of wildlife, like moose and fisher, to New England — though, in contrast, along the lake a few miles downhill, cottages perch atop one another, motorboats and water-skiers buzz around, and trollers use radar fish-finders to trace the final sanctuaries of the schools that the lake still holds.

Just as habitat is the central factor in whether birds and animals can survive, what *we* are able to do in the woods will be determined by land regulation or taxing policy and public purchases. Maine's private timberlands have remained unpopulated because of America's lavish need for toilet paper — as Vermont's trees too make paper, cotton-mill bobbins, cedar fencing, and yellow-birch or maple dowels that become furniture legs. Any day, I watch truckloads of pulpwood go by. And in the California Sierras above Lake Tahoe, or on the pristine sea island of Ossabaw, off Savannah, Georgia, I've devoted lovely, utterly timeless hours to exploring refuges that seem quite empty of people but are actually allotted in careful fashion by state or federal agencies for intensive recreational use. The animals hide while the sun is up and feed when it's down. This is the way it will have to work. Levels of life on the same acreage. Or else it won't work at all.

I can be as jubilant indoors, listening to Schubert or Scott Joplin, as when sauntering underneath a mackerel sky on a day striped yellow, red, and green. Indeed, the density of sensations in which we live is such that one can do both — enjoy a virtuoso pianist through a headset outside. We live two lives or more in one nowadays, with our scads of travel, absurd excesses of unread informational material, the barrage of Internet and TV screens, wallpaper music, the serializing of polygamy and the elongation of youth blurring old age. A sort of mental gridlock sometimes blocks out the amber pond, the mackerel sky, the seething leaves in a fresh breeze up in a canopy of trees, and the Walkman's lavish outpouring of genius too. Even when we just go for a walk, the data jam.

Verisimilitude, on computer screens or in pictorial simulation, is carrying us we don't entirely know where. I need my months each year without electricity and a telephone, living by the sun and looking down the hill a hundred times a day at the little pond. The toads sing passionately when breeding, observing a hiatus only at midmorning when the moose descends from the woods for his therapeutic wallow, or when a heron sails in for a meal. I see these things so clearly I think our ears have possibly changed more than our eyes under the impact of civilization — both the level of noise and subtleties of sound are so different from hunter-gatherer whisperings. I'm a worrier, if not a Luddite. The gluttonies that are devouring nature are remorseless, and the imbalances within the human family give me vertigo. The lovely old idea that human life is sacred, each soul immortal, is in the throes of a grand mal seizure; overpopulation is doing it in. I didn't believe that anyway, but did adhere to the transcendental idea that heaven is right here on earth, if we perceive and insist on it. And this faith is also becoming harder to sustain.

"Religion is what the individual does with his own solitariness," as A. N. Whitehead said. ("Thus religion is solitariness; and if you are never solitary, you are never religious," he added.) I fall back on elemental pleasures like my love of ponds, or how my first sight of any river invariably leaves me grinning. And the sheen of rainwater on a bare black field in March. The thump of surf, combed in the wind and foaming, glistening, yet humping up again like a dinosaur. Yet fish don't touch me as much as animals, perhaps because they never leave the water. Frogs *do;* and I seem to like frog songs even more than bird songs, maybe because they're two-legged like us but can't fly either and were the first vertebrate singers. But I especially respond to them because they live a good deal more than we do in the water.

Frogs are disappearing worldwide in a drastic fashion, perhaps because of ultraviolet rays or acid rain; and I may finally cease to believe that heaven is on earth, if they do. Water without dolphins, frogs, pelicans, cormorants will not mean much to me. But in the meantime I like to search out springs in the high woods where brooks begin — a shallow sink in the ground, perpetually filling. If you carefully lift away the bottom covering of waterlogged leaves, you'll see the penny-sized or pencil-point sources of the groundwater welling up, where it all originates — the brook, the pond, the stream, the lake, the river, and the ocean, till rain brings it back again.

JAMAICA KINCAID

Those Words That Echo . . . Echo . . . Echo Through Life

FROM THE NEW YORK TIMES

HOW DO I WRITE? Why do I write? What do I write? This is what I am writing: I am writing "Mr. Potter." It begins in this way; this is its first sentence: "Mr. Potter was my father, my father's name was Mr. Potter." So much went into that one sentence; much happened before I settled on those eleven words.

Walking up and down in the little room in which I write, sitting down and then getting up out of the chair that is in the little room in which I write, I wanted to go to the bathroom. In the bathroom Mr. Potter vanished from my mind; I examined the tiles on the floor in front of me and found them ugly, worn out.

I looked at the faucet and the sink in front of me, but not too closely; I did not examine those. I flushed the toilet and I thought: Will the plumbing now just back up? Does the septic need pumping? Should I call Mr. A. Aaron? But Mr. A. Aaron's name is not that at all. His real name is something quite far from that. His real name is something like Mr. Christian or Mr. Zenith, though I cannot remember exactly. He only calls himself A. Aaron so he can be the first listing in the telephone book under the heading "Septic Tanks & Systems — Cleaning." I come back and look at Mr. Potter.

"Mr. Potter," I write, and I put clothes on him, even though I do not see him naked, for he was my father, and just now he is not yet dead. He is a young man, and I am not yet born. Oh, I believe I am seeing him as a little boy; as a little boy he has clothes, but he has not shoes. I do not place him in shoes until he is — I have not decided when exactly I shall allow him to wear shoes.

And then after many days of this and that and back and forth, I wrote, with a certainty that I did not necessarily intend to last, "Mr. Potter was my father, my father's name was Mr. Potter." And Mr. Potter remained my father, and Mr. Potter remained my father's name for a long time, even up to now.

And then? I grew tired of that sentence and those eleven words just sitting there all alone followed by all that blank space. I grew sad at seeing that sentence and those eleven words just sitting there followed by nothing, nothing, and nothing again. After many days it frightened me to see nothing but that one sentence and those eleven words and nothing, nothing, and nothing again came after them. "Say something," I said to Mr. Potter. To myself I had nothing to say.

Speaking no longer to Mr. Potter, speaking no longer to myself in regard to Mr. Potter, I got up at five o'clock in the morning and at half-past five o'clock went running with my friend Meg and a man named Dennis Murray; he builds houses of every kind in the city of Bennington in the state of Vermont.

"My father is dead," I said to Dennis one morning as we were just past the Mahar funeral parlor on Main Street. I never make an effort to speak before the funeral parlor. I despise death and consider it a humiliation and in any case much overdone and so plan never to do it myself and plan never to have anything at all to do with it, for it is so contagious. I have noticed that when you know people who die, you catch it and end up dead too.

"My father is dead," I said to Dennis, but he could not hear me for he was far ahead. He runs at a faster pace than I do, and he thought I was agreeing with something he had just said about the weekend he had just spent hiking into the woods and spending the night and fishing with a friend whose name I cannot remember and catching many trout and cooking them and eating them and going to sleep in a tent while there was a great downpour of rain outside and waking up the next morning and having the best pancakes and fishing again and doing everything again and all of it as perfect as it had been before and then coming home to his wife who loves him very much.

And the perfect narrative of Dennis's life, uninterrupted by any feelings of approaching and then leaving behind the Mahar funeral parlor, did not make me envious or make me grieve that Mr. Potter's life remained frozen in the vault that was his name and the vault of being only my father.

The days then rapidly grew thick into all darkness with only small spaces of light (that is autumn) and then remained solidly all darkness with only small patches of light (that is winter), and then the darkness slowly thinned out (that is spring), but the light was never as overwhelming in its way as the darkness was overwhelmingly dark in its way (that is summer). So too was the night dark except for when the moon was full and the day bright with light except for when clouds blocked out the sun. And Mr. Potter remained my father, and my father's name remained Mr. Potter for a very long time.

One day when I seemed uncertain about which foot to put first, the one in front of the other, my husband said to me, "Mrs. S., Mrs. S., how are you doing?" and "Are you okay?" The first letter in his family's chosen name is S. Our children go to school every day on a great big bus that was painted yellow and driven by a woman named Verta. A man named Mr. Sweet came and picked up our rubbish.

In the American way we have much rubbish, and Mr. Sweet is hard of hearing. Saying to him, as I feel I must if I see him, I must say to him, "Hallo, Mr. Sweet." And since he cannot hear me, he is deaf, he looks at me and then holds his ear forward, cupping it in the palm of his hand, as if it were a receptacle, for he wants it to receive the sounds that I am making.

"What?" says Mr. Sweet. "Hallo," I say again, and Mr. Sweet is then very nice and sincerely so, and he asks if I could pay him for the eight weeks he has picked up the rubbish without being paid.

"But no," I say to him, and then I explain that I am not allowed to write checks because I never put the debits and balances in their proper columns, and I make a mess of the household accounts. Mr. Sweet says, "Yep, yep," and then Mr. Sweet says he will see me next week. Mr. Sweet does not know about Mr. Potter, not in the way of my writing about him, not in the way of Mr. Potter as a real person.

And one day, after all sorts of ups and downs and many travails that are interesting, especially to me, Mr. Potter was driving a motorcar and dressing in a way imitative of men who had enormous amounts of money. And of course Mr. Potter was right to imitate the wardrobe of men who had enormous amounts of money, for without the existence of Mr. Potter and people like him, working very hard and being paid a mere pittance, there can be no enormous amounts of money. And I am Mr. Potter's daughter, so I know this.

But that "and one day" left me bereft and exhausted and feeling empty; and that "and one day" is just what I want when in the process of encountering a certain aspect of my world.

And then that one day, that one day after Mr. Potter's life advanced and exploded on the page, I had to have my lunch, but I could not eat too much of anything, not even plain green leaves. I could only eat very small amounts of anything, for I wanted to fit into my nice blue (tilting to lavender) silk taffeta skirt, a skirt that has box pleats. And I so love my nice blue (tilting to lavender) silk taffeta skirt with the box pleats and will not eat too much of anything, even just plain green leaves, for I look very beautiful in it. I look most beautiful in it when I am in a room all by myself, just alone with only my reflection, no one at all there to observe me.

In the early afternoon, just after I have eaten my lunch, I look at Mr. Potter, in my own way, a way I am imagining, a way that is most certainly true and real. (His name really was Roderick Potter; he really was my father.) He cannot look back at me unless I make him do so, and I shall never make him do so.

The telephone rings, and I do not answer it. The telephone rings, and I do not answer it. The telephone rings, I answer it, and on the other end is someone employed by one of my many creditors asking me to satisfy my debt. I promise to do so in a given time, but I have no money. I like having no money. I do not like having no money. I only like to have contempt for people who have a great deal of money and are unhappy even so, or are happy with money in a way that I find contemptible.

Driving past a sign that says YIELD, driving past the house where a dentist lives, driving past the house where the chiropractor I see from time to time lives, swiftly I pass by a sloping moist field that in spring is filled up with marsh marigolds. Swiftly I go past the home for delinquent children. Swiftly I go to await my children getting off the bus with Verta.

My children will soon get off the schoolbus, the one painted a harsh yellow, and it is driven by Verta. "Mr. Shoul," I say to myself, for I am all alone in the car, having driven so swiftly. "Mr. Shoul," I say, for I now can see that I have saddled Mr. Potter with this personality, Mr. Shoul. And Mr. Shoul is a merchant, an ordinary merchant, specializing in nothing particular; he sells anything. Mr. Shoul sells everything. Mr. Shoul might sell Mr. Potter; on the other hand, he might draw the line at selling Mr. Potter. And I have saddled Mr. Potter with Mr. Shoul.

Mr. Potter does not know the world. He is produced by the world, but he is not familiar with the world. He does not know its parameters. Mr. Potter was my father, my father's name was Mr. Potter. My children pour out of the bus. My daughter (she is fourteen) hurls an insult at my son (he is ten). His small self (the self that is not seen) crumbles to the ground; I rush to pick up his self that is not seen but has fallen to the ground and bring it back together again with his self that I can see.

I look at her, my daughter. What should I do? For her selves (one or two or three or more) are not all in one bundle, tied up together, either.

"Mr. Shoul," I say to myself, for I am at the bus stop and can tell no one what I am really thinking. "Mr. Shoul," I say. What to tell Mr. Potter about Mr. Shoul, where to begin?

"Mr. Shoul!" I shout at Mr. Potter, but Mr. Potter cannot hear me. I have left him at home on the page, the white page, the clean white page, all alone with Mr. Shoul. "Mr. Shoul," I will write, "Mr. Shoul," I will tell Mr. Potter, "Mr. Shoul comes from Lebanon."

GEETA KOTHARI

If You Are What You Eat, Then What Am I?

FROM THE KENYON REVIEW

To belong is to understand the tacit codes of the people you live with.
— Michael Ignatieff, *Blood and Belonging*

I

THE FIRST TIME my mother and I open a can of tuna, I am nine years old. We stand in the doorway of the kitchen, in semidarkness, the can tilted toward daylight. I want to eat what the kids at school eat: bologna, hot dogs, salami — foods my parents find repugnant because they contain pork and meat byproducts, crushed bone and hair glued together by chemicals and fat. Although she has never been able to tolerate the smell of fish, my mother buys the tuna, hoping to satisfy my longing for American food.

Indians, of course, do not eat such things.

The tuna smells fishy, which surprises me because I can't remember anyone's tuna sandwich actually smelling like fish. And the tuna in those sandwiches doesn't look like this, pink and shiny, like an internal organ. In fact, this looks similar to the bad foods my mother doesn't want me to eat. She is silent, holding her face away from the can while peering into it like a half-blind bird.

"What's wrong with it?" I ask.

She has no idea. My mother does not know that the tuna everyone else's mothers made for them was tuna *salad*.

"Do you think it's botulism?"

I have never seen botulism, but I have read about it, just as I have read about but never eaten steak and kidney pie.

There is so much my parents don't know. They are not like other parents, and they disappoint me and my sister. They are supposed to help us negotiate the world outside, teach us the signs, the clues to proper behavior: what to eat and how to eat it.

We have expectations, and my parents fail to meet them, especially my mother, who works full-time. I don't understand what it means, to have a mother who works outside and inside the home; I notice only the ways in which she disappoints me. She doesn't show up for school plays. She doesn't make chocolate-frosted cupcakes for my class. At night, if I want her attention, I have to sit in the kitchen and talk to her while she cooks the evening meal, attentive to every third or fourth word I say.

We throw the tuna away. This time my mother is disappointed. I go to school with tuna eaters. I see their sandwiches, yet cannot explain the discrepancy between them and the stinking, oily fish in my mother's hand. We do not understand so many things, my mother and I.

II

On weekends, we eat fried chicken from Woolworth's on the back steps of my father's first-floor office in Murray Hill. The back steps face a small patch of garden — hedges, a couple of skinny trees, and gravel instead of grass. We can see the back window of the apartment my parents and I lived in until my sister was born. There, the doorman watched my mother, several months pregnant and wearing a sari, slip on the ice in front of the building.

My sister and I pretend we are in the country, where our American friends all have houses. We eat glazed doughnuts, also from Woolworth's, and french fries with ketchup.

III

My mother takes a catering class and learns that Miracle Whip and mustard are healthier than mayonnaise. She learns to make egg salad with chopped celery, deviled eggs dusted with paprika, a cream cheese spread with bits of fresh ginger and watercress, chicken liver pâté, and little brown-and-white checkerboard sandwiches that we have only once. She makes chicken à la king in puff pastry shells and eggplant Parmesan. She acquires smooth wooden paddles, whose purpose is never clear, two different egg slicers, several wooden spoons, icing tubes, cookie cutters, and an electric mixer.

IV

I learn to make tuna salad by watching a friend. My sister never acquires a taste for it. Instead, she craves

bologna
hot dogs
bacon
sausages

and a range of unidentifiable meat products forbidden by my parents. Their restrictions are not about sacred cows, as everyone around us assumes; in a pinch, we are allowed hamburgers, though lamb burgers are preferable. A "pinch" means choosing not to draw attention to ourselves as outsiders, impolite visitors who won't eat what their host serves. But bologna is still taboo.

V

Things my sister refuses to eat: butter, veal, anything with jeera. The baby-sitter tries to feed her butter sandwiches, threatens her with them, makes her cry in fear and disgust. My mother does not disappoint her; she does not believe in forcing us to eat, in using food as a weapon. In addition to pbj, my sister likes pasta and marinara sauce, bologna and Wonder Bread (when she can get it), and fried egg sandwiches with turkey, cheese, and horseradish. Her tastes, once established, are predictable.

VI

When we visit our relatives in India, food prepared outside the house is carefully monitored. In the hot, sticky monsoon months in New Delhi and Bombay, we cannot eat ice cream, salad, cold food, or any fruit that can't be peeled. Definitely no meat. People die from amoebic dysentery, unexplained fevers, strange boils on their bodies. We drink boiled water only, no ice. No sweets except for jalebi, thin fried twists of dough in dripping hot sugar syrup. If we're caught outside with nothing to drink, Fanta, Limca, Thums Up (after Coca-Cola is thrown out by Mrs. Gandhi) will do. Hot tea sweetened with sugar, served with thick creamy buffalo milk, is preferable. It should be boiled, to kill the germs on the cup.

My mother talks about "back home" as a safe place, a silk cocoon frozen in time where we are sheltered by family and friends. Back home, my sister and I do not argue about food with my parents. Home is where they know all the rules. We trust them to guide us safely through the maze of city streets for which they have no map, and we trust them to feed and take care of us, the way parents should.

Finally, though, one of us will get sick, hungry for the food we see our cousins and friends eating, too thirsty to ask for a straw, too polite to insist on properly boiled water.

At my uncle's diner in New Delhi, someone hands me a plate of aloo tikki, fried potato patties filled with mashed channa dal and served with a sweet and a sour chutney. The channa, mixed with hot chilies and spices, burns my tongue and throat. I reach for my Fanta, discard the paper straw, and gulp the sweet orange soda down, huge drafts that sting rather than soothe.

When I throw up later that day (or is it the next morning, when a stomachache wakes me from deep sleep?), I cry over the frustration of being singled out, not from the pain my mother assumes I'm feeling as she holds my hair back from my face. The taste of orange lingers in my mouth, and I remember my lips touching the cold glass of the Fanta bottle.

At that moment, more than anything, I want to be like my cousins.

VII

In New York, at the first Indian restaurant in our neighborhood, my father orders with confidence, and my sister and I play with the silverware until the steaming plates of lamb biryani arrive.

What is Indian food? my friends ask, their noses crinkling up.

Later, this restaurant is run out of business by the new Indo-Pak-Bangladeshi combinations up and down the street, which serve similar food. They use plastic cutlery and Styrofoam cups. They do not distinguish between North and South Indian cooking, or between Indian, Pakistani, and Bangladeshi cooking, and their customers do not care. The food is fast, cheap, and tasty. Dosa, a rice flour crepe stuffed with masala potato, appears on the same trays as chicken makhani.

Now my friends want to know, Do you eat curry at home?

One time my mother makes lamb vindaloo for guests. Like dosa, this is a South Indian dish, one that my Punjabi mother has to learn from a cookbook. For us, she cooks everyday food — yellow dal, rice, chapati, bhaji. Lentils, rice, bread, and vegetables. She has never referred to anything on our table as "curry" or "curried," but I know she has made chicken curry for guests. Vindaloo, she explains, is a curry too. I understand then that curry is a dish created for guests, outsiders, a food for people who eat in restaurants.

VIII

I have inherited brown eyes, black hair, a long nose with a crooked bridge, and soft teeth with thin enamel. I am in my twenties, moving to a city far from my parents, before it occurs to me that jeera, the spice my sister avoids, must have an English name. I have to learn that haldi = turmeric, methi = fenugreek. What to make with fenugreek, I do not know. My grandmother used to make methi roti for our breakfast, cornbread with fresh fenugreek leaves served with a lump of homemade butter. No one makes it now that she's gone, though once in a while my mother will get a craving for it and produce a facsimile ("The cornmeal here is wrong") that only highlights what she's really missing: the smells and tastes of her mother's house.

I will never make my grandmother's methi roti or even my mother's unsatisfactory imitation of it. I attempt chapati; it takes six hours, three phone calls home, and leaves me with an aching back. I have to write translations down: jeera = cumin. My memory is unreliable. But I have always known garam = hot.

IX

My mother learns how to make brownies and apple pie. My father makes only Indian food, except for loaves of heavy, sweet brown bread that I eat with thin slices of American cheese and lettuce.

The recipe is a secret, passed on to him by a woman at work. Years later, when he finally gives it to me, when I finally ask for it, I end up with three bricks of gluten that even the birds and my husband won't eat.

X

My parents send me to boarding school, outside of London. They imagine that I will overcome my shyness and find a place for myself in this all-girls' school. They have never lived in England, but as former subjects of the British Empire, they find London familiar, comfortable in a way New York — my mother's home for over twenty years by now — is not. Americans still don't know what to call us; their Indians live on reservations, not in Manhattan. Because they understand the English, my parents believe the English understand us.

I poke at my first school lunch — thin, overworked pastry in a puddle of lumpy gravy. The lumps are chewy mushrooms, maybe, or overcooked shrimp.

"What is this?" I don't want to ask, but I can't go on eating without knowing.

"Steak and kidney pie."

The girl next to me, red-haired, freckled, watches me take a bite from my plate. She has been put in charge of me, the new girl, and I follow her around all day, a foreigner at the mercy of a reluctant and angry tour guide. She is not used to explaining what is perfectly and utterly natural.

"What, you've never had steak and kidney pie? Bloody hell."

My classmates scoff, then marvel, then laugh at my ignorance. After a year, I understand what is on my plate: sausage rolls, blood pudding, Spam, roast beef in a thin, greasy gravy, all the bacon and sausage I could possibly want. My parents do not expect me to starve.

The girls at school expect conformity; it has been bred into them, through years of uniforms and strict rules about proper behavior. I am thirteen and contrary, even as I yearn for acceptance. I declare myself a vegetarian and doom myself to a diet of cauliflower cheese and baked beans on toast. The administration does not question my decision; they assume it's for vague, undefined religious reasons, although my father, the doctor, tells them it's for my health. My reasons, from this distance of many years, remain murky to me.

Perhaps I am my parents' daughter after all.

XI

When she is three, sitting on my cousin's lap in Bombay, my sister reaches for his plate and puts a chili in her mouth. She wants to be like the grownups, who dip green chilies in coarse salt and eat them like any other vegetable. She howls inconsolable animal pain for what must be hours. She doesn't have the vocabulary for the oily heat that stings her mouth and tongue, burns a trail through her small tender body. Only hot, sticky tears on my father's shoulder.

As an adult, she eats red chili paste, mango pickle, kimchee, foods that make my eyes water and my stomach gurgle. My tastes are milder. I order raita at Indian restaurants and ask for food that won't sear the roof of my mouth and scar the insides of my cheeks. The waiters nod, and their eyes shift — a slight once-over that indicates they don't believe me. I am Indian, aren't I? My father seems to agree with them. He tells me I'm asking for the impossible, as if he believes the recipes are immutable, written in stone during the passage from India to America.

XII

I look around my boyfriend's freezer one day and find meat: pork chops, ground beef, chicken pieces, Italian sausage. Ham in the refrigerator, next to the homemade bolognese sauce. Tupperware filled with chili made from ground beef and pork.

He smells different from me. Foreign. Strange.

I marry him anyway.

He has inherited blue eyes that turn gray in bad weather, light brown hair, a sharp pointy nose, and excellent teeth. He learns to make chili with ground turkey and tofu, tomato sauce with red wine and portobello mushrooms, roast chicken with rosemary and slivers of garlic under the skin.

He eats steak when we are in separate cities, roast beef at his mother's house, hamburgers at work. Sometimes I smell them on his skin. I hope he doesn't notice me turning my face, a cheek instead of my lips, my nose wrinkled at the unfamiliar, musky smell.

XIII

And then I realize I don't want to be a person who can find Indian food only in restaurants. One day my parents will be gone and I will long for the foods of my childhood, the way they long for theirs. I prepare for this day the way people on TV prepare for the end of the world. They gather canned goods they will never eat while I stockpile recipes I cannot replicate. I am frantic, disorganized, grabbing what I can, filing scribbled notes haphazardly. I regret the tastes I've forgotten, the meals I have inhaled without a thought. I worry that I've come to this realization too late.

XIV

Who told my mother about Brie? One day we were eating Velveeta, the next day Brie, Gouda, Camembert, Port Salut, Havarti with caraway, Danish fontina, string cheese made with sheep's milk. Who opened the door to these foreigners that sit on the refrigerator shelf next to last night's dal?

Back home, there is one cheese only, which comes in a tin, looks like Bakelite, and tastes best when melted.

And how do we go from Chef Boyardee to fresh pasta and homemade sauce, made with Redpack tomatoes, crushed garlic, and dried oregano? Macaroni and cheese, made with fresh cheddar and whole milk, sprinkled with bread crumbs and paprika. Fresh eggplant and ricotta ravioli, baked with marinara sauce and fresh mozzarella.

My mother will never cook beef or pork in her kitchen, and the foods she knew in her childhood are unavailable. Because the only alternative to the supermarket, with its TV dinners and canned foods, is the gourmet Italian deli across the street, by default our meals become socially acceptable.

XV

If I really want to make myself sick, I worry that my husband will one day leave me for a meat-eater, for someone familiar who doesn't sniff him suspiciously for signs of alimentary infidelity.

XVI

Indians eat lentils. I understand this as absolute, a decree from an unidentifiable authority that watches and judges me.

So what does it mean that I cannot replicate my mother's dal? She and my father show me repeatedly, in their kitchen, in my kitchen. They coach me over the phone, buy me the best cookbooks, and finally write down their secrets. Things I'm supposed to know but don't. Recipes that should be, by now, engraved on my heart.

Living far from the comfort of people who require no explanation for what I do and who I am, I crave the foods we have shared. My mother convinces me that moong is the easiest dal to prepare, and yet it fails me every time: bland, watery, a sickly greenish yellow mush. These imperfect imitations remind me only of what I'm missing.

But I have never been fond of moong dal. At my mother's table it is the last thing I reach for. Now I worry that this antipathy toward dal signals something deeper, that somehow I am not my parents' daughter, not Indian, and because I cannot bear the touch and smell of raw meat, though I can eat it cooked (charred, dry, and overdone), I am not American either.

I worry about a lifetime purgatory in Indian restaurants where I will complain that all the food looks and tastes the same because they've used the same masala.

XVII

About the tuna and her attempts to feed us, my mother laughs. She says, "You were never fussy. You ate everything I made and never complained."

My mother is at the stove, wearing only her blouse and petticoat, her sari carefully folded and hung in the closet. She does not believe a girl's place is in the kitchen, but she expects me to know that too much hing can ruin a meal, to know without being told, without having to ask or write it down. Hing = asafetida.

She remembers the catering class. "Oh, that class. You know, I had to give it up when we got to lobster. I just couldn't stand the way it looked."

She says this apologetically, as if she has deprived us, as if she suspects that having a mother who could feed us lobster would have changed the course of our lives.

Intellectually, she understands that only certain people regularly eat lobster, people with money or those who live in Maine, or both. In her catering class there were people without jobs for whom preparing lobster was a part of their professional training as caterers. Like us, they wouldn't be eating lobster at home. For my mother, however, lobster was just another American food, like tuna — different, strange, not natural yet somehow essential to belonging.

I learned how to prepare and eat lobster from the same girl who taught me tuna salad. I ate bacon at her house too. And one day this girl, with her houses in the country and Martha's Vineyard, asked me how my uncle was going to pick me up from the airport in Bombay. In 1973, she was surprised to hear that he used a car, not an elephant. At home, my parents and I laughed, and though I never knew for sure if she was making fun of me, I still wanted her friendship.

My parents were afraid my sister and I would learn to despise the foods they loved, replace them with bologna and bacon and lose our taste for masala. For my mother, giving up her disgust of lobster, with its hard exterior and foreign smell, would mean renouncing some essential difference. It would mean becoming, decidedly, definitely, American — unafraid of meat in all its forms, able to consume large quantities of protein at any given meal. My willingness to toss a living being into boiling water and then get past its ugly appearance to the rich meat inside must mean to my mother that I am somehow someone she is not.

But I haven't eaten lobster in years. In my kitchen cupboards, there is a thirteen-pound bag of basmati rice, jars of lime pickle, mango pickle, and ghee, cans of tuna and anchovies, canned soups, coconut milk, and tomatoes, rice noodles, several kinds of pasta, dried mushrooms, and unlabeled bottles of spices: haldi, jeera, hing. When my husband tries to help me cook, he cannot identify all the spices. He gets confused when I forget their English names and remarks that my expectations of him are unreasonable.

I am my parents' daughter. Like them, I expect knowledge to pass from me to my husband without one word of explanation or translation. I want him to know what I know, see what I see, without having to tell him exactly what it is. I want to believe that recipes never change.

RICHARD McCANN

The Resurrectionist

FROM TIN HOUSE

HERE IS what happened:

I was cut apart.

The liver of a dead person was placed inside me so I might live again. This took twelve hours and thirty-three units of blood.

But who was I afterward?

I could still recall the body I'd had when I was ten, the body in which I carried what I called "myself," walking along the C&O Railroad tracks or crossing the divided highway that separated our house from the woods; a heavy, modest body, dressed in husky-size jeans from Monkey Ward and a brown corduroy car coat that my mother chose, identical to those my uncles wore back in the mining towns they lived in. I could recall the body I'd had, nervous and tentative, when I first made love at seventeen. But these bodies were gone, as was the body into which I'd been born, these bodies I'd called "mine" without hesitation, intact and separate and entire.

Three months after my liver transplant I flew to Nashville to visit my mother in the nursing home. She sat in a blue housecoat at a folding card table, slowly spooning a Dixie cup of ice cream to her mouth. "Marie, your son's here," the nurse kept telling her. But my mother wouldn't look up except to look through me. She'd begun her own metamorphosis since the last time I'd seen her, withdrawing into the form of a bony old woman who only sometimes recognized my brother or me.

"Is this your son Richard?" the nurse asked, a grade-school teacher prompting a forgetful pupil. My mother shook her head: no, no.

At night I sat at her bedside. "I'm here," I whispered as she slept. "I made it through. I'm here."

I didn't know if she could hear me. For a while I tried to work on the letter of gratitude I was planning to send to the strangers the transplant coordinator referred to as my "donor family," though I knew nothing about them or their loved one whose liver I'd received. I couldn't figure what to write to them that would seem neither too rehearsed nor too intimate, though I planned to repeat some remarks I'd heard in a support group meeting, thanking them for "the gift of life" and assuring them that the highest form of giving occurred, as theirs had, when neither the donor nor the recipient were known to one another.

For a moment my mother shifted beneath her blanket, murmuring in her sleep. I put down the pencil and closed my eyes. *In just a second,* I thought, *she'll say my name.*

"Mother," I said, though she said nothing further. I wanted us back as we had been, restored to what I felt were our real and original bodies, my mother smoking a cigarette on the stoop of our old house in Silver Spring and me beside her with a bottle of Pepsi in my hand, though I knew if my mother were able to ask what had happened to the liver I was born with — the one she'd given me, I sometimes imagined, for it had once been a part of her as well as of me — I could have told her only what the surgeon had told me: "It was sent to pathology and burned."

I flew home the next morning. On the plane I noticed the man beside me staring as one by one I swallowed the half-dozen immunosuppressants that kept my body from rejecting the organ it would forever perceive as foreign, and for a moment I felt my own sudden strangeness, even to myself, as if I were a distinct biological phenomenon, constructed in a manner different from that of my fellow passengers hurtling though space in a pressurized cabin, drinking coffee and reading their magazines.

"I'm a liver transplant recipient," I told my seatmate.

He wanted to know if my new liver was male or female or white or black.

I said I didn't know; he said that if it were him, he'd sure want to find out.

But I didn't, or at least I didn't think so, and I was relieved when the plane began its descent. Somewhere over the Alleghenies my seatmate had asked if I'd heard about a man with AIDS who'd gotten a liver from a baboon.

No, I hadn't.

But in my transplant support group I had heard of recipients who'd waived their rights to anonymity to arrange what they sometimes called "reunions," inviting their donor families over for *yahrzeit* rituals and barbecues, and I'd heard of donor families who'd secured the names of recipients, showing up unannounced on their doorsteps, bearing bouquets of mixed flowers and brightly colored Mylar balloons.

"Maybe it's kind of like discovering you're adopted or finding your birth mother," one woman said, confiding to our support group her anxious plans for meeting the mother of the teenage boy whose lungs she'd received.

No one dared the obvious: the mother was the mother of a child who was dead, even if his lungs were still drawing breath on earth.

Sometimes I too fantasized that I had an alternate family that was eager to receive me as flesh and blood, especially as my mother retreated further and further into a world from which I was excluded, as when she imagined that I was her dead brother and called me by his name. But my fantasies of a happy meeting with a donor family were vague and unspecific, even less concrete than the fantasies I'd concocted as a child, waiting for George Maharis from *Route 66* to pull up to the house in his Corvette, ready to speed me away to what I felt sure was my real future.

My fantasies of a painful meeting, however, were explicit and detailed with dread. What would I say if my donor family were to ask to place their hands on my belly so they could feel the liver softly pulsing within?

How could I refuse them? I owed these people everything. I was alive because of a decision they'd made while standing in the bright fluorescence of a hospital corridor. Wasn't the liver more theirs than mine?

I imagined myself hesitating when they reached to touch me, and I imagined them demanding of me, with what I would have agreed was a rightful anger, "Who do you think you are?"

We are made of the dust of old stars, our grade-school teacher told us; we are made of leaves and sediment and the mulch of life. But I was made also of something rescued from the graveyard, I realized after the transplant, and if I was now among the resurrected, I was also the resurrectionist — the name given in the nineteenth century to the grave robbers who sold corpses for dissection to physicians and anatomists, trafficking in bodies and parts.

I don't recall when I began to think of what is medically called "the non–heart-beating cadaver donor" as neither a noble but faceless benefactor nor a nonhuman organ source, but rather as someone particular and separate who'd lived his own life before he died. I don't recall when I began to think of a donor organ as a bearer of its own set of cellular memories and not just as some sort of bloodied and perishable apparatus that one could airlift a great distance in an Igloo cooler marked HUMAN HEART or HUMAN EYES. In the eleven months I spent waiting for a transplant, I could barely acknowledge what was happening to my own body as my liver rapidly failed: abdomen grossly distended from accumulated fluids; muscle wasting as my body cannibalized itself for nutrients and proteins; pale stools streaked with bile; profound and constant exhaustion; brief spells of aphasia; cramps and sudden hemorrhages, blood puddling in my mouth from ruptured esophageal varices; skin the color of copper and eyes the color of urine.

I do recall a spring afternoon a month before my transplant, when I was lying on the grass in Rock Creek Park, back from the transplant clinic, where I'd overheard a nurse telling someone in the next room — I couldn't see who — that a high number of teenage donors die not from car wrecks but from suicide.

I didn't want to know this, not as I myself was growing so desperate for a donor. As soon as I left the clinic, I asked a taxi driver to take me to Rock Creek Park — "Are you all right?" he kept asking, afraid of my appearance — where I'd often gone when I was well to sunbathe with my friends, though now I was alone. I paid the fare; then I was lying on the unmowed grass, attempting to lose myself in the song I could hear playing on a far-off radio, pretending that my whole life consisted of just one word: *sunny, sunny . . .*

But it didn't work. My donor had begun to claim me, or so it seemed; I felt as if he'd somehow been constructing himself inside me without my knowledge as I was dying, though he was still alive and waiting for nothing unforeseen. *Perhaps he's here right now in this park,* I thought, *or perhaps he's in another part of the city, crossing a street against traffic or standing at a pay phone or waiting for the bus that will bear him home from work.* For a moment it seemed as if there were but the two of us left in the world, me and my blood brother, though one of us would soon be dying.

Don't die, I wanted to whisper, though I didn't know if I was speaking to him or myself.

I suppose I found out four weeks later: the hospital paged me past midnight to say they'd located a suitable donor.

My friend Sarah drove me to the ER. The whole way I kept checking and rechecking the contents of the small suitcase I'd packed six months before — silk dressing gown, twenty-dollar bill, packet of Dentyne, razor and toothbrush and comb; I couldn't stop touching these things, as if they were all that was left holding me to earth.

I knew what would happen when we got to the hospital — X-ray, EKG, and enema; introduction of IV lines, one in the left hand and another beneath the collarbone, for sedatives and cyclosporine and antibiotics. For months I'd been trying to prepare myself for the transplant surgery, studying the booklets the doctor had given me, one with drawings of abdomens marked with dotted lines to represent incision sites and another with a diagram showing how a pump-driven external system of plastic tubing would route my blood outside my body during the time when I would have no liver.

I was prepared to wake in the ICU, as in fact I did, unable to speak or move, brain buzzing like high voltage from prednisone.

But I was not prepared for what came the week after that: the impact of the realization that I had participated in the pain and violence and grief of a human death. *You have to face what you've done,* I kept telling myself as each day I watched myself in the mirror, growing healthier, until even my jaundiced eyes were white again: I had taken a liver from a brain-dead corpse that had been maintained on a ventilator during the removal of its organs, so that it looked like a regular surgical patient, prepped and draped, with an anesthesiologist standing by its head to monitor blood pressure and maintain homeostasis, its chest visibly rising and falling with regulated breath.

"It's not like you killed him," my friends kept telling me.

"I know, I know," I said to quiet them, though I didn't know, not really. But I did know, as perhaps my friends did not, that it isn't just children who believe they can kill with the power of a thought or a word. After all, I had sat in the clinic waiting room with other transplant candidates, joking that we should take a rifle up to the roof to shoot some people whose organs we might like. "I wish we'd been at the Texas Book Depository with Oswald," one man had said.

At night in bed I often thought of the person who'd died; when I was quiet, I could feel myself quietly grieving for him, just as I was grieving for my own body, so deeply wounded and cut apart, though still alive.

"I'm sorry," I wanted to tell him.

Sometimes I woke in the middle of the night, troubled to realize that I had taken a piece of him inside me, as if I had eaten him to stay alive. When this happened, I often forced myself to think of it longer, though I didn't want to, as if I were a member of a tribe I'd read about a long time before in an old ethnographic text that described how the bereaved dripped the bodily fluids of the dead into their rice, which they then made themselves eat as an act of reverence and love.

In this state, I could not console myself. I got up and sat on the sofa. *So here I am,* I thought, *right on the edge of the unspeakable . . .*

Other nights I thought of the donor with a great tenderness, sometimes perceiving him as male and sometimes as female. These nights, I placed my hand over what seemed to be still her liver, not mine, and slowly massaged the right side of my body — a broken reliquary with a piece of flesh inside — all the way from my hip to the bottom of my ribcage. "It's okay, it's okay," I whispered over and over, as if I were attempting to quiet a troubled spirit not my own.

If I could, I would undo what I have done, I thought, though I knew that if I had to, I would do it again.

I wasn't new to survivor guilt. After all, I'd been living for a long time in the midst of the AIDS epidemic while so many of my close friends died: Larry, Ed, Darnell, Allen, Ricardo, Paul, George, Arcadio, Jaime, Wally, Billy, Victor, and David.

In this sense, it had been a relief to be diagnosed, to have a progressive disease that threatened my life, to be bivouacked with the others. "It's like you're one of us now," my friend Kenny had told me. "It's like you've got AIDS."

But I couldn't tell him it wasn't true, at least not after the transplant; it wasn't the same at all. I'd outlived everyone, even myself.

What did Lazarus want after he stumbled from the cave, tied hand and foot with graveclothes, his face bound about with a napkin? *Loose him,* Jesus said, and *Let him go.*

I survived. It's two years since the transplant. Here I am, in my new life.

I want to unfurl.

I want to become my gratitude.

I want to fly around the world.

I want to be a man with a suntan. The man in the Arrow shirt.

And above all, this: I want to complete what I've written here — these fragments, these sticky residues of trauma — by adding just one more line before the words THE END: "It's a miracle."

It is a miracle, of course. I know that. Just the other day, for instance, stopping at a sidewalk fruit stand and buying a blood orange: *Oh,* I thought, *this will replace the blood I lost.* I carried the orange to the park, where I sat in the sun, lazily devouring its juicy flesh, its piercing wine-red tartness. *There's nothing more than this I need,* I thought. *I'm alive. I'm alive.*

But what happens after the miracle? What happens after the blinding light of change withdraws and the things of the earth resume their shadows?

What happened to Lazarus after his resurrection? On this, the Gospel according to Saint John is silent. Did Lazarus speak after he was commanded from the grave and his shroud was loosed? Did he thank the one who was his savior and then walk back into the house with his sisters Mary and Martha so they could wash him clean? Or did he turn in anger toward his savior, demanding to know why he had tarried so long with his apostles before coming? *If thou hadst been here, I had not died.*

Where did he go afterward? Did he live a long life? Did he forget his time in the grave? Here is where I went after my resurrection: Miami Beach, Sarasota, Raleigh, Nashville, Peterborough, Madrid, Barcelona, New York City, and Provincetown.

And I went back as an inpatient to the hospital — five more times, at least to date. The hepatitis goes on, the doctor tells me. The transplant doesn't cure it. It gives the virus a new liver to infect and feast upon. *(Dear donor, forgive me, I can't save your life . . .)*

A year after the transplant, just after the anniversary the social worker called my "first birthday," these things happened: low-grade fever; weight gain; edema; jaundice; sudden and unwanted elevations in alkaline phosphatase, bilirubin, and liver enzymes. *This can't be happening,* I thought, *not again.*

"We need to biopsy the liver," the doctor said. He said we needed to measure the progression of the disease by assessing the extent of new cirrhotic scarring. I knew what that meant: it meant the story wasn't over, as I so badly wanted it to be. It meant that things were uncertain.

"Don't worry," the doctor said as he sorted through my file. "We can always discuss retransplantation."

No, I thought, *I can't hear that word, not ever again, especially if it's applied to me.* Where was the miracle now? I was supposed to have been restored. I was supposed to have been made whole. I wanted to loose the graveclothes; I wanted to unbind the napkin from my face; I wanted to be through with death forever.

Instead I was sitting in a windowless medical office, waiting for the phlebotomist to come and draw more blood. I wasn't sure I had the heart for more miracles.

Did Lazarus believe he was done with death after his resurrection? There's no record of whether Christ cured him of the sickness that had killed him in the first place, before he rose again; there's no record of the pain his body must have felt after having lain four days in its grave — long enough to have begun to decompose and (as the Gospel says) *to stinketh.*

As for me: for three weeks I got worse, then I slowly got better. A few months later the doctor said there'd be no need to discuss retransplantation, at least not yet, at least not in the immediate future.

It wasn't a miracle that pulled me back, at least not then: I was saved not by a sudden and divine intervention but by the persistent and real efforts of physicians, some with Cartier watches and others wearing scuffed shoes. The story didn't end with a tongue of flame or a blinding light. Each morning and evening I monitor myself for organ rejection, as I'll do for the rest of my life: blood pressure, temperature, weight. I go to the clinic for blood draws; I await faxes detailing test results.

Here is what happens after the resurrection:

Your body hurts, because it's hard to come to life again after lying so long in a grave, but you set goals and you labor to meet them, holding yourself up with your IV pole as you shuffle down the hospital corridor, slowly building back your strength. You learn your medications; you learn to pack your wounds with sterile gauze; you learn to piss into a bottle and shit into a pan. It's work, preparing yourself for sunlight.

Then the day comes when you are allowed to wash your hair and shower. A little while later you're walking down a street.

People you've not seen in ages stop to ask how you're doing; you say you're doing fine, you're doing great. It's life again, dear ordinary life! Life as you hungered for it, with its pleasures and its requirements.

Yes, it's life again, your life, but it's not the same, not quite. Or so it seems, because you can't forget how it felt to lie in the close darkness of that grave; you can't forget the acrid smell of the earth or the stink of the moldering graveclothes, especially now that you know, as you never did before, that you're headed back to the grave again, as is everyone, and you know this with a clarity you cherish and despise.

The gift of life is saturated with the gift of death.

Sometimes, sleepless at night, I imagine I'm back in the hospital the night of my transplant, lying naked in a cubicle behind a thin curtain, waiting for a nurse to prep me for surgery. *This is how it feels to lie in a cold room,* I tell myself, because this might be my last night on earth and I want to feel everything, to feel once more how life feels, each breath in and each breath out.

The nurse comes in and instructs me to lie on my side. She administers an enema. *This is how it feels to be filled with warm water.* I go to the toilet and afterward I look at myself for a moment in the bathroom mirror. When I return to the cubicle and lie down, the nurse says she must shave the hair from my abdomen, all the way from my groin to my chest. "I hope my hands are warm enough," she says, spreading the shaving soap across my stomach. She touches the cold razor to my belly, and I think, *This is how it feels to be alive.*

CYNTHIA OZICK

The Synthetic Sublime

FROM THE NEW YORKER

MORE THAN any other metropolis of the Western world, New York disappears. It disappears and then it disappears again; or say that it metamorphoses between disappearances, so that every seventy-five years or so another city bursts out, as if against nature — new shapes, new pursuits, new immigrants with their unfamiliar tongues and worried uneasy bustle. In nature, the daffodil blooms, withers, vanishes, and in the spring returns — always a daffodil, always indistinguishable from its precursor. Not so New York, preternatural New York! Go to Twenty-third Street and Eighth Avenue: where is the Grand Opera House, with its statuary and carvings, its awnings and Roman-style cornices? Or reconnoitre Thirteenth Street and Broadway: who can find Wallack's Theatre, where the acclaimed Mrs. Jennings, Miss Plessy Mordaunt, and Mr. J. H. Stoddart once starred, and where, it was said, "even a mean play will be a success"? A hundred years ago, no one imagined the dissolution of these dazzling landmarks; they seemed as inevitable, and as permanent, as our Lincoln Center, with its opera and concerts and plays and its lively streaming crowds.

Yet catapult us forward another hundred years, and (though we won't recognize the place) it is certain to be, uninterruptedly, New York, populous, evolving, faithfully inconstant, magnetic, man-made, unnatural — the synthetic sublime. If you walk along Lexington Avenue, say, it isn't easy to be reminded that Manhattan is an island, or even that it lies, like everything else, under an infinitude of sky. New York's sky is jigsawed, cut into geometric pieces glimpsed between towers or caught slantwise across a granite-and-glass ravine. There is no horizon; the lucky penthouses and fifteenth-floor apartments and offices may have long views, but the streets have almost none. At night, the white glow that fizzes upward from the city — an inverted electric Niagara — obscures the stars, and except for the planetarium's windowless mimicry New York is oblivious of the cosmos. It is nearly as indifferent, by and large, to its marine surround. Walt Whitman once sang of the "tall masts of Mannahatta" and of the "crested and scallop-edg'd waves," but the Staten Island ferry and the Circle Line beat on mastless, and the drumming ribbon of the West Side Highway bars us from the sound and smell of waters rushing or lapping. New York pretends that it is inland and keeps dry indoors and feels shoreless; New York water means faucets and hidden pipes and, now and then, a ceiling leak or the crisis of a burst main. Almost in spite of itself, Riverside Drive looks out on the Hudson and can, if it likes, remember water. On Manhattan's other flank, the FDR Drive swims alongside the East River like a heavy-chuffing landlubber crocodile, unmindful of the moving water nearby. New York domesticates whatever smacks of sea. And when the two rivers, the Hudson and the East, converge and swallow each other at the Battery's feet, it is the bays alone, the Upper and the Lower, that hurry out to meet the true deep. New York turns its back on the Atlantic. The power and the roar New York looks to are its own.

The Russian poet Joseph Brodsky — born in Leningrad, exiled to New York, buried in Venice — used to say that he wrote to please his predecessors, not his contemporaries. Often enough, New York works toward the opposite: it means to impress the here-and-now, which it autographs with an insouciant wrecking ball. For New Yorkers, a millennium's worth of difference can be encompassed in six months. Downtown lofts on spooky dark blocks that once creaked under the weight and thunder and grime of industrial machinery are suddenly filled with sofas upholstered in white linen and oak bars on wheels and paintings under track lighting and polyurethaned coffee tables heaped with European magazines. Bryant Park, notorious shady hangout, blossoms into a cherished noonday amenity. Or else the deserted tenements along the Metro-North line, staring out eyeless and shamefaced at the commuters' train down from Stamford, will, overnight, have had their burned-out hollows covered over with painted plywood — trompe l'oeil windows and flowerpots pretending, Potemkin-like, and by municipal decree, that human habitation has resumed.

Despite New York's sleight-of-hand transmutations and fool-the-eye pranks, the lady isn't really sawed in half: she leaps up, alive and smiling. If physical excision is the city's ongoing principle, there are, anyhow, certain surprising tenacities and keepsake intuitions. Wait, for instance, for the downtown No. 104 at the bus stop on Broadway at Seventy-second Street, look across the way, and be amazed — what Renaissance palazzo is this? A tall facade with draped female sculptures on either side, arched cornices, patterned polychrome bricks: ornamental flourish vying with ornamental flourish. And then gaze down the road to your right: one vast slab after another, the uncompromising severity of straight lines, brilliantly winking windows climbing and climbing, not a curve or entablature or parapet or embrasure ruffling the sleek skin of these new residential monoliths. In sharp winter light, a dazzling juxtaposition, filigreed cheek by modernist jowl. The paradox of New York is that its disappearances contain constancies — and not only because some buildings from an earlier generation survive to prod us toward historical self-consciousness. What is most steadfast in New York has the fleet look of the mercurial: the city's persistent daring, vivacity, enchantment, experiment; the marvel of new forms fired by old passions, the rekindling of the snuffed.

The Lower East Side, those tenement-and-pushcart streets of a century ago, once the venue of synagogues and sukkahs and religious-goods stores and a painful density of population, and later the habitat of creeps and druggies, is now the neighborhood of choice for the great-grandchildren of earlier tenants who were only too happy to escape to the Bronx. At the nearby Knitting Factory and in other clubs, you may catch up with Motel Girl, a band specializing in "Las Vegas stripper *noir*" — avant-garde jazz described as jarring, flashy, seedy, sexy, Movietone-violent, dark. Many of the singers and musicians live in the old tenement flats (toilet down the hall) on Avenue B, with rents as high as a thousand dollars. Broadway and Prince, where Dean & Deluca boasts three hundred varieties of cheese, was home to a notions shop two generations ago; not far away, on Orchard Street, the Tenement Museum stands as an emblem of nostalgic consecration, ignored by its trendy neighbors. You can still buy pickles out of the barrel at Guss's, but the cutting-edge young who come down to Ludlow and Stanton for the music or the glitz rarely find those legendary greenhorn warrens of much historic interest; their turf is the East Village. The Lower East Side's current inhabitants, despite their fascination with the louche, are educated and middle-class, with mothers back on Long Island wishing their guitar-playing daughters had gone to medical school. What these seekers on A, B, and C are after — like their aunts and uncles gyrating in the talismanic Rainbow Room, or like Scott and Zelda plunging into fountains to jump-start the Jazz Age — is New York's insuperable constant: the sense of belonging to the glamorous marrow of one's own time.

Uptown's glamour drive is more domestic. On the Upper West Side, the great style emporia dominate, behemoths of food, cooking devices, leather accessories, "natural" cosmetics, no-color cotton sheets, Mission furniture. Zabar's, the Fairway, Barney Greengrass, Citarella, H & H Bagels — dizzyingly flooded with epicurean getters and spenders — harbor prodigalities of dimpled breads, gourmet coffees, the right kind of polenta, the right kind of rice and salsa, the right kind of coffeemaker. Across town, the Upper East Side seems, in contrast, staid, reserved, nearly quiet. The streets are less peopled. The wind is colder. A hauteur lurks in the limestone. If the West Side is a roiling marketplace, the East Side is a marble lobby presided over by a monarchical doorman. Fifth Avenue can be tacky here and there, but Madison, with its rows of elite European designers, grows more and more burnished, New York's version of the Rue du Faubourg-Saint-Honoré. On Park and Madison, affluence reigns, and with it a certain neighborhood serenity — a privacy, a regal intimacy. (Over on Lexington and Third, the city's rush begins again.)

Posh East and extravagant West dislike each other, with the ingrained antipathy of restraint and profusion, calm and bustle; nor are they likely, except for an audacious handful of crosstown adventurers, to rub elbows in the shops. A silent cold war chills Manhattan. Its weapons are Zabar's in the West, Versace in the East. There is no hot line between them.

Who lives in New York? E. B. White, mulling the question fifty years ago, imagined "a farmer arriving from Italy to set up a small grocery store in a slum, or a young girl arriving from a small town in Mississippi to escape the indignity of being observed by her neighbors, or a boy arriving from the Corn Belt with a manuscript in his suitcase and a pain in his heart." This has a musty if sweetish scent for us now — eau de Jimmy Stewart, perhaps. The circumstances of the arrivals were generally not so benign; neither was their reception. In a 1922 address before the New York–based American Academy of Arts and Letters, Owen Wister, the author of *The Virginian,* said of the newcomers, "Recent arrivals pollute the original spring. . . . It would be well for us if many recent arrivals would become departures." He meant the immigrants who were just then inundating Ellis Island; but the children of those immigrants would soon be sorting out the dilemmas of welcome and unwelcome by other means.

I remember a ferocious street game that was played in the northeast Bronx long ago, in the neighborhood known as Pelham Bay. It was called war, and it was exclusively a girls' game. With a piece of colored chalk you drew a small circle, in which you placed a pink rubber ball. Then you drew a second circle around it, concentric but far larger. This second circle you divided into as many pie slices as there were players. Each player was assigned a pie slice as her designated territory and wrote in it the name of a country she felt to be her own. So it went like this: Peggy Scanlon chose Ireland; Dorothy Wilson, Scotland; Hilda Weber, Germany; Carolyn Johnson, Sweden; Maria Viggiano (whose Sicilian grandmothers yearly wrapped their fig trees in winter canvas), Italy; Allegra Sadacca (of a Sephardic family recently from Turkey, a remnant of the Spanish Jews exiled by Ferdinand and Isabella in 1492), Spain; Madge Taylor (an immigrant from Iowa), America; and I (whose forebears had endured the despots of Russia for nearly a thousand years), Palestine. So much for the local demographics. Immediately after these self-defining allegiances were declared, someone would shriek "War!" and the asphalt mayhem of racing and tackling and tumbling would begin, with the pink rubber globe as prize. I don't suppose little girls anywhere in New York's boroughs nowadays play this disunited-nations game, but if they do, surely the pie slices are chalked up with preferences for Trinidad, Jamaica, Haiti, Puerto Rico, the Dominican Republic, Colombia, Mexico, Peru, Greece, Lebanon, Albania, Pakistan, India, China, and, of course

— for antecedents who were never willing immigrants — Africa. In New York, origins still count, and not always benevolently.

Though proletarian and patrician may inhabit adjoining streets, it is the upper crust that runs the city. This stratum of the social order was once dubbed the Four Hundred, but New York's current patriciate, however it may have multiplied, escapes being counted — though it counts as heavily as ever and remains as conscientiously invisible. Elitism of this kind is rarely political; it almost never becomes mayor. In a democratic ambience, New York's potentates and nabobs have no easy handle; no one names them, not even in tabloid mockery. Then let us call them, collectively, by what they possess: Influence. Influence is financial, corporate, loftily and discreetly legal; Influence is power and planning and money. And money is the armature on which the mammoth superstructure that is New York is sculptured: architecture and philanthropy, art galleries and libraries and foundations, zoos and conservatories and museums, concert halls and universities and houses of worship. The tallest buildings — the Chrysler, the Empire State, the risen polyhedrons of Rockefeller Center, the Twin Towers, assorted old spires — all have their ankles in money. Influence *means* money, whether in the making of it, the spending, or the giving. Influence is usually private and guarded; it may shun celebrity; it needs no public face; its precincts are often reclusive. You are not likely to follow Influence in its daily maneuvers — though you can, all week long, observe the subway riders as they patiently swarm, intent on getting in and getting out and getting there. The jerky cars grind out their wild sawing clamor; locked inside the racket, the passengers display a Buddhist self-forgetfulness. Noiseless Influence, meanwhile, is driven in smoked-glass limousines, hidden, reserved, arcane. If all the rest of the citizenry were carted off and only Influence were left, the city would be silent. But if Influence were spirited away in some grand and ghostly yacht, a kind of Flying Dutchman, say, the men in their dinner jackets, the women in their gowns, what would happen to New York? The mysterious and mazy coursings of money would dry up. The city would come to a halt.

Old money — New York's old muse — made the palaces; time impaired them. Grand Central Terminal, Cornelius Vanderbilt's embellished paragon of a transport temple, by the 1950s had declined into a routinely seedy train depot. But what old money brought into being, new money, along with civic determination, refurbishes. New York, the Eraser and the Renewer, with a sweep of its resuscitating will, has cleansed the temple's degradation. The gawky advertising signs are banished and the constellations on the vaulted horizon scrubbed until their stars glitter. The theme is artful mirroring: the existing grand stair engenders an answering grand stair on the opposite end of the great concourse. Grand Central has no fear of the ornamental; it revels in breadth and unstinting scale; it intends to inspire. The idea of the publicly palatial — unashamed lavishness — has returned.

And not only here. Follow Forty-second Street westward to Fifth Avenue and enter the most illustrious temple of all, the lion-sentried library, where the famed third-floor reading room has just undergone its own rebirth — both in homage to and in dissent from the modern. High-tech computers parade across vast polished tables under a gilded rococo ceiling, a beaux-arts confection frosted with floral arabesques. Whatever the mavens may say and however the critics may scowl, New York (in at least one of its multiple manifestations) thirsts for intimations of what the Victorians did not hesitate to invoke: Noble Beauty. New York has learned to value — though never to venerate — its old robber-baron muses, not for their pre–income-tax devourings but for their appetite for the baronial: the Frick Collection, the Morgan Library, the Cooper-Hewitt (housed in Andrew Carnegie's sixty-four-room mansion). The vanished Pennsylvania Station, the original — razed a generation ago as an elaborate eyesore, now regretted, its bargain-basement replacement a daily discouragement — will soon rise again, in the nearby body of the superannuated General Post Office (Roman, kingly, columned). Fancy, then, a soaring apparition of the Metropolitan Museum of Art, that prototype of urban palace, and of its philosophical rival, the Museum of Modern Art, hovering over the city, scanning it for symptoms of majesty — the Met and MOMA, joined by spectral flights of the City Ballet, the serious little theaters, and Carnegie Hall, all whispering, "Aspire, aspire!"

But grandeur of this style is a neighborhood of the mind, and a narrow one at that. Real neighborhoods and psychological neighborhoods may in fact overlap — literary Greenwich Village being the most storied case in point. Nowadays, Village literariness (Hart Crane, Marianne Moore, and all the rest of the enshrined) hangs as a kind of tattered nimbus not over the old, mostly temporary residences of the celebrated but over the bars, cellars, and cafés they once frequented. Neighborhoods of the mind, though, are rarely so solidly placed in a single site. Of actual neighborhoods (or "sections," in moribund New Yorkese) — SoHo, Tribeca, Chinatown, Little Italy, Chelsea, Gramercy Park, Harlem, Murray Hill, South Street Seaport — only a few are as determinedly self-defined as the Village. But a denizen of any of them can venture out to a collectivity of taste and imagination and familiarity unconstrained by geography. Jazz and blues and nightlife aficionados, movie buffs, gays, rap artists, boxing and wrestling zealots, singles, esoteric-restaurant habitués, Central Park joggers, marathon runners, museum addicts, lovers of music or theater or dance, lonelyhearts, shoppers, hotel weekenders, barflies, churchgoers, Talmud enthusiasts, Bronx-born Tibetan Buddhists, students of Sufism, kabbalists, theosophists, voice or ski coaches, SAT and LSAT crammers, amateur painters, union members, members of boards and trustees, Internet devotees, fans of the Yankees or the Mets or the Jets or the Knicks, believers in psychics and tea-leaf readers, streetwalkers and their pimps, antiques fanciers, art collectors, philanthropists, professors of linguistics, lexicographers, copy editors, librarians, kindergarten teachers, crossing guards, wine votaries, storefront chiropractors, Chinese or Hebrew or Arabic calligraphers — all these, and inconceivably more, can emerge from any locality to live, if only for a few hours, in a sympathetic neighborhood of affinity. Expertise and idiosyncrasy and bursting desire burn and burn in New York: a conflagration of manifold, insatiable, tumultuous will.

I was born in a brownstone on East Eighty-eighth Street, between First and York Avenues — but both the latter avenue and the area have since altered their designations and their character. York was once Avenue A, and the neighborhood, populated largely by German immigrants, was called Yorkville. It was here before my birth that my infant brother was kidnapped by a madwoman. The story as it was told to me is set in a certain year but not in any special weather; it seems to me that it must have been summer. I see my mother, hot, sleeveless, breathless, frantic, running through the night streets of Yorkville to find the kidnapper and snatch her baby back. He had been sleeping in his wicker carriage in a nook among rows of brown bottles and drawers filled with maple-flavored rock candy on strings, not four yards from where my young father, in his pharmacist's jacket, a fountain pen always in its pocket, stood tending to his mortar and pestle, working up a medicinal paste. Into my parents' drugstore the madwoman flew, seizing baby and carriage and all, and out into the dark she fled, only to be discovered some hours later in nearby Carl Schurz Park, disheveled and undone by furious infantile howls, and grateful to relinquish the captive screamer.

In my half-dreaming recreation of this long-ago scene — the stolen child, the fleeing madwoman — why must it be summertime? I think I know why. New York in summer is another sort of city; in mood and weight it has nothing in common with wintry New York. A New York summer is frenetic, syncopated, blistered, frayed, dusty. There is a desperation in its heat, and a sense of letdown, despite relief, in its air-conditioned indoors. Melting squads of tourists, in shorts and open shirts or halters, sweat pooling under their camera straps, their heads swiveling from one gaudy carnival sight to the next, push through Times Square in anxious quick march. Smells of perspiring hot dogs under venders' grease-lined umbrellas mingle with the exhaust fumes of heaving buses. There is nothing relaxed about the summer city. New York's noise is louder, New York's toughness is brasher, New York's velocity is speedier. Everything — stores, offices, schedules, vacations, traffic — demands full steam ahead; no one can say the livin' is easy. New York in July is out of sync, not quite itself, hoping for ransom, kidnapped by midsummer frolicking: picnickers awaiting free twilight performances of Shakespeare in Central Park; street parades of nighttime swelterers along Museum Mile, where tappers and clappers gather before the Jewish Museum to salute the tootling klezmer players; break-dancers down from Harlem, twelve-year-olds effortless and expert and little and lithe, who spin on their heels across from the hive of Madison Square Garden. In the American heartland in summer, babies fall down wells and pipes, and that is news. In New York — fidgety, frittering, frenzied, boiling New York — summer itself is news.

The true city is the winter city. The woolly enchantment of a population swaddled and muffled, women and men in long coats, eccentric boots, winding scarves; steam sculptures forming out of human breath; hushed streets; tiny white electric points on skeletal trees! The icy air like a scratch across a sheet of silver, the smoky chestnut carts, the foggy odor of hot coffee when you open a door, a bakery's sweet mist swirling through its transom, a glimpse of rosy-nosed skaters in the well of the Rockefeller stelae, the rescuing warmth of public lobbies — New York in February is a city of grateful small shocks. And just as in an antiquated English novel of manners, New York has its "season" — lectures, readings, rallies, dinner parties, chamber music in someone's living room. While in summer you cannot rely on the taxis to turn on their air-conditioning, in winter each yellow capsule is a hot little bullet; the driver in his turban remembers his subcontinental home. There is no dusk like a New York winter dusk: the blurry gray of early evening, when the lone walker, ferried between day and night, jostled by strangers in packs, feels most desolate, and when the privacy of burrowing into a coat collar brings on a nameless loss. At such a moment, the forest of flowering lights (a brilliance suddenly apprehended) makes its cheering claim: that here, right here, is importance, achievement, delight in the work of the world; that here, right here, is the hope of connection, and life in its fulfillment. In a gregarious New York winter, especially in restaurants at eight o'clock, you will hear jokes, stories with amazing climaxes, futures plotted out, jealousies retailed, gossip above all: who's up, who's down, what's in, what's out. Central heating never abolished the theory and practice of the fireside.

What Manhattan talks about, obliquely or openly — what it thinks about, whatever the season — is ambition. Europeans always make much of this: how *hard* New Yorkers work, the long days, the paltry vacations, the single-minded avarice for status, the obsessiveness, the terrible drive. What? No *dolce far niente*? But only an outsider would remark on the city's striving; for New Yorkers it is ingrained, taken for granted, valued. Unlike Bartleby, downtown's most distinctive imaginary inhabitant, New York never prefers not to. New York prefers and prefers and prefers — it prefers power and scope to tranquillity and intimacy, it prefers crowds and tumult to gardens and ease, it prefers struggle and steel to acquiescence and cushions. New York is where you go to seize the day, to leave your mark, to live within the nerve of your generation. Some might say that there is nothing new in this — why else did Willa Cather begin in Red Cloud, Nebraska, and end on Bank Street? Why else did Jackson Pollock, born in Cody, Wyoming, land in New York?

Yet there is a difference. New York ambition has changed its face. Fifty years ago, when postal clerks and bank tellers wearing vests were what were still called "family men," the hankering young were on the lowest rung of any hierarchy. Their patience was commanded; their deference was expected. It was understood that power and position were the sovereign right of middle age, and that a twenty-three-year-old would have to wait and wait. Opportunity and recognition were light-years away. A few — writers mostly — broke out early: Mary McCarthy at twenty-two, Norman Mailer at twenty-five, Philip Roth and John Updike at twenty-six. Leonard Bernstein and Bobby Fischer were youthful stars. Still, these were all prodigies and exceptions. In the run-of-the-mill world of getting ahead, the young were at the bottom, and stayed there until judged — by their elders at the top — to be sufficiently ripe. The Information Age, with its ear to the ground, reverses all that. The old ways are undone. A twenty-something young woman in publishing keeps a television set on in her office all day, monitoring possible acquisitions: what sells, who's cool. The auditory and the visual, in whatever mode, belong almost exclusively to the newest generation. Everywhere in New York, the knowledgeable young are in charge of the sound, the image, the latest word; ambition need no longer stand in line and wait its graying turn. Fifty-somethings, their passion still unspent, and recalling the slower passages of long ago, may be a little wistful.

Now and then, heartstruck, I pass the crenellated quasi-Gothic building that once housed my high school, where latecomers, myself among them, would tremble before its great arched doorway, fearing reprimand; but the reprimanders are all dead. My Latin teacher is dead. My German teacher is dead. My biology teacher is dead. It is only the city itself that lives on, half amnesiac, hardly ever glancing back, reinventing its fabric, insisting on being noticed for what it is now. There is no grief for what precedes the common memory, and ultimately the fickle urban tide, as mutable as the Nile, accommodates every disappearance.

In May of 1860, when Frederick Law Olmsted's Central Park

was just in the making, a forty-year-old Wall Street lawyer named George Templeton Strong recorded in his diary his own wistfulness:

> The park below the reservoir begins to look intelligible. Unfinished still, and in process of manufacture, but shewing the outline now of what it is to be. Many points are already beautiful. What will they be when their trees are grown and I'm dead and forgotten?
>
> One thinks sometimes that one would like re-juvenescence, or a new birth. One would prefer, if he could, to annihilate his past and commence life, say in this A.D. 1860, and so enjoy longer acquaintance with this era of special development and material progress, watch the splendid march of science on earth, share the benefits of the steam engine and the electric telegraph, and grow up with this park — which is to be so great a fact for the young men and maidens of New York in 1880, if all goes well and we do not decompose into anarchy meanwhile. . . . Central Park and Astor Library and a developed Columbia University promise to make the city twenty years hence a real center of culture and civilization, furnishing privileges to youth far beyond what it gave me in my boyhood.

A century and a half on, Strong's "era of special development and material progress" may seem quaint to us, for whom fax and e-mail and jets and microwaves are everyday devices, and whose moonwalkers are already old men. By now, the park below the reservoir, the library on Fifth Avenue, and the university on Morningside Heights are seasoned inheritances — established components of the city's culture and civilization. But even standing as we do on the lip of the next millennium, who can resist falling into George Templeton Strong's wishful dream of a new birth and a longer acquaintance? His New York of steam engine and telegraph, as ephemeral as the May clouds of 1860, has ceased to be. Our New York too will melt away, and a renewed and clarified city will lift out of the breathing breast of the one we know. New York, Enemy of the Merely Picturesque, Headquarters of Misery and Marvel, Eraser and Renewer, Brain and Capital of the Continent!

The immigrants will come — what language will they speak? The towers will climb to the sky — what shapes will they have? The crowds will stream in the streets — what thoughts will they think? Will they think our outworn thoughts, or imaginings we cannot imagine?

SCOTT RUSSELL SANDERS

The Force of Spirit

FROM ORION

My wife's father is dying, and I can think of little else, because I love him and I love my wife. Once or twice a week, Ruth and I drive the forty miles of winding roads to visit him in the nursing home. Along the way we pass fields bursting with new corn, stands of trees heavy with fresh leaves, pastures deep in grass. In that long grass the lambs and calves and colts hunt for tender shoots to nibble and for the wet nipples of their mothers to suck. The meadows are thick with flowers, and butterflies waft over the blossoms like petals torn loose by wind. The spring this year was lavish, free of late frosts, well soaked with rain, and now in early June the Indiana countryside is all juiced up.

On our trip to the nursing home this morning, I drive while Ruth sits beside me, knitting. Strand by strand, a sweater grows under her hands. We don't talk much, because she must keep count of her stitches. To shape the silence, we play a tape of Mozart's *Requiem* from a recent concert in which Ruth sang, and I try to detect her clear soprano in the weave of voices. The car fills with the music of sorrow. The sound rouses aches in me from earlier losses, the way cold rouses pain from old bone breaks.

Yet when I look out through the windows at the blaze of sunlight and the blast of green, I forget for minutes at a time where we're going and what we're likely to see when we get there. Ruth must forget as well, because every now and again she glances up from her knitting to recall a story or a task or some odd discovery she's read about recently.

As we slow down for a hamlet named Cope — a cluster of frame houses gathered at a bend in the road — she describes a scientific article that she came across at the lab this past week. After puzzling over what distinguishes living organisms from dead matter, the author, a biologist, had concluded that the vital secret is the flow of electrons in association with oxygen.

I tell her that all sounds reasonable enough, but I wonder why oxygen goes hauling electrons around in the first place.

"He hasn't figured that out yet," she replies.

"Wouldn't it be easier," I say, "for oxygen to sit still and leave matter alone? Why stir things up?"

"In other words, why life?"

"Yeah, why life?"

She laughs. "Ask me an easy one."

"All right," I say. "Why corn? Why shagbark hickories? Why moss and wolves? Why not just rock and dust?"

Used to my pestering her with questions, she normally answers with good humor and patience. But now she merely says, "You'll have to read the article."

A fly beats against the inside of the windshield. Suddenly the crazed, buzzing bit of stuff seems bizarre and precious. I lift one hand from the steering wheel, crank down a window, shoo the fly to freedom, then grip the wheel once more. Now my fingers seem utterly strange. How can they curl so exactly in the shape of my thoughts? The lurching of my heart surprises me, as if a desperate animal has crawled inside my chest. All at once my whole body feels like an implausible contraption, and my skin barely contains the storm of electrons.

What I feel is not exactly panic, because I'm spared for the moment the chill of knowing I will die. What I feel right now is amazement that anything lives, fly or hawk, virus or man. I stare at the radiant fields and woods flowing past our windows, and they seem far-fetched, outrageous. Why all those leaves waving? Why all those juicy stems thrusting at the sky? Why those silky black wings of crows slicing the air? And why am I set moving through this luminous world, only to feel such grief when some patch of woods falls before the saw, when a farm vanishes beneath the pavement of a shopping mall or a valley beneath a reservoir, when a man withers in a nursing home bed?

"What are you thinking?" I ask Ruth, just to make sure my voice works.

"I'm thinking I only need two more inches to finish the front of this sweater."

"About your dad, I mean."

She turns her brown eyes on me, reading my face, which has grown transparent to her gaze over thirty years of marriage. Her own heart-shaped face draws into a frown. "I'm wondering if he'll still know us."

"Surely he's not that far gone," I say.

"Maybe not yet," she agrees.

I turn my attention back to the music, and gradually Mozart restores my composure.

After a while Ruth sets down her knitting and takes up a stack of her father's insurance papers. She's been working on them for months, but the stack keeps growing thicker, each layer of papers recording another bout in the hospital, another round of tests. She circles numbers, places checkmarks beside dates, compares one statement with another, imposing order on this chronicle of illness. Congestive heart failure is the short name for what afflicts him. After coronary seizures, quadruple bypass surgery, the insertion of a pacemaker, and several strokes, and after seventy-eight years of faithfully pumping blood, Earl McClure's heart is simply wearing out.

Near a tiny settlement called Bud, we pass a white barn that bears a warning in letters six feet high: AT THE END THERE IS JUDGMENT! One side of the barn is painted with the silhouette of a man hanging on a cross, the figure entirely black except for two white rings marking the eyes, which glare out like searchlights. A caption explains, "He died for you."

Ruth and I have known since childhood who he is, this dangling man, for we both spent nearly all of our childhood Sundays in Methodist churches, singing hymns, memorizing Bible verses, listening to sermons, learning that Jesus saves. Although Ruth still sings regularly in a church choir and I sit in a pew on the occasional Sunday morning with a Bible in my lap, neither of us any longer feels confident that the man on the cross will preserve us from annihilation, nor that he will reunite us with our loved ones in heaven. The only meetings we count on are those we make in the flesh. The only time we're sure about is right now.

"Whenever we pass by here," Ruth says, "I wonder why anybody would paint such a scary picture on a barn. Who'd want to look every day at those awful eyes?"

"They're meant to keep your mind on ultimate things as you milk the cows."

"They're creepy," she insists.

I agree, but I also understand the attraction of a faith that eases the sting of loss, including the loss of one's own precious life. Until I was twenty or so I embraced that faith, hoping for heaven; then I gradually surrendered it under the assault of science, and in dismay over witnessing so much evil carried out in Christ's name. I no longer believe that Jesus can do our dying for us; we must do that for ourselves, one by one. Yet I've not given up believing in the power that was supposed to have sent him to redeem us, the Creator who laid the foundations of the world.

For the last few miles of our drive to the nursing home, I study the land. There's a shaping intelligence at work here, I feel sure of it. I sense a magnificent energy in the grasses bowing beneath the wind, in the butterflies flouncing from blossom to blossom, in the trees reaching skyward and the jays haranguing from the topmost branches and the clouds fluffing by. I sense in this rippling countryside a tremendous throb and surge, the same force that squeezes and relaxes my heart. Everything rides on one current. As I listen to the music of grief filling the car, as I go with my wife to visit her dying father, the world, for all its density and weight, seems made of breath.

Legend has it that Mozart died while composing the *Requiem,* a few measures into the section beginning with the Latin word *Lacrimosa,* which means tearful or weeping. "On that day of weeping," the verse proclaims,

> again from the ashes will arise
> guilty mankind, to be judged.

That much he orchestrated, but he never completed the remainder of the verse:

> Therefore, spare this one, O God,
> Merciful Lord Jesus,
> And grant them rest.

Officially, the one to be spared from God's wrath was the dearly departed wife of the count who had commissioned this mass for the dead, but the ailing Mozart must also have been mourning himself. Another scrap of legend claims that in those final days he said, "It is for myself that I am writing this." I suspect he was grieving as well for his own dearly departed, especially his mother, who had died some years earlier in Paris while he was there looking for work.

Ruth's mother died last October, not long before the chorus began rehearsing the *Requiem.* By the time of her death, Dessa McClure had been whittled away by Alzheimer's disease for half a dozen years, losing her memory, speech, balance, and strength, becoming again as a little child. This was not the sort of child she had aspired to become, for she meant to find her way to heaven by achieving a clear vision and a simple heart. Toward the end, her vision grew cloudy, and the world became a blur of strange rooms and unknown faces. And at the very end, while she was rising from a bath, her heart quit.

The nurse who'd been helping her at the time told us afterward, "She went limp all of a sudden and dropped right down and was gone."

Ruth's father, still able to get around fairly well back then, had just been to see Dessa in the special care unit, where patients suffering from various forms of dementia drifted about like husks blown by an idle breeze. She had seemed almost happy, he recalled. She even whistled a bit, and showed no signs of pain. And he was sure she'd recognized him by the way she squeezed his finger and smiled. He let that be his last glimpse of her, for he chose not to look at his wife's body after the nurses brought him news of her death.

But Ruth saw her laid out in the nursing home, still crumpled, as if, when breath departed, the body had collapsed like an empty sack. Ruth was so appalled by the image that she insisted on seeing her mother's body one more time before the cremation. And so, after we had finished our business in the funeral home, she and I slipped into a back room to gaze for a moment at the shell of her mother resting on a cart, all but the face hidden by a white sheet, the skin pale except for dark rings under the shut eyes. We knew this face, yet it seemed aloof and slack, for it had been peeled away from the person to whom it once belonged. Beneath the sheet, the body lay as motionless as a piece of furniture covered with drapery in a vacant house. I put my arm around Ruth, not so much to comfort her as to comfort me, to feel the warmth and weight of her. She tilted her head against my shoulder and stood there for a long while without speaking. Then she leaned forward, ran a hand over that forsaken face, and turned to go.

The heart is only a muscle. It's a meaty pump that shoves and sucks the blood that carries the oxygen that carries the electrons that keep us alive. It beats forty or a hundred and forty times a minute, hour after hour, day after day, until, between one contraction and the next, it falters and stops. When surgeons lay the heart open to repair valves and carve out damaged tissue, they find no spirit hiding there, no seat of the soul. Biologists can trace it back down the evolutionary path to the earliest twitchings of life in the sea.

Yet who can accept that we're merely meat? Who can shake the suspicion that we're more than two-legged heaps of dust accidentally sprung into motion? Whatever the doctors and biologists claim, we go on using the word "heart" as if it pointed to an emotional center, a core of integrity. We trust those who speak from the heart. We're wary of those who are heartless and hardhearted. Have a heart, we say, begging for kindness. Home is where the heart is, we say.

We're drawn irresistibly to our heartthrob, who knows how to pluck our heartstrings. We long to feel heart's-ease by fulfilling our heart's desire. In our earnest pronouncements, we appeal to hearts and minds, heart and soul. Swearing most solemnly, we cross our hearts and hope to die, if what we say should be a lie. Heartfelt and heartsick, heartland and heartache, heartwood and heartbreak: the word, like the muscle beating in our chest, is indispensable. The beliefs we truly live by, the ones we'll die for, are those we hold in our heart of hearts.

At the nursing home, we find Ruth's father drowsing on his bed, arms outstretched as if he has fallen there from a great height. He wears a white shirt, brown dress pants, low knit socks that leave his ankles bare, and lace-up leather shoes. His hair, still dark and full, is neatly combed. Except for his gauntness, he might be a man resting after a day at the office. Yet he's too frail even to stand up for more than a few minutes at a time. His wrists are sticks. His cheeks are hollow. Blue veins show through the translucent skin of his jaw.

I can see Ruth hesitate before waking him, because she wonders if he will recognize her. So long as he sleeps, she remains his daughter. At last she lightly touches one of those out-flung arms, and he startles awake. Behind thick spectacles, his eyes are milky and uncertain. He looks bewildered for a moment, and then he beams, reaching out to grasp Ruth's hand.

"Hey, there," he says. "I'd about given up on you."

"Don't you worry," she answers. "If I say I'm coming, I'm coming."

"Well, I was thinking —" he begins, then loses his way and falls silent with an embarrassed little shrug.

But he has said enough to assure Ruth that he knows her, that he's still there in his withered body. She asks how he's feeling, how he's eating, whether he's had any visitors, whether the nurses have been treating him well, and he answers each question in two or three words, staring up into her face and squeezing her hand.

To say that he is dying makes it sound as though he's doing something active, like singing or dancing, but really something's being done to him. Life is leaving him. From one visit to the next we can see it withdrawing, inch by inch, the way the tide retreating down a beach leaves behind dry sand. With each passing day he has more and more trouble completing sentences, as if words too were abandoning him.

I hang back, awkward before his terrible weakness. Eventually he notices me standing near the foot of his bed.

"Why, here's Scott," he says.

I step closer. "Came to see if you're behaving yourself."

"I am, pretty much," he says. "How was the drive over?"

"It was beautiful," I tell him, lifting my voice because I can see he's chosen not to wear his hearing aids. "Everything's blooming. The corn's shooting up. Some of the hay is cut and drying."

"Good, good," he murmurs. Then he asks if I've been watching the NBA tournament, which I haven't, and so he tells me, pausing for breath between sentences, how the Indiana Pacers lost to the New York Knicks. The Pacers had a lead going into the fourth quarter, but their legs gave out. "I understand tired legs," he says, and gives a rheumy laugh.

Ruth and I exchange looks, amazed that he's following basketball. He's also following our children, Eva and Jesse, for now he asks what they've been up to since our last visit. After we've told him, he repeats bits of what we've said, as if to pin memory down: "So Jesse's working in the restaurant. Is that right? And Eva's studying birds? She bought a new computer?" His voice is thin and soft, like a trickle of water over smooth stone.

Since we saw him last, Ruth and I have attended a college graduation in Ohio. He remembers this as well, and asks if we had a good time. We did, I answer. And then I tell him about watching the graduates troop across the stage as each name was called, most of them so young and spry they fairly danced in their black robes, while parents and friends and fellow students cheered. A few waddled heavily or limped stiffly. Two scooted across in electric chairs. Then, near the end of the ceremony, one slight woman who'd been waiting in line among those receiving degrees in nursing rose from a wheelchair, labored up the stairs, and slowly crossed the stage while holding on to the arm of a young man. When the president gave her the diploma and shook her hand, the audience broke out in the loudest applause of the afternoon. We clapped because many of us knew she was gravely ill with cancer, she'd not been expected to live until commencement, and yet she'd refused to give up. Now here she was, onstage for a moment, drawing our praise.

When I finish my story, which poured out of me before I thought how it might sound in the ears of a dying man, Ruth's father says, "She's got spunk."

"She does," I answer.

"I like that," he says. "You can never have too much spunk." He rouses a bit to report that he's going once a day to physical therapy. They wheel him down there in his chair, but then they make him stand up and push a walker across the room to build up his legs and make him lift dumbbells to build up his arms.

"Pumping iron, are you?" I say.

"I need to get my strength back." He raises an arm and the sleeve droops down, revealing the tender bruised skin of his wrist.

We learned from a doctor this week that his heart now pumps blood at 20 percent of the normal rate, and it will keep on dwindling. His eyes close, but he doesn't let go of Ruth's hand. She says we'd better let him get some rest. Does he need anything before we go? Yes, he answers, three things: his bathrobe, an extra pair of trousers, and his electric shaver.

I go to fetch them from his apartment on the floor below, a comfortable suite of rooms where he'll never be able to stay by himself again. Going there and coming back, I take the stairs two at a time. I rush down the halls past elderly residents who look at me as if I'm a lunatic. There's no reason to race, except that I still can, and so I do, savoring the bounce in my legs and the wild flutter in my chest.

I want a name for the force that keeps Earl McClure asking questions while the tide of life withdraws from him. I want a name for the force that abandoned the body of Dessa McClure and left it like a piece of shrouded furniture on a cart in the funeral home. I want a name for the force that carried a woman dying of cancer through her studies and across a stage to claim her diploma. I want a name for the force that binds me to Ruth, to her parents, to my parents, to our children, to neighbors and friends, to the land and all its creatures.

This power is larger than life, although it contains life. It's tougher than love, although it contains love. It's akin to the power I sense in lambs nudging the teats of their dams to bring down milk, in the raucous tumult of crows high in trees, in the splendor of leaves gorging on sun. I recognize this force at work in children puzzling over a new fact, in grownups welcoming strangers, in our capacity, young and old, for laughter and kindness, for mercy and imagination.

No name is large enough to hold this power, but of all the inadequate names, the one that comes to me now is spirit. I know the risks of using such a churchy word. Believers may find me blasphemous for speaking of the wind that blows through all things without tracing the breath to God. Nonbelievers may find me superstitious for invoking any force beyond gravity, electromagnetism, and the binding energy of atoms. But I must run those risks, for I cannot understand the world, cannot understand my life, without appealing to the force of spirit. If what I feel for my wife or her father and mother is only a byproduct of hormones, then what I feel for swift rivers or slow turtles, for the shivering call of a screech owl or the green thrust of bloodroot breaking ground, is equally foolish. If we and the creatures who share the earth with us are only bundles of quarks in motion, however intricate or clever the shapes, then our affection for one another, our concern for other species, our devotion to wildness, our longing for union with the Creation are all mere delusions.

I can't prove it, but I believe we're more than accidental bundles of quarks, more than matter in motion. Our fellowship with other creatures is real, our union with the Creation is already achieved, because we all rise and fall on a single breath. You and I and the black-footed ferret, the earth, the sun, and the far-flung galaxies, are dust motes whirling in the same great wind. Whether we call that magnificent energy Spirit or Tao, Creator or God, Allah or Atman, or some other holy name, or no name at all, makes little difference, so long as we honor it. Wherever it flows — in person or place, in animal or plant or the whole of nature — we feel the pressure of the sacred, and that alone deserves our devotion.

A gusty breeze is pawing the grass and churning the ponds as Ruth and I drive back from the nursing home over the winding roads. Neither of us can bear to hear the *Requiem* again right now, so we talk. She remembers stories of her father from when he was strong — how he lifted her in and out of bed when she was down with rheumatic fever, how he laid fires in a charcoal grill when the family went camping, how he dug up the yard to plant roses. She recalls how, in their last house before the nursing home, her father and mother used to stand spellbound at the dining room window and watch birds at the feeders. And she recalls how, even in the final stark days, her mother shuffled to the birdcage in the special care unit and watched the fierce, tiny finches darting about, squabbling and courting. From inside the Alzheimer's daze, her mother would say nothing, but sometimes she whistled at the finches, and sometimes she laughed.

As if summoned by these memories of Dessa and Earl McClure, birds fill this blustery June afternoon here in southern Indiana. We see goldfinches dipping and rising as they graze among the waving seedheads of the tall grasses. We see red-winged blackbirds clinging to the tops of cattails that sway in the breeze. We see a kettle of hawks, a swirl of starlings, a fluster of crows. A great blue heron goes beating by, and six or eight geese plow the ruffled waters of a lake. Near the barn that's painted with the crucified man, more than a dozen turkey vultures spiral over a field, a lazy black funnel pointing down toward carrion.

There's an abundance in this teeming land that promises to make up for anything lost to vultures. The corn seems to have shot up higher since our drive over this morning. In the afternoon heat the woods bristle and the pastures heave and the fields are charged with light.

After a while Ruth takes up her knitting, clacks along for a few stitches, then puts it down again. Gazing out the window, she recalls in a soft voice how she thought of her mother at every rehearsal of the *Requiem,* and how moved she was at the performance itself when the conductor announced that the concert would be given in memory of Dessa McClure. Ruth had been forewarned of this gesture, but still she had to blink hard to read the opening measures.

We pass a hayfield where a tractor is rolling the cut grass into fat round bales, and I can't help thinking of the verse in Isaiah:

> All flesh is grass,
> and all its beauty is like the flower of the field.
> The grass withers, the flower fades,
> when the breath of the Lord blows upon it;
> surely the people is grass.

These days, I'm in no danger of forgetting how swiftly every living thing withers. But I also remember that grass, once cut, sprouts up again from the roots. Whatever Lord breathes upon this world of crickets and constellations blows beginnings as well as endings. The Latin word for breath is *spiritus,* which also means courage, air, and life. Our own word "spirit" carries all those overtones for me when I use it to speak of the current that lifts us into this life and bears us along and eventually lets us go.

We pass more fields scattered with round bales of hay like herds of slow, ungainly beasts. When we come up behind a truck on the road sagging under the weight of a single great bale, a stream of chaff comes blowing back at us, and loose bits float in through our open windows.

I reach over to brush some straw from Ruth's lap. She grabs my hand and holds on.

"I hate to think of clearing out Daddy's things," she says. "We'll have to find who wants what, then get rid of the rest."

"Let's hope that won't be for a while yet," I say.

She doesn't answer. We drive on through the lush green countryside. I remember when we cleared out Dessa's things, how we found more than forty Bibles and hundreds of religious books, which she had long since lost the ability to read. In drawers and cupboards we found entry forms for sweepstakes, because she had decided, as her mind began to go, that winning some game of chance might set things right. And we found lists she had made of crucial events in her life — her marriage, her children's births, her surgeries, her husband's heart attack, the death of her parents, the moves from house to house — all the personal history that was slipping away from her. On page after page in a spiral notebook she wrote down in broken phrases what mattered to her, what defined her life, as if words on paper might preserve what the mind no longer could hold.

I make my own lists, in sentences and paragraphs rather than broken phrases, because language has not yet abandoned me. I am making such a list now, here in these pages. You've seen the long version. A short version of the story I've been telling you might say only:

Ruth, Earl, Dessa,
corn, crow, grass,
wind, dirt, sun.

LYNNE SHARON SCHWARTZ

At a Certain Age

FROM THE THREEPENNY REVIEW

WHEN I WAS YOUNG I was a fairly good judge of age. No longer. Everyone between twenty and forty looks more or less the same to me, and so does everyone between forty and sixty. But for some reason I can tell the ages of children very accurately: I can see the difference between three and a half and four, or eight and nine.

Also, my friends do not age. They all seem around forty-five. Some are in fact around forty-five and some are less: over the years I've made several young friends, partly with selfish calculation — in case I live long, I won't find myself friendless, the friends of my age having died off. But even the older ones seem around forty-five. If I make a serious effort to recall their age, I always come up with the age they were when I first learned it, as if our friendship has persisted in a timeless medium. This is true even of the friends who are what is called "a certain age" — the women, that is, for it is invariably women who attain a certain age; men have a number.

"A certain age." As if the actual number were too shameful to utter. A phrase rich with contempt in the guise of deference. A condescending phrase. Cancer was spoken of that way not so long ago. People didn't want to embarrass the poor sufferer by speaking the word. And they were superstitious — it might happen to them if they let the word so much as float over their tongues. "He has a growth," they would say. "It's malignant," if they were brave. A certain age is malignant too. I will surely die of it in time.

Now that I myself may be a certain age — I'm not sure when it starts, since it is never specified — I think about age all the time. I think about age the way younger people think about sex. I haven't stopped thinking about sex, but its mysteries no longer tease me. I know a lot about sex at my certain age. But age is still a mystery, so I think about it. I watch for its signs. Not so much the tangible signs, though those are appalling in their sneaky gradualness and irreversibility, and I work hard at staving them off. I imagine a contest between my efforts and age's incursions. I know, of course, who the winner will be; the thrill of the contest is seeing how long I can delay its victory. The signs I watch for more closely are not the obvious ones but the negative ones, the little things I can no longer do, or do as well. The diminishments. So far they are few and I would not, at this point at least, dream of naming them.

Thinking about age has borne prejudices, alas. I have preconceptions about people depending on their ages; I like to ascertain people's ages so I can judge them properly. I favor the old. I have always had an affinity for the old, even when I was young. I like the way they look. I've never especially connected beauty with youth and am always surprised when someone says of an older woman, a woman of a certain age, *She must have been a great beauty,* since to me she still is. But then I'm not looking the way men look, with "beauty" meaning they'd like to sleep with her. I'm looking at the aesthetic object.

The old are more substantial, even when physically frail. Time has textured their nature and their words along with their skin and their voices. I tend to think the opinions of people under thirty-five are negligible; by the time they're forty or so they may be worth paying attention to. People over fifty are trustworthy; over sixty, they're either wise or they should be. All this is very wrong, I know. Older people tolerated me and listened to me when I was young. I appreciate now how tolerant they were. And yet, like racists or sexists who also should know better, I cling to my prejudices as truth.

Even worse, I feel the only people who can understand and properly appreciate me are around my age. I used to allow a ten-year range for this understanding, then a five-year range. Now I feel the most kinship for people within two or three years of my age, and the time may come when I can speak freely and wholeheartedly only to people born in the same month as I was.

One of the many things young people don't know is that everyone no longer chronologically young is privately young, or at least younger; we all have an age at which, subjectively, we stopped aging. We were comfortable there and remained: perhaps it's the age at which we felt fully ourselves, or felt finally grown up. But if we each have an optimum age, what happens when we pass it? We lead a kind of double life, one life in the actual world, where the numbers accumulate, and the other in a temporal no man's land.

I regret that my children will not often think of me as I was at thirty-eight, say, or even forty-one, but most likely as I am just before death. That is how I most often recall my mother. It's hard to keep in mind, when picturing the dead, that they spent only a short time in that worn state in which we picture them, and that for most of their life they were younger and more vigorous, blessed with an uncertain future.

As a child, when I asked my mother her age she was coy and evasive: in our family, the ages of women were never spoken aloud. My father liked to boast of his age in company, as if the combination of his years and his vigor were noteworthy, and my mother would fret and try to make him stop, for if he announced he was sixty, could she be far behind? As an adult, I didn't dream of asking her age — it would have been an immense breach of courtesy. I figured I'd find out when she died. I didn't have to wait that long. At some point, she wanted us to open a joint bank account, and I saw her year of birth on the cards the bank had us fill out. Had she really cared about concealing her age, she could have had me fill out my section of the cards first, when they were blank. I took this oversight or perhaps nonchalance about her age as itself a sign of age: either she had lost the acuity to be devious, or else she was giving in, her vanity depleted. Her age surprised me — my guesses had been off by about six years; her past evasions had been successful.

I think I may begin lying about my age too. I can imagine times when it would be advantageous. Or just for the hell of it. I can probably get away with about five or six years, like my mother. For now, at any rate. But if I start now and later on begin to look my actual age, people will think I have aged prematurely or look old for my age. That is not desirable either. A dilemma to ponder — but not for too long.

Why lie? Despite the encouraging books on aging which proclaim its great gifts, old age is an embarrassment, both for those who have it and for those who regard it. If its gifts were so great, there would be no need for books to proclaim them. The old, however beautiful and substantial, are disconcerting. They mar the *tableau vivant,* not by their appearance but by what they signify, the nearness of death. Mortality embarrasses us; the notion that notwithstanding all our efforts we must die is literally mortifying. The old, in all their gallantry, signify our common helplessness: the more gallant they are in the face of approaching death, the more vividly they denote our plight.

Thinking about age is thinking about death. Approaching death: how to parse the phrase? Is it approaching me, or am I approaching it? Either way, will we come face to face in ten minutes or ten months or ten years, and what exactly will be the form of our greeting? Which indignities are in store? Once I thought I'd rather die than live with certain physical humiliations; now I'm more amenable. I could manage, given the alternative.

For the most part death seems an outrage, the rudest of interruptions. But at times it seems not so bad — a relief, even, to have the whole business over with. There are a few things I'd like to get done first, though. Also a few things I'd like to live to see. Still, it is some consolation to think that if I died in ten minutes, or even ten months, I'd be considered young to die, even if I'm not considered young to be alive.

I may not even be considered truly alive; I can't be sure. I recently had an intense, intimate, and mildly sexually charged conversation with a man I assumed was my own age. He had that nice, substantial, slightly worn look. Later I discovered he was quite a bit younger. Maybe I had mistaken the sexual charge; maybe he was talking so intimately because he felt the freedom of talking to an "older" woman. Not a happy thought. At this certain age, when I make such a discovery, I cannot say with confidence exactly what the air was charged with.

This is because a certain age engenders the famous invisibility. I've observed it, naturally: men digging up the street no longer stop eating their sandwiches to gawk at me. But I'm not invisible to everyone. Older men look at me, men over fifty, that is. We look at each other. There's an implicit and amused recognition along with the sexual flicker: *Those kids must be blind!* we say. *Yes, it's not that we're invisible, but that they're blind!* This is pleasant, especially as I've always been drawn to older, even old, men. Despite this penchant,

I married a man who is a mere four years older, which at the time I married him was an appropriate and conventional age difference. I was incapable then of doing anything so unconventional as marrying an "older" man, and at this point it's a good thing I didn't, for he might well be dead. Out in the world, I would look at old men, then think, *This is silly, why am I looking at these old guys when I have this attractive and virile youngish man right at home?* Now, with time, he has become just the sort of older man I always liked. This is one of the unanticipated rewards of age. Not a reward that would be granted to old men who like young women, and if I had in fact broken with convention to marry one of those, as time passed he might have become increasingly disenchanted and left me for someone younger.

It's assumed that women who like older men are thinking of their fathers. This is true only in a very small way, like most psychological explanations. I loved my father, but he was not really my type. I enjoy seeing one of his features, a tone of voice or a gesture, turn up in some stranger, but apart from the little gust of nostalgia, the intriguing thing is how my father's familiar tone of voice or gesture meshes into the unfamiliar configuration of a stranger who is unlike my father in every other way. I would not like the stranger any better were he more like my father; I might like him less.

But this may be taking the psychological explanation too literally. Apart from their specific features, fathers, ideally, are people who take care of you, and perhaps women who like older men want to be taken care of. That would be appealing, I grant, but in fact at a certain age one no longer expects it to happen — one has become so accustomed to taking care of others — and besides, the ways I would enjoy being taken care of are not at all the ways — quite solid, honorable, and uninteresting — I recall my father taking care of me.

Obviously this could lead to further thickets of the psyche, but psychological explanations are among the many sets of belief I've shed with age. I hardly believe in anything anymore except the brutality, greed, stupidity, and capacity for destruction of the human race and the need to counteract them by doing good. I'm not much interested in personal improvement either, as I was when young. I thought of myself and my life as a kind of giant sculpture I worked on patiently day by day, chipping away here, adding there, forever remodeling with a view to perfection. No longer. I may still chip and model, but more in a spirit of curiosity than of perfectability.

Age itself, in the encouraging books, is considered ameliorative, bringing wisdom, acceptance, and freedom from petty vanities. It's true that at a certain age a certain wise and philosophical acceptance settles over you, like a cloud. That is inevitable, considering all we've seen, and one should never scorn wisdom. Still, my own acceptance seems a loss of vitality. No doubt I'm obtuse in thinking so, but I would rather retain the qualities that need to vanish in order for wisdom, acceptance, and freedom from vanity to take their place, qualities like impulsiveness and struggle and energy and endless hope. The thing about fighting and struggle that philosophical and accepting people don't grasp is that we fighters and strugglers enjoy it. Luckily I can still struggle to accept my acceptance.

My mother, were she still alive, would be horrified at my setting down these thoughts. Not horrified at the thoughts themselves. No. She would say, *You're telling the whole world how old you are.* But now that I may be a certain age, it may be time to stop thinking about what my mother would say.

PETER SINGER

The Singer Solution to World Poverty

FROM THE NEW YORK TIMES MAGAZINE

IN THE BRAZILIAN FILM *Central Station,* Dora is a retired schoolteacher who makes ends meet by sitting at the station writing letters for illiterate people. Suddenly she has an opportunity to pocket a thousand dollars. All she has to do is persuade a homeless nine-year-old boy to follow her to an address she has been given. (She is told he will be adopted by wealthy foreigners.) She delivers the boy, gets the money, spends some of it on a television set, and settles down to enjoy her new acquisition. Her neighbor spoils the fun, however, by telling her that the boy was too old to be adopted — he will be killed and his organs sold for transplantation. Perhaps Dora knew this all along, but after her neighbor's plain speaking, she spends a troubled night. In the morning Dora resolves to take the boy back.

Suppose Dora had told her neighbor that it is a tough world, other people have nice new TVs too, and if selling the kid is the only way she can get one, well, he was only a street kid. She would then have become, in the eyes of the audience, a monster. She redeems herself only by being prepared to bear considerable risks to save the boy.

At the end of the movie, in cinemas in the affluent nations of the world, people who would have been quick to condemn Dora if she had not rescued the boy go home to places far more comfortable than her apartment. In fact, the average family in the United States spends almost one third of its income on things that are no more necessary to them than Dora's new TV was to her. Going out to nice restaurants, buying new clothes because the old ones are no longer stylish, vacationing at beach resorts — so much of our income is spent on things not essential to the preservation of our lives and health. Donated to one of a number of charitable agencies, that money could mean the difference between life and death for children in need.

All of which raises a question: in the end, what is the ethical distinction between a Brazilian who sells a homeless child to organ peddlers and an American who already has a TV and upgrades to a better one, knowing that the money could be donated to an organization that would use it to save the lives of kids in need?

Of course, there are several differences between the two situations that could support different moral judgments about them. For one thing, to be able to consign a child to death when he is standing right in front of you takes a chilling kind of heartlessness; it is much easier to ignore an appeal for money to help children you will never meet. Yet for a utilitarian philosopher like myself — that is, one who judges whether acts are right or wrong by their consequences — if the upshot of the American's failure to donate the money is that one more kid dies on the streets of a Brazilian city, then it is in some sense just as bad as selling the kid to the organ peddlers. But one doesn't need to embrace my utilitarian ethic to see that at the very least, there is a troubling incongruity in being so quick to condemn Dora for taking the child to the organ peddlers while at the same time not regarding the American consumer's behavior as raising a serious moral issue.

In his 1996 book, *Living High and Letting Die,* the New York University philosopher Peter Unger presented an ingenious series of imaginary examples designed to probe our intuitions about whether it is wrong to live well without giving substantial amounts of money to help people who are hungry, malnourished, or dying from easily treatable illnesses like diarrhea. Here's my paraphrase of one of these examples:

Bob is close to retirement. He has invested most of his savings in a very rare and valuable old car, a Bugatti, which he has not been able to insure. The Bugatti is his pride and joy. In addition to the pleasure he gets from driving and caring for his car, Bob knows that its rising market value means that he will always be able to sell it and live comfortably after retirement. One day when Bob is out for a drive, he parks the Bugatti near the end of a railway siding and goes for a walk up the track. As he does so, he sees that a runaway train, with no one aboard, is running down the railway track. Looking farther down the track, he sees the small figure of a child very likely to be killed by the runaway train. He can't stop the train and the child is too far away to warn of the danger, but he can throw a switch that will divert the train down the siding where his Bugatti is parked. Then nobody will be killed — but the train will destroy his Bugatti. Thinking of his joy in owning the car and the financial security it represents, Bob decides not to throw the switch. The child is killed. For many years to come, Bob enjoys owning his Bugatti and the financial security it represents.

Bob's conduct, most of us will immediately respond, was gravely wrong. Unger agrees. But then he reminds us that we too have opportunities to save the lives of children. We can give to organizations like UNICEF or Oxfam America. How much would we have to give one of these organizations to have a high probability of saving the life of a child threatened by easily preventable diseases? (I do not believe that children are more worth saving than adults, but since no one can argue that children have brought their poverty on themselves, focusing on them simplifies the issues.) Unger called up some experts and used the information they provided to offer some plausible estimates that include the cost of raising money, administrative expenses, and the cost of delivering aid where it is most needed. By his calculation, $200 in donations would help a sickly two-year-old transform into a healthy six-year-old — offering safe passage through childhood's most dangerous years. To show how practical philosophical argument can be, Unger even tells his readers that they can easily donate funds by using their credit card and calling one of these toll-free numbers: (800) 367-5437 for UNICEF; (800) 693-2687 for Oxfam America.

Now you too have the information you need to save a child's life. How should you judge yourself if you don't do it? Think again about Bob and his Bugatti. Unlike Dora, Bob did not have to look into the eyes of the child he was sacrificing for his own material comfort. The child was a complete stranger to him and too far away to relate to in an intimate, personal way. Unlike Dora too, he did not mislead the child or initiate the chain of events imperiling him. In all these respects, Bob's situation resembles that of people able but unwilling to donate to overseas aid and differs from Dora's situation.

If you still think that it was very wrong of Bob not to throw the switch that would have diverted the train and saved the child's life, then it is hard to see how you could deny that it is also very wrong not to send money to one of the organizations listed above. Unless, that is, there is some morally important difference between the two situations that I have overlooked.

Is it the practical uncertainties about whether aid will really reach the people who need it? Nobody who knows the world of overseas aid can doubt that such uncertainties exist. But Unger's figure of $200 to save a child's life was reached after he had made conservative assumptions about the proportion of the money donated that will actually reach its target.

One genuine difference between Bob and those who can afford to donate to overseas aid organizations but don't is that only Bob can save the child on the tracks, whereas there are hundreds of millions of people who can give $200 to overseas aid organizations. The problem is that most of them aren't doing it. Does this mean that it is all right for you not to do it?

Suppose that there were more owners of priceless vintage cars — Carol, Dave, Emma, Fred, and so on, down to Ziggy — all in exactly the same situation as Bob, with their own siding and their own switch, all sacrificing the child in order to preserve their own cherished car. Would that make it all right for Bob to do the same? To answer this question affirmatively is to endorse follow-the-crowd ethics — the kind of ethics that led many Germans to look away when the Nazi atrocities were being committed. We do not excuse them because others were behaving no better.

We seem to lack a sound basis for drawing a clear moral line between Bob's situation and that of any reader of this article with $200 to spare who does not donate it to an overseas aid agency. These readers seem to be acting at least as badly as Bob was acting when he chose to let the runaway train hurtle toward the unsuspecting child. In the light of this conclusion, I trust that many readers will reach for the phone and donate that $200. Perhaps you should do it before reading further.

*

Now that you have distinguished yourself morally from people who put their vintage cars ahead of a child's life, how about treating yourself and your partner to dinner at your favorite restaurant? But wait. The money you will spend at the restaurant could also help save the lives of children overseas! True, you weren't planning to blow $200 tonight, but if you were to give up dining out just for one month, you would easily save that amount. And what is one month's dining out compared to a child's life? There's the rub. Since there are a lot of desperately needy children in the world, there will always be another child whose life you could save for another $200. Are you therefore obliged to keep giving until you have nothing left? At what point can you stop?

Hypothetical examples can easily become farcical. Consider Bob. How far past losing the Bugatti should he go? Imagine that Bob had got his foot stuck in the track of the siding, and if he diverted the train, then before it rammed the car it would also amputate his big toe. Should he still throw the switch? What if it would amputate his foot? His entire leg?

As absurd as the Bugatti scenario gets when pushed to extremes, the point it raises is a serious one: only when the sacrifices become very significant indeed would most people be prepared to say that Bob does nothing wrong when he decides not to throw the switch. Of course, most people could be wrong; we can't decide moral issues by taking opinion polls. But consider for yourself the level of sacrifice that you would demand of Bob, and then think about how much money you would have to give away in order to make a sacrifice that is roughly equal to that. It's almost certainly much, much more than $200. For most middle-class Americans, it could easily be more like $200,000.

Isn't it counterproductive to ask people to do so much? Don't we run the risk that many will shrug their shoulders and say that morality, so conceived, is fine for saints but not for them? I accept that we are unlikely to see, in the near or even medium-term future, a world in which it is normal for wealthy Americans to give the bulk of their wealth to strangers. When it comes to praising or blaming people for what they do, we tend to use a standard that is relative to some conception of normal behavior. Comfortably off Americans who give, say, 10 percent of their income to overseas aid organizations are so far ahead of most of their equally comfortable fellow citizens that I wouldn't go out of my way to chastise them for not doing more. Nevertheless, they should be doing much more, and they are in no position to criticize Bob for failing to make the much greater sacrifice of his Bugatti.

At this point various objections may crop up. Someone may say, "If every citizen living in the affluent nations contributed his or her share, I wouldn't have to make such a drastic sacrifice, because long before such levels were reached the resources would have been there to save the lives of all those children dying from lack of food or medical care. So why should I give more than my fair share?" Another, related objection is that the government ought to increase its overseas aid allocations, since that would spread the burden more equitably across all taxpayers.

Yet the question of how much we ought to give is a matter to be decided in the real world — and that, sadly, is a world in which we know that most people do not, and in the immediate future will not, give substantial amounts to overseas aid agencies. We know too that at least in the next year, the United States government is not going to meet even the very modest United Nations–recommended target of 0.7 percent of gross national product; at the moment it lags far below that, at 0.09 percent, not even half of Japan's 0.22 percent or a tenth of Denmark's 0.97 percent. Thus, we know that the money we can give beyond that theoretical "fair share" is still going to save lives that would otherwise be lost. While the idea that no one need do more than his or her fair share is a powerful one, should it prevail if we know that others are not doing their fair share and that children will die preventable deaths unless we do more than our fair share? That would be taking fairness too far.

Thus, this ground for limiting how much we ought to give also fails. In the world as it is now, I can see no escape from the conclusion that each one of us with wealth surplus to his or her essential needs should be giving most of it to help people suffering from poverty so dire as to be life-threatening. That's right: I'm saying that you shouldn't buy that new car, take that cruise, redecorate the house, or get that pricy new suit. After all, a thousand-dollar suit could save five children's lives.

So how does my philosophy break down in dollars and cents? An American household with an income of $50,000 spends around

$30,000 annually on necessities, according to the Conference Board, a nonprofit economic research organization. Therefore, for a household bringing in $50,000 a year, donations to help the world's poor should be as close as possible to $20,000. The $30,000 required for necessities holds for higher incomes as well. So a household making $100,000 could cut a yearly check for $70,000. Again, the formula is simple: whatever money you're spending on luxuries, not necessities, should be given away.

Now, evolutionary psychologists tell us that human nature just isn't sufficiently altruistic to make it plausible that many people will sacrifice so much for strangers. On the facts of human nature, they might be right, but they would be wrong to draw a moral conclusion from those facts. If it is the case that we ought to do things that, predictably, most of us won't do, then let's face that fact head-on. Then, if we value the life of a child more than going to fancy restaurants, the next time we dine out we will know that we could have done something better with our money. If that makes living a morally decent life extremely arduous, well, then that is the way things are. If we don't do it, then we should at least know that we are failing to live a morally decent life — not because it is good to wallow in guilt but because knowing where we should be going is the first step toward heading in that direction.

When Bob first grasped the dilemma that faced him as he stood by that railway switch, he must have thought how extraordinarily unlucky he was to be placed in a situation in which he must choose between the life of an innocent child and the sacrifice of most of his savings. But he was not unlucky at all. We are all in that situation.

FLOYD SKLOOT

Gray Area: Thinking with a Damaged Brain

FROM CREATIVE NONFICTION

I USED TO BE ABLE to think. My brain's circuits were all connected and I had spark, a quickness of mind that let me function well in the world. There were no problems with numbers or abstract reasoning; I could find the right word, could hold a thought in mind, match faces with names, converse coherently in crowded hallways, learn new tasks. I had a memory and an intuition that I could trust.

All that changed on December 7, 1988, when I contracted a virus that targeted my brain. A decade later, my cane and odd gait are the most visible evidence of damage. But most of the damage is hidden. My cerebral cortex, the gray matter that MIT neuroscientist Steven Pinker likens to "a large sheet of two-dimensional tissue that has been wadded up to fit inside the spherical skull," has been riddled with tiny perforations. This sheet and the thinking it governs are now porous. Invisible to the naked eye, but readily seen through brain imaging technology, are areas of scar tissue that constrict blood flow. Anatomic holes, the lesions in my gray matter, appear as a scatter of white spots like bubbles or a ghostly pattern of potshots. Their effect is dramatic; I am like the brain-damaged patient described by neuroscientist V. S. Ramachandran in his book *Phantoms in the Brain:* "Parts of her had forever vanished, lost in patches of permanently atrophied brain tissue." More hidden still are lesions in my Self, fissures in the thought process that result from this damage to my brain. When the brain changes, the mind changes — these lesions have altered who I am.

Neurologists have a host of clinical tests that let them observe what a brain-damaged patient can and cannot do. They stroke his sole to test for a spinal reflex known as Babinski's sign or have him stand with feet together and eyes closed to see if the ability to maintain posture is compromised. They ask him to repeat a set of seven random digits forward and four in reverse order, to spell *world* backward, to remember three specific words such as *barn* and *handsome* and *job* after a spell of unrelated conversation. A new laboratory technique, positron emission tomography, uses radioactively labeled oxygen or glucose that essentially lights up specific and different areas of the brain being used when a person speaks words or sees words or hears words, revealing the organic location for areas of behavioral malfunction. Another new technique, functional magnetic resonance imaging, allows increases in brain blood flow generated by certain actions to be measured. The resulting computer-generated pictures, eerily colorful relief maps of the brain's lunar topography, pinpoint hidden damage zones.

But I do not need a sophisticated and expensive high-tech test to know what my damaged brain looks like. People living with such injuries know intimately that things are awry. They see it in activities of daily living, in the way simple tasks become unmanageable. This morning, preparing oatmeal for my wife, Beverly, I carefully measured out one-third cup of oats and poured them onto the pan's lid rather than into the bowl. In its absence, a reliably functioning brain is something I can almost feel viscerally. The zip of connection, the shock of axon-to-axon information flow across a synapse, is not simply a textbook affair for me. Sometimes I see my brain as a scalded pudding, with fluky dark spots here and there through its dense layers and small scoops missing. Sometimes I see it as an eviscerated old TV console, wires all disconnected and misconnected, tubes blown, dust in the crevices.

Some of this personal, low-tech evidence is apparent in basic functions like walking, which for me requires intense concentration, as does maintaining balance and even breathing if I am tired. It is apparent in activities requiring the processing of certain fundamental information. For example, no matter how many times I have been shown how to do it, I cannot assemble our vacuum cleaner or our poultry shears or the attachments for our hand-cranked pasta maker. At my writing desk, I finish a note and place the pen in my half-full mug of tea rather than in its holder, which quite obviously teems with other pens. I struggle to figure out how a pillow goes into a pillowcase. I cannot properly adjust Beverly's stereo receiver in order to listen to the radio; it has been and remains useful to me only in its present setting as a CD player. These are all public, easily discernible malfunctions.

However, it is in the utterly private sphere that I most acutely experience how changed I am. Ramachandran compares this to harboring a zombie, playing host to a completely nonconscious being somewhere inside yourself. For me, being brain-damaged also has a physical, conscious component. Alone with my ideas and dreams and feelings, turned inward by the isolation and timelessness of chronic illness, I face a kind of ongoing mental vertigo in which thoughts teeter and topple into those fissures of cognition I mentioned earlier. I lose my way. I spend a lot of time staring into space, probably with my jaw drooping, as my concentration fragments and my focus dissolves. Thought itself has become a gray area, a matter of blurred edges and lost distinctions, with little that is sharp about it. This is not the way I used to be.

In their fascinating study, *Brain Repair,* an international trio of neuroscientists — Donald G. Stein from America, Simon Brailowsky from Mexico, and Bruno Will from France — report that after injury, "both cortical and subcortical structures undergo dramatic changes in the pattern of blood flow and neural activity, even those structures that do not appear to be directly or primarily connected with the zone of injury." From this observation, they conclude that "the entire brain — not just the region around the area of damage — reorganizes in response to brain injury." The implications of this are staggering; my entire brain, the organ by which my very consciousness is controlled, was reorganized one day ten years ago. I went to sleep *here* and woke up *there;* the place looked the same, but nothing in it worked the way it used to.

If Descartes was correct, and to think is to be, then what happens when I cannot think, or at least cannot think as I did, cannot think well enough to function in a job or in the world? Who am I?

You should hear me talk. I often come to a complete stop in midsentence, unable to find a word I need, and this silence is an apt reflection of the impulse blockage occurring in my brain. Sitting next to Beverly as she drives our pickup truck through Portland traffic at six P.M., I say, "We should have gone for pizza to avoid this blood . . ." and cannot go on. I hear myself; I know I was about to say "blood tower traffic" instead of "rush hour traffic." Or I manifest staggered speech patterns — which feels like speaking with a limp — as I attempt to locate an elusive word. "I went to the . . . *hospital* yesterday for some . . . *tests* because my head . . . *hurt.*" Or I blunder on, consumed by a feeling that something is going wrong, as when I put fresh grounds into the empty carafe instead of the filter basket on my coffeemaker, put eyedrops in my nose, or spray the cleaning mist into my face instead of onto the shower walls. So at the dinner table I might say "Pass the sawdust" instead of "Pass the rice," knowing even as it happens that I am saying something inappropriate. I might start a conversation about "Winston Salem's new CD" instead of Wynton Marsalis's or announce that "the shore is breaking" when I mean to say "the shower is leaking." There is nothing smooth or unified anymore about the process by which I communicate; it is disintegrated and unpredictably awkward. My brain has suddenly become like an old man's. Not gradually, the way such changes occur naturally, but overnight, I was geezered.

It is not just about words. I am also *dyscalculic,* struggling with the math required to halve a recipe or to figure out how many more pages are left in a book I'm reading. If we are on East 82nd and Third Avenue in Manhattan, staying with my childhood friend Larry Salander for the week, it is very difficult for me to compute how far away the Gotham Book Mart is over on West 47th between Fifth and Sixth, though I spent much of my childhood in the city.

Because it is a place where I still try to operate normally, the kitchen is an ideal neurological observatory. After putting the leftover chicken in a plastic bag, I stick it back in the oven instead of the refrigerator. I put the freshly cleaned pan in the refrigerator, which is how I figure out that I must have put the chicken someplace else, because it's missing. I pick up a chef's knife by its blade. I cut off an eighth of a giant white onion and then try to stuff the remainder into a recycled sixteen-ounce yogurt container that might just hold the small portion I set aside. I assemble ingredients for a vinaigrette dressing, pouring the oil into an old olive jar, adding balsamic vinegar, mustard, a touch of fresh lemon juice, and spices. Then I screw the lid on upside down and shake vigorously, spewing the contents everywhere. I stack the newspaper in the wood stove for recycling. I walk the garbage up our two-hundred-yard-long driveway and try to put it in the mailbox instead of the trash container.

At home is one thing; when I perform these gaffes in public, the effect is often humiliating. I can be a spectacle. In a music store last fall, I was seeking an instruction book for Beverly, who wanted to relearn how to play her old recorder. She informed me that there were several kinds of recorders; it was important to buy exactly the right category of book, since instructions for a soprano recorder would do her no good while learning on an alto. I made my way up to the counter and nodded when the saleswoman asked what I wanted. Nothing came out of my mouth, but I did manage to gesture over my right shoulder like an umpire signaling an out. I knew I was in trouble, but forged ahead anyway, saying, "Where are the books for sombrero reporters?" Last summer in Manhattan, I routinely exited from the subway stations and led Beverly in the wrong direction, no matter which way we intended to go. She kept saying things like "I think west is *that* way, sweetie" while I confidently and mistakenly headed east, into the glare of the morning sun, or "Isn't that the river?" as I led her away from our riverside destination. Last week, in downtown Portland on a warm November morning, I stopped at the corner of 10th and Burnside, one of the busiest crossings in the city, carefully checked the traffic light (red) and the traffic lanes (bus coming), and started to walk into the street. A muttering transient standing beside me on his way to Powell's Books, where he was going to trade in his overnight haul of tomes for cash, grabbed my shoulder just in time.

At home or not at home, it ultimately makes no difference. The sensation of dysfunctional mentation is like being caught in a spiral of lostness. Outside the house, I operate with sporadic success, often not knowing where I am or where I'm going or what I'm doing. Inside the house, the same feelings often apply, and I find myself standing at the top of the staircase wondering why I am going down. Even inside my head there is a feeling of being lost, thoughts that go nowhere, emptiness where I expect to find words or ideas, dreams I never remember.

Back in the fall, when it was Beverly's birthday, at least I did remember to go to the music store. More often, I forget what I am after within seconds of beginning the search. As she gets dressed for work, Beverly will tell me what she wants packed for lunch, and I will forget her menu by the time I get up the fourteen stairs. Now I write her order down, like a waiter. Sometimes I think I should carry a pen at all times. In the midst of preparing a salad, I stop to walk the four paces over to the little desk where we keep our shopping list and forget "tomatoes" by the time I get there. So I should also have paper handy everywhere. Between looking up a phone number and dialing it, I forget the sequence. I need the whole phone book on my speed-dial system.

Though they appear without warning, these snafus are no longer strange to me. I know where they come from. As Dr. Richard M. Restak notes in *The Modular Brain,* "a common error frequently resulting from brain damage involves producing a semantically related word instead of the correct response." But these paraphasias and neologisms, my expressive aphasias, and my dyscalculas and my failures to process — the rapids of confusion through which I feel myself flailing — though common for me and others with brain damage, are more than symptoms to me. They are also more than what neurologists like to call "deficits," the word of choice when describing impairment or incapacity of neurological function, as Oliver Sacks explains in his introduction to *The Man Who Mistook His Wife for a Hat.* These "deficits" have been incorporated into my very being, my consciousness. They are now part of my repertoire. Deficits imply losses; I have to know how to see them as gains.

Practitioners of neuroscience call the damage caused by trauma, stroke, or disease "an insult to the brain." So pervasive is this language that the states of Georgia, Kentucky, and Minnesota, among others, incorporate the phrase "insult to the brain" in their statutory definitions of traumatic brain injury for disability determinations. Such insults, according to the Brain Injury Association of Utah, "may produce a diminished or altered state of consciousness, which results in an impairment of cognitive abilities or physical functioning." The death of one Miles Dethmuffen, front man and founding member of the Boston rock band Dethmuffen, was attributed in news reports to "an alcoholic insult to the brain." The language used is so cool. There is this sentence from the Web site

NeuroAdvance.com: "When there is an insult to the brain, some of the cells die." Yes.

"Insult" is an exquisitely zany word for the catastrophic neurological event it is meant to describe. In current usage, of course, "insult" generally refers to an offensive remark or action, an affront, a violation of mannerly conduct. To insult is to treat with gross insensitivity, insolence, or contemptuous rudeness. The medical meaning, however, as with so many other medical words and phrases, is different, older, linked to a sense of the word that is some two or three centuries out of date. "Insult" comes from the Latin compound verb *insultare,* which means "to jump on" and is also the root word for "assault" and "assail." It's a word that connotes aggressive physical abuse, an attack. Originally it suggested leaping upon the prostrate body of a foe, which may be how its link to contemptuous action was forged.

Though "an insult to the brain" (a blow to the head, a metal shard through the skull, a stroke, a viral "attack") is a kind of assault, I am curious about the way contempt has found its way into the matter. Contempt was always part of the meaning of insult, and now it is primary to the meaning. Certainly a virus is not acting contemptuously when it targets the brain; neither is the pavement nor steering wheel nor falling wrench nor clot of blood nor most other agents of insult. But I think society at large, medical scientists, insurers, legislators, and the person on the street do feel a kind of contempt for the brain-damaged, with their comical way of walking, their odd patterns of speech or ways in which neurological damage is expressed, their apparent stupidity, their abnormality. The damage done to a brain seems to evoke disdain in those who observe it and shame or disgrace in those who experience it.

The poet Peter Davison has noticed the resonant irony of the phrase "an insult to the brain" and made use of it in his poem "The Obituary Writer." Thinking about the suicide of John Berryman, the heavily addicted poet whose long-expected death in 1972 followed years of public behavior symptomatic of brain damage, Davison writes that "his hullabaloos/of falling-down drunkenness were an insult to the brain." In this poem, toying with the meaning of the phrase, Davison suggests that Berryman's drinking may have been an insult to his brain, technically speaking, but that watching him was, for a friend, another kind of brain insult. He has grasped the fatuousness of the phrase as a medical term, its inherent judgment of contempt, and made use of it for its poetic ambiguity.

But I have become enamored of the idea that my brain has been insulted by a virus. I use it as motivation. There is a long tradition of avenging insults through duels or counterinsults, through litigation, through the public humiliation of the original insult. So I write. I avenge myself on an insult that was meant, it feels, to silence me by compromising my word-finding capacity, my ability to concentrate and remember, to spell or conceptualize, to express myself, to think.

The duel is fought over and over. I have developed certain habits that enable me to work — a team of seconds, to elaborate this metaphor of a duel. I must be willing to write slowly, to skip or leave blank spaces where I cannot find words that I seek, compose in fragments and without an overall ordering principle or imposed form. I explore and make discoveries in my writing now, never quite sure where I am going, but willing to let things ride and discover later how they all fit together. Every time I finish an essay or poem or piece of fiction, it feels as though I have faced down the insult.

In his book *Creating Mind,* the Harvard neurobiologist John E. Dowling says "the cerebral cortex of the human brain, the seat of higher neural function — perception, memory, language, and intelligence — is far more developed than is the cerebral cortex of any other vertebrate." Our gray matter is what makes us human. Dowling goes on to say that "because of the added neural cells and cortical development in the human brain, new facets of mind emerge." Like the fractured facet of a gemstone or crystal, like a crack in the facet of a bone, a chipped facet of mind corrupts the whole, and this is what an insult to the brain does.

Though people long believed, with Aristotle, that the mind was located within the heart, the link between brain and mind is by now a basic fact of cognitive science. Like countless others, I am living proof of it. Indeed, it is by studying the behavior of brain-damaged patients like me that medical science first learned, for example, that the brain is modular, with specific areas responsible for specific functions, or that functions on one side of the body are controlled by areas on the opposite side of the brain. "The odd behavior of these patients," says Ramachandran, speaking of the brain-damaged, "can help us solve the mystery of how various parts of the brain create a useful representation of the external world and generate the illusion of 'self' that endures in space and time." Unfortunately, there is ample opportunity to observe this in action, since, according to the Brain Injury Association, more than two million Americans suffer traumatic brain injury every year, a total that does not include damage by disease.

No one has yet explained the way a brain produces what we think of as consciousness. How does the firing of an electrical impulse across a synapse produce love, math, nightmare, theology, appetite? Stated more traditionally, how do brain and mind interact? Bookstore shelves are now filled with books, like Steven Pinker's brilliant 1997 study, *How the Mind Works,* that attempt to explain how a three-pound organ the consistency of Jell-O makes us see, think, feel, choose, and act. "The mind is not the brain," Pinker says, "but what the brain does."

And what the brain does, according to Pinker, "is information processing, or computation." We think we think with our brain. But in doing its job of creating consciousness, the brain actually relies upon a vast network of systems and is connected to everything — eyes, ears, skin, limbs, nerves. The key word is "processing." We actually think with our whole body. The brain, however, takes what is shipped to it, crunches the data, and sends back instructions. It converts; it generates results. Or, when damaged, does not. There is nothing wrong with my sensory receptors, for instance. I see quite well. I can hear and smell; my speech mechanisms (tongue, lips, nerves) are intact. My skin remains sensitive. But it's in putting things together that I fail. Messages get garbled, blocked, missed. There is, it sometimes seems, a lot of static when I try to think, and this is the gray area where nothing is clear any longer.

Neurons, the brain's nerve cells, are designed to process information. They "receive, integrate, and transmit," as Dowling says, receiving input from dendrites and transmitting output along axons, sending messages to one another across chemical passages called synapses. When there are lesions like the ones that riddle my gray matter, processing is compromised. Not only that, certain cells have simply died and with them the receiving, integrating, and transmitting functions they performed.

My mind does not make connections because, in essence, some of my brain's connectors have been broken or frayed. I simply have less to work with, and it is no surprise that my IQ dropped measurably in the aftermath of my illness. Failing to make connections, on both the physical and metaphysical levels, is distressing. It is very difficult for me to free-associate; my stream of consciousness does not absorb runoff or feeder streams well, but rushes headlong instead. Mental activity that should follow a distinct pattern does not, and indeed, I experience my thought process as subject to random misfirings. I do not feel in control of my intelligence. Saying "Pass me the tracks" when I intended to say "Pass me the gravy" is a nifty example. Was it because "gravy" sounds like "grooves," which led to "tracks," or because my tendency to spill gravy leaves tracks on my clothes? A misfire, a glitch in the gray area that thought has become for me, and as a result my ability to express myself is compromised. My very nature seems to have altered.

I am also easily overloaded. I cannot read the menu or converse in a crowded, noisy restaurant. I get exhausted at Portland Trailblazers basketball games, with all the visual and aural imagery, all the manufactured commotion, so I stopped going nine years ago. My hands are scarred from burns and cuts that occurred when I tried to cook and converse at the same time. I cannot drive in traffic, especially in our standard-transmission pickup truck. I cannot talk about, say, the fiction of Thomas Hardy while I drive; I need to be given directions in small doses rather than all at once and need those directions to be given precisely at the time I must make the required turn. This is, as Restak explains, because driving and talking about Hardy, or driving and processing information about where to turn, are handled by different parts of the brain, and my brain's parts have trouble working together.

I used to write accompanied by soft jazz, but now the least pattern of noises distracts me and shatters concentration. My entire writing process, in fact, has been transformed as I learned to work with my newly configured brain and its strange snags. I have become an avid note-taker, a jotter of random thoughts that might or might not find their way together or amount to anything, a writer of bursts instead of steady work. A slight interruption — the movement of my cat across my window view, the call of a hawk, a spell of coughing — will not just make me lose my train of thought, it will leave me at the station for the rest of the day.

I have just finished reading a new book about Muhammad Ali, *King of the World,* by David Remnick. I anticipated identifying a bit with Ali, now suffering from Parkinson's disease, who shows so strikingly what brain damage can do, stripped as he is of so many of the functions — speech, movement, spontaneity — that once characterized him. But it was reading about Floyd Patterson that got me.

Patterson was a childhood hero of mine. Not only did we share a rare first name, we lived in neighboring towns — he was in Rockville Center, on Long Island, while I was five minutes away in Long Beach, just across the bridge. I was nine when he beat Archie Moore to take the heavyweight championship belt, almost twelve when he lost it to Ingemar Johannson, and almost thirteen when he so memorably won it back. The image of Johannson's left leg quivering as he lay unconscious on the mat is one of those vivid memories that endures (because, apparently, it is stored in a different part of the brain from other, less momentous memories). That Floyd, like me, was small of stature in his world, was shy and vulnerable, and I was powerfully drawn to him.

During his sixty-four professional fights, his long amateur career, his many rounds of sparring to prepare for fights, Patterson absorbed a tremendous amount of damage to his brain. Now, in his sixties, his ability to think is devastated. Testifying in court earlier this year in his capacity as head of the New York State Athletic Commission, Patterson "generally seemed lost," according to Remnick. He could not remember the names of his fellow commissioners, his phone number or secretary's name or lawyer's name. He could not remember the year of his greatest fight, against Archie Moore, or "the most basic rules of boxing (the size of the ring, the number of rounds in a championship fight)." He kept responding to questions by saying, "It's hard to think when I'm tired."

Finally, admitting "I'm lost," he said, "Sometimes I can't even remember my wife's name, and I've been married thirty-two, thirty-three years." He added again that it was hard for him to think when he was tired. "Sometimes I can't even remember my own name."

People often ask if I will ever "get better." In part, I think what they wonder about is whether the brain can heal itself. Will I be able, either suddenly or gradually, to think as I once did? Will I toss aside the cane, be free of symptoms, have all the functions governed by my brain restored to smooth service, rejoin the world of work and long-distance running? The question tends to catch me by surprise, because I believe I have stopped asking it myself.

The conventional wisdom has long been that brains do not repair themselves. Other body tissue, other kinds of cells, are replaced after damage, but we have as many brain cells at age one as we will ever have. This has been a fundamental tenet of neuroscience, yet it has also long been clear that people do recover, fully or in part, from brain injury. Some stroke victims relearn to walk and talk; feeling returns in once numb limbs. Children — especially children — recover and show no lasting ill effects from catastrophic injuries or coma-inducing bouts of meningitis.

So brain cells do not get replaced or repaired, but brain-damaged people occasionally do regain function. In a sense, then, the brain heals, but its cells do not.

There are in general five theories about the way people might recover function lost to brain damage. One suggests that we do not need all of our brain because we only use a small part of it to function. Another is that some brain tissue can be made to take over functions lost to damage elsewhere. Connected to this is the idea that the brain has a backup mechanism in place allowing cells to take over like understudies. Rehabilitation can teach people new ways to perform some old tasks, bypassing the whole damaged area altogether. And finally, there is the theory that in time, and after the chemical shock of the original injury, things return to normal and we just get better.

It is probably true that for me, a few of these healing phenomena have taken place. I have, for instance, gotten more adept at tying my shoes, taking a shower, driving for short periods. With careful preparation, I can appear in public to read from my work or attend a party. I have developed techniques to slow down my interactions with people or to incorporate my mistakes into a longer-term process of communications or composition. I may not be very good in spontaneous situations, but given time to craft my responses I can sometimes do well. But I still can't think.

A recent development promises to up the ante in the game of recovery from brain damage. The *New York Times* reported in October of 1998 that "adult humans can generate new brain cells." A team at the Salk Institute for Biological Studies in La Jolla, California, observed new growth in cells of the hippocampus, which controls learning and memory in the brain. The team's leader, Dr. Fred Gale, expressed the usual cautions; more time is needed to "learn whether new cell creation can be put to work" and under what conditions. But the findings were deemed both "interesting" and "important."

There is only one sensible response to news like this. It has no personal meaning to me. Clinical use of the finding lies so far in the future as to be useless, even if regenerating cells could restore my lost functions. Best not to think about this sort of thing.

Because in fact, the question of whether I will ever get better is meaningless. To continue looking outside for a cure, a "magic bullet," some combination of therapies and treatments and chemicals to restore what I have lost, is to miss the point altogether. Certainly if a safe, effective way existed to resurrect dead cells or generate replacements, and if this somehow guaranteed that I would flash back or flash forward to "be the person I was," it would be tempting to try.

But how would that be? Would the memories that have vanished reappear? Not likely. Would I be like the man, blind for decades, who had sight restored and could not handle the experience of vision, could not make sense of a world he could see? I am, in fact, who I am now. I have changed. I have learned to live and live richly as I am now. Slowed down, softer, more heedful of all that I see and hear and feel, more removed from the hubbub, more internal. I have made certain decisions, such as moving from the city to a remote rural hilltop in the middle of acres of forest, that have turned out to be good for my health and even my soul. I have gained the love of a woman who knew me before I got sick and likes me much better now. Certainly I want to be well. I miss being able to think clearly and sharply, to function in the world, to move with grace. I miss the feeling of coherence or integrity that comes with a functional brain. I feel old before my time.

In many important respects, then, I have already gotten better. I continue to learn new ways of living with a damaged brain. I continue to make progress, to avenge the insult, to see my way around the gray area. But no, I am not going to be the man I was. In this, I am hardly alone.

MARK SLOUKA

Listening for Silence

FROM HARPER'S MAGAZINE

MUSIC, Claude Debussy once famously remarked, is the stuff between the notes, an observation that resonates, pardon the pun, from the flawless spacing of a Billie Holiday tune to the deletions — whether generous or cruel — in our daily lives. Essentially neuter, neither balm nor curse, silence, like light or love, requires a medium to give it meaning, takes on the color of its host, adapts easily to our fears and needs. Quite apart from whether we seek or shun it, silence orchestrates the music of our days.

I'm well aware, of course, that one man's music is another man's noise, that the primary differences between a cork-lined room and solitary confinement are the lock on the door and the sensibility of the inmate. I wish not to define silence but to inquire about its absence, and I ask the question not to restate the obvious — that silence, in its way, is fundamental to life, the emotional equivalent of carbon — but because everywhere I turn I see a culture willing to deny that essential truth. In my idle moments I picture a god from my son's book of myths (with an Olympian straw and sucked-in cheeks) drawing the silence out of the land, and if the conceit is fanciful, the effect, sadly, is not: as silence disappears, the world draws tighter, borders collapse, the public and the private bleed and intermix. Victim to the centripetal pull, the imagination crackles with the static of outside frequencies, while somewhere in the soul — listen! — a cell phone is chirping. Answer it quickly, before someone else does.

*

At the close of the millennium, a new Tower of Babel, monolingual (despite the superficial mixture of tongues), homogeneous (because almost invariably pitched in the vernacular of the marketplace), casts its shadow over the land. Ubiquitous, damn near inescapable, it is rearranging the way we live, forcing crucial adjustments in our behavior, straining our capacity for adaptation. If it continues to grow, as I believe it will, future generations may one day distinguish our age not for its discovery of Elsewhere, as E. B. White called the world beyond the television screen, but for its colonization of silence.

Ensnared in webs of sound, those of us living in the industrialized West today must pick our way through a discordant, infinite-channeled auditory landscape. Like a radio stuck on permanent scan, the culture lashes us with skittering bits and bytes, each dragging its piece of historical or emotional context: a commercial overheard in traffic, a falsely urgent weather report, a burst of canned laughter, half a refrain. The pager interrupts lectures, sermons, second acts, and funerals. Everywhere a new song begins before the last one ends, as though to guard us against even the potential of silence. Each place we turn, a new world — synthetic, fragmented, often as not jacked into the increasingly complex grid that makes up the global communications network — encroaches on the old world of direct experience, of authentic, unadorned events with their particular, unadorned sounds.

Although a great deal has been said about our increasingly visual age, the changes to our aural landscape have gone relatively unremarked. The image has grown so voracious that any child asked to sum up the century will instantly visualize Einstein's hair and Hitler's mustache, mushroom clouds and moon landings; this despite the fact that each of these visual moments has its aural correlative, from the blast over Hiroshima to the high-pitched staccato ravings of the Führer, to Neil Armstrong's static-ridden "giant leap for mankind."

But make no mistake: sound will have its dominion. The aural universe, though subtler than the one that imprints itself on our retina, is more invasive, less easily blocked. It mocks our sanctuaries as light never can. If my neighbor decides to wash his car in front of my study window, as he does often, I can block out the uninspiring sight of his pimpled posterior by drawing the shades; to block out his stereo, I must kill noise with noise. We hear in our sleep. There is no aural equivalent for the eyelid. In our day, when the phone can ring, quite literally, anywhere on the planet, this is not necessarily good news.

I have nothing against my aural canal. I adore music (though I make it badly). I have nothing against a good party, the roar of the crowd. But I make a distinction between nourishment and gluttony: the first is a necessity, even a pleasure; the second, a symptom. Of what? In a word, fear. One of the unanticipated side effects of connectedness. Perhaps because it's never enough, or because, having immersed ourselves in the age of mediation (as Bill Gates refers to it), accustomed ourselves to its ways and means, we sense our dependency. Or because, finally, like isolated apartment dwellers running the TV for company, we sense a deeper isolation beneath the babble of voices, the poverty of our communications. So, adaptable to a fault, we embrace this brave new cacophony, attuned, like apprentice ornithologists, to the distinguishing calls of a mechanical phylum. Capable of differentiating between the cheeps and chimes of the cell phones, portable phones, baby monitors, pagers, scanners, personal digital assistants, laptop computers, car alarms, and so on that fill our lives, we've grown adept, at the same time, at blocking them out with sounds of our own, at forcing a privacy where none exists.

At the supermarket, a middle-aged man in a well-cut suit is calling someone a bitch on the phone. Unable to get to the ricotta cheese, I wait, vaguely uncomfortable, feeling as though I'm eavesdropping. At the gym, the beeps of computerized treadmills clash with the phones at the front desk, the announcements of upcoming discounts, the disco version of Gordon Lightfoot's "If You Could Read My Mind." A number of individuals in Walkman earphones, unaware that they've begun to sing, bellow and moan like the deaf.

"I love a wide margin to my life," Thoreau remarked, quaintly, referring to the space — the silence — requisite for contemplation, or, more quaintly, the forming of a self. A century and a half later, aural text covers the psychic page, spills over; the margin is gone. Walking to work, we pass over rumbling pipes and humming cables, beneath airplane flight corridors and satellite broadcasts, through radio and television transmissions whose sounds, reconstituted from binary code, mix and mingle, overlap and clash, and everywhere drifts the aural refuse of our age.

Thus may the stuff between the discordant notes of our lives require — and I'm not unaware of the irony here — a few words in its defense. Begin anywhere. The cottage in which I spend my summers is silent yet full of sound: the rainy hush of wind in the oaks, the scrabble of a hickory nut rolling down the roof, the slurp of the dog in the next room, interminably licking himself . . . I've never known perfect silence. I hope to avoid making its acquaintance for some time to come, yet I court it daily.

My ambivalence toward silence is natural enough: the grave, the scythe, the frozen clock, all the piled symbols of death, reinforce an essential truth, a primal fear: beneath the sloping hood, death is voiceless. Silence spits us out and engulfs us again, one and all, and all the noisemakers on Bourbon Street, all the clattering figurines in Cuernavaca, can't undo the unpleasant fact that *el día,* properly understood, always ends in *la muerte,* that quiet, like a pair of great parentheses around a dependent clause, closes off our days. Sorry.

But if it's true that all symphonies end in silence, it's equally true that they begin there as well. Silence, after all, both buries and births us, and just as life without the counterweight of mortality would mean nothing, so silence alone, by offering itself as the eternal Other, makes our music possible. The image of Beethoven composing against the growing void, like all clichés, illuminates a common truth: fear forces our hand, inspires us, makes visible the things we love.

But wait. Does this mean that all is well? That the pendulum swings, the chorus turns in stately strophe and antistrophe, the buds of May routinely answer winter's dark aphelion? Not quite. We are right to be afraid of silence, to resist that sucking vacuum — however much we depend on it — to claw and scratch against oblivion. The battle is in deadly earnest. And therein lies the joke. Resistance is one thing, victory another.

Left partially deaf by a childhood inflammation of the mastoid bones, Thomas Edison throughout his life embraced the world of silence, reveled in its space, allowed it to empower him; as much as any man, perhaps, he recognized silence as the territory of inspiration and cultivated its gifts. Deafness, his biographers agree, acted like an auditory veil, separating him from the world's distractions, allowing him to attend to what he called his business: thinking.

I mention these facts, however, not for the small and obvious irony — that a man so indebted to silence should do more than any other to fill the world with noise — but to set the context for a scene I find strangely compelling. In June 1911, hard at work on what would eventually become the disk phonograph, Edison hired a pianist to play for him (as loudly as possible) the world's entire repertoire of waltzes. And there, in the salon at Glenmont, either out of frustration at not being able to hear the music to his satisfaction or, as I'd like to believe, out of sudden desperate love for the thing he'd missed (as charged as any of love's first fumblings), the sixty-four-year-old Edison got on his hands and knees and bit into the piano's wood, the better to hear its vibrations. Will Edison's fate be our own? Afloat in the river of sound loosed upon the world by Edison's inventions, having drunk from it until our ears ring, we now risk a similar thirst.

Tacked to the wall above my desk, staring out from a page torn from the back of the *New York Times Magazine,* are the faces of seventeen men and women whose portraits were taken by KGB photographers more than half a century ago, then filed, along with hundreds of thousands like them, in the top-secret dossiers of Stalin's secret police. Over the years, I've come to know the faces in these photographs nearly as well as I know those of the living. I study them often — the woman at the left whose graying hair has begun to loosen, the beautiful young man at the right, the fading lieutenant at the bottom corner whose cheeks, I suspect, had the same roughness and warmth as my father's — because each and every one of them, within hours of having his or her picture taken, was driven to a forest south of Moscow and executed; because all, or nearly all, knew their fate at the time their pictures were taken; and because, finally, having inherited a good dose of Slavic morbidity (and sentimentalism), I couldn't bear to compound the silence of all of those lives unlived by returning them — mothers and fathers, sons and lovers — to the oblivion of yet another archive, the purgatory of microfiche. On my wall, in some small measure, they are not forgotten; they have a voice.

Today, as the panopticon reveals to us as never before the agony of our species, the lesson is repeated daily. We read it in the skulls of Srebrenica, growing out of the soil, in the open mouths of the dead from Guatemala to the Thai-Cambodian border, whose characteristic posture — head back, neck arched — seems almost a universal language: the harvest of dictatorship, properly understood, is not death, but silence. Mr. Pinochet's *los desaparecidos* (like Slobodan Milosevic's, or Heinrich Himmler's) are really *los callados* (the silenced), the snuffing of their voices only the last, most brutal expression of a system dependent on silence as a tool of repression. The enforced quiet of censorship and propaganda, of burning pages and jammed frequencies, is different from the gun to the temple only in degree, not in kind.

And yet who could deny that silence, though both the means and the end of totalitarian repression, is also its natural enemy? That silence, the habitat of the imagination, not only allows us to grow the spore of identity but, multiplied a millionfold, creates the rich loam in which a genuine democracy thrives? In the silence of our own minds, in the quiet margins of the text, we are made different from one another as well as able to understand others' differences from us.

In the famous John Cage composition *4′33″*, the pianist walks onstage, bows, flips the tail of his tuxedo, and seats himself at the piano. Taking a stopwatch out of his vest pocket, he presses the start button, then stares at the keys for precisely four minutes and thirty-three seconds. When the time is up, he closes the piano and leaves the stage.

Nearly half a century after it was first performed, *4′33″* rightly strikes us as hackneyed and worn, a postmodern cliché intent on blurring a line (between art and non-art, order and disorder, formal structure and random influence) that has long since been erased. As simple theater, however, it still has power. Cage's portrait of the artist frozen before his medium, intensely aware of his allotted time, unable to draw a shape out of the universe of possibilities, carries a certain allegorical charge, because we recognize in its symbolism — so apparently childlike, so starkly Manichaean — a lesson worthy of Euripedes: art, whatever its medium, attempts to force a wedge beneath the closed lid of the world, and fails; the artist, in his or her minutes and seconds, attempts to say — to paint, to carve; in sum, to communicate — what ultimately cannot be communicated. In the end, the wedge breaks; the lid stays shut. The artist looks at his watch and leaves the stage, his "success" measurable only by the relative depth of his failure. Too bad. There are worse things.

But if silence is the enemy of art, it is also its motivation and medium: the greatest works not only draw on silence for inspiration but use it, flirt with it, turn it, for a time, against itself. To succeed at all, in other words, art must partake of its opposite, suggest its own dissolution. Examples are legion: once attuned to the music of absence, the eloquence of omission or restraint, one hears it everywhere — in the sudden vertiginous stop of an Elizabeth Bishop poem; in the space between souls in an Edward Hopper painting; in Satchmo's mastery of the wide margins when singing "I'm Just a Lucky So and So." In the final paragraph of Frank O'Connor's small masterpiece "Guests of the Nation," an Irish soldier recalls looking over a patch of bog containing the graves of two British soldiers he's just been forced to execute and observes simply, "And anything that happened to me afterwards, I never felt the same about again." Such a black hole of a line, dense with rejected possibilities, merciless in its willingness to sacrifice everything for a quick stab at truth.

"Silence," wrote Melville, only five years before withdrawing from writing more or less for good, "is the only Voice of our God." The assertion, like its subject, cuts both ways, negating and affirming, implying both absence and presence, offering us a choice; it's a line that the Society of American Atheists could put on its letterhead and the Society of Friends could silently endorse while waiting to be moved by the spirit to speak. What makes the line particularly notable, however, is that it appears in *Pierre, or, the Ambiguities,* a novel that, perhaps more than any other in American literature, calls attention to its own silences, its fragility. Offering us a hero who is both American Christ and Holy Fool, martyr and murderer, writer and subject, Melville propels him toward his death with such abandon, with such a feel for what Thomas Mann would one day call "the voluptuousness of doom," that even his language gets caught in the vortex: in one particularly eerie passage we watch the same sentence, repeated four times, pruned of adverbs, conjunctions, dependent clauses, until it very nearly disappears before our eyes.

There's nothing safe about this brinksmanship, nothing of the deconstructionists' empty posturings. "He can neither believe," Hawthorne wrote, "nor be comfortable in his unbelief." Melville had simply allowed his doubts to bleed into his art. As they will. Having "pretty much made up his mind to be annihilated," he quite naturally took his writing with him.

Reading *Pierre* is an uncomfortable business, akin to watching an artist painstakingly put the finishing touches on his own epitaph. One naturally hopes for a slightly more redemptive vision, a vision that shifts the stress from the inevitability of doom and the triumph of silence to the creative energy these release to the living. Within Melville's own work, we don't have far to look. In *Moby-Dick,* the book he wrote just before *Pierre,* Melville also engineered an apocalypse yet managed to remain far enough away to avoid its pull, to save something, to offer us a metaphor that captures perfectly the tensions essential to our work and our lives. Something survives the *Pequod*'s sinking; though silence may reign over the waters, the vortex eventually slows. The coffin bursts to the surface. And on that coffin are the hieroglyphics of our art.

If one of the characteristics of capitalism is that it tends to shut down options, narrow the margins, then perhaps what we are seeing these days is one of the side effects of the so-called free market: most of the noises we hear are the noises of buying and selling. Even the communication between individuals has been harnessed to the technologies that make them possible: to be deprived of the fax machine, the cell phone, the TV, the pager, etc., is to be relegated to silence. Communication, having been narrowed into whatever can be squeezed into binary code, has been redefined by the marketplace into a commodity itself.

Yet capitalism, we know, always tries to feed the hungers it creates, to confect its own antidotes — so long as the price is right. As the vast silences of the republic are paved over by designer outlets and shopping malls, a kind of island ecosystem remains, self-conscious in its fragility, barely viable. The proof is detectable in any upscale travel magazine: there you will find exclusive spas advertising the promise of silence — no pagers, no cell phones, just the sounds of lakewater lapping — as though silence were a rare Chardonnay or an exclusive bit of scenery, which, of course, is precisely what it now is.

That silence, like solitude, is now a commodity should not surprise us. Money buys space, and space buys silence; decibels and dollars are inversely proportional. Lacking money, I've lived with noise — with the sounds of fucking and feuding in the airshaft, MTV and Maury Povitch coming through the walls, in apartments with ceilings so thin I could hear the click of a clothes hanger placed on a rod or the lusty stream of an upstairs neighbor urinating after a long night out. I've accepted this, if not gracefully, at least with a measure of resignation. The great advantage that money confers, I now realize, is not silence per se but the *option* of silence, the privilege of choosing one's own music, of shutting out the seventeen-year-old whose boombox nightly rattles my panes.

But if the ability to engineer one's own silence has been one of the age-old prerogatives of wealth, it's also true that the rapidly changing aural landscape of the late twentieth century has raised the status (and value) of silence enormously. As the world of the made, to recall e. e. cummings, replaces the world of the born, as the small sounds of fields at dusk or babies crying in the next apartment are erased by the noise of traffic and Oprah, as even our few remaining bits of wilderness are pressed thin and flat beneath satellite transmissions, Forest Service bulldozers, and airplane flight corridors, we grow sentimental for what little has escaped us and automatically reach for our wallets. Like a telltale lesion that appears only on those who are desperately ill, value — even outrageous value — often blossoms on things just before they leave us, and if the analogy is an ugly one, it is also appropriate; the sudden spasm of love for the thing we're killing, after all, is as obscene as it is human. As we continue to pave the world with sound, we will continue to crave what little silence escapes us, an emptiness made audible by its disappearance.

CHERYL STRAYED

Heroin/e

FROM DOUBLETAKE

WHEN MY MOTHER DIED, I stripped her naked. Plush round belly and her pale breasts rising above. Her arms were black-and-blue from all the needles going in. Needles with clear liquid and needles that only the nurses had a hold of and other needles gripping constantly into her, held tight with tape to the translucent skin of her hand or the silk skin of her wrist. And not one of those needles trying to save her. I picked her dead hand up, the arm slack and draping below. It did not want to be held. Her skin was dry and cracked and stabbed. When she died the nurse took the needle out forever. But I wanted it back, and eventually I would get it.

The day they told us my mother had cancer I was wearing green. Green pants, green shirt, green bow in my hair. My mother had sewn this outfit for me. I did not like such a themed look, but I wore it anyway, to the Mayo Clinic, as a penance, an offering, a talisman. We found a vacant wheelchair, and I got into it and raced and spun down the hallway. Cancer, at this point, was something we did not have to take seriously. My mother was forty-five. She looked fine, beautiful, I would later think, *alive.* It was just the two of us, me and my mother. There were others too, my stepfather working his job, wondering, my grandparents waiting by the phone, wanting to know if it was true, if perhaps the oncologist in Duluth had been mistaken after all. But now, as before, as it would always be, it was only me and my mother. In the elevator she sat in the wheelchair and reached out to tug at my pants. She rubbed the fabric between her fingers proprietarily. "Perfect," she said.

I was twenty-two. I believed that if a doctor told you that you were going to die soon, you'd be taken to a room with a gleaming wooden desk. This was not so. My mother sat with her shirt off on top of the table with paper stretched over it. When she moved, the room was on fire with the paper ripping and crinkling beneath her. She wore a pale yellow smock with strings meant to be tied. I could see her soft back, the small shelf of flesh that curved down at her waist. The doctor said she'd be lucky if she lived a year. My mother blinked her wet eyes but did not cry. She sat with her hands folded tightly together and her ankles hooked one to the other. Shackled to herself. She'd asked the doctor if she could continue riding her horse. He then took a pencil in his hand and stood it upright on the edge of the sink and tapped it down on the surface hard. "This is your spine after radiation," he said. "One jolt and your bones will crumble like a dry cracker."

First we went to the women's restroom. Each of us locked in a separate stall, weeping. We didn't say a word. Not because we felt alone in our grief, but because we were so together in it, as if we were one body instead of two. I could feel her weight leaning against the door, her hands slapping slowly against it, causing the entire frame of the bathroom stalls to shake. Later we came out to wash our hands and faces, standing side by side in the ladies' room mirror.

We were sent to the pharmacy to wait. I sat next to my mother in my green pantsuit. There was a big bald boy in an old man's lap. There was a woman who had an arm that swung wildly from the elbow. She held it stiffly with the other hand, trying to calm it. She waited. We waited. There was a beautiful dark-haired woman who sat in a wheelchair. She wore a purple hat and a handful of diamond rings. We could not take our eyes off her. She spoke in Spanish to the people gathered around her, her family and perhaps her husband. "Do you think she has cancer?" my mother whispered loudly to me. There was a song coming quietly over the speakers. A song without words, but my mother knew the words anyway and sang them softly to herself. "Paper roses, paper roses, oh they're only paper roses to me," she sang. She put her hand on mine and said, "I used to listen to that song when I was young. It's funny to think of that. To think about listening to the same song now. I would've never known." My mother's name was called then: her prescriptions were ready. "Go get them for me," she said. "Tell them who you are. Tell them you're my daughter."

My mother said I could have her jewelry box. She said, "When I am done with it." She was lying in the bed my stepfather had made for her, for them, with branches twisting and arching up behind her, leaves and jumping bugs carved discreetly into them. There was a dancing pink girl who lived in the jewelry box. She stood and twirled around to the song that played when you wound it up and opened the box. The song changed as it slowed, became sorrowful and destitute. The girl tottered and then stopped as if it hurt her. She had lips the size of a pinhead painted red and a scratchy pink tutu. When we shut the box she went down into it, stiff as a board, bending at the feet.

"I always wonder what the ballerina is thinking," my mother said dreamily.

When my mother got cancer I'd folded my life down. I was a senior in college in Minneapolis, and I'd convinced my professors to allow me to be in class only two days each week. As soon as those days were over, I drove north to the house in rural Minnesota where I had grown up, racing home, to my mother. I could not bear to be away from her. Plus I was needed. My stepfather was with my mother when he could be, when he wasn't working as a carpenter in an attempt to pay the bills. I cooked food that my mother tried to eat. She'd say: pork chops and stuffed green peppers, cherry cheesecake and chicken with rice, and then holler the recipes out to me from her bed. When I'd finished she'd sit like a prisoner staring down at her steaming plate. "It smells good," she'd say. "I think I'll be able to eat it later." I scrubbed the floors. I took everything from the cupboards and put new paper down. My mother slept and moaned and counted and swallowed her pills, or on good days she sat in a chair and talked to me, she paged through books.

"Put these on for me." My mother sat up and reached for a pair of socks. It had been a few weeks since we'd learned of her cancer, and already she could not reach her own feet without great pain. I bent at my mother's feet. She held the ball of socks in her hand. "Here," she said. I had never put socks onto another person, and it was harder than you might think. They don't slide over the skin.

They go on crooked and you have to work to get them right. I became frustrated with my mother, as if she were holding her foot in a manner that made it impossible for me. She sat back with her body leaning on her hands on the bed, her eyes closed. I could hear her breathing deeply, slowly. "Goddammit," I said, "help me." My mother looked down at me, silently.

We didn't know it then, but this would be the last time she was home. Her movements were slow and thick as she put her coat on, and she held on to the walls and edges of doors as she made her way out of the house. On the drive to the hospital in Duluth she looked out the window. She said, "Look at the snow there on those pines." She told me to toot my horn when we went past Cindy's house in Moose Lake. She said, "Be careful of the ice. It's black ice." She held an old plastic milk jug with the top cut off so she could vomit into it during the drive. My mother put one hand up to her ribs, where the cancer lived, and pressed gently. "Wouldn't that be something, to get into an accident now?"

Three years after my mother died I fell in love with a man who had electric blue hair. I'd gone to Portland, Oregon, to visit a friend, seeking respite from the shambles my life had become. I had thought that by then I'd have recovered from the loss of my mother and also that the single act of her death would constitute the only loss. It is perhaps the greatest misperception of the death of a loved one: that it will end there, that death itself will be the largest blow. No one told me that in the wake of that grief other griefs would ensue. I had recently separated from the husband I loved. My stepfather was no longer a father to me. I was alone in the world and acutely aware of that. I went to Portland for a break.

We'll call the man with electric blue hair Joe. I met him on his twenty-fourth birthday and drank sangria with him. In the morning he wanted to know if I'd like some heroin. He lived on a street called Mississippi, in North Portland. There was a whole gathering of people who'd rigged up apartments above what thirty years before had been a thriving Rexall drugstore. Within days I lived there with him. In the beginning, for about a week, we smoked it. We made smooth pipes out of aluminum foil and sucked the smoke of burning black tar heroin up into them. "This is called chasing the dragon!" Joe said, and clapped his hands. The first time I smoked heroin it was a hot, sunny day in July. I got down on my knees in front of Joe where he sat on the couch. "More," I said, and laughed like a child. "More, more, more," I chanted. I had never cared much for drugs. I'd experimented with each kind once or twice, and drank alcohol with moderation and reserve. Heroin was different. I loved it. It was the first thing that worked. It took away every scrap of hurt that I had inside of me. When I think of heroin now, it is like remembering a person I met and loved intensely. A person I know I must live without.

The first time they offered my mother morphine, she said no. "Morphine is what they give to dying people," she said. "Morphine means there is no hope."

We were at the hospital in Duluth. We could not get the pillows right. My mother cried in pain and frustration when the nurses came into the room. The doctor told her that she shouldn't hold out any longer, that he had to give her morphine. He told her she was *actively dying*. He was young, perhaps thirty. He stood next to my mother, a gentle hairy hand slung into his pocket, looking down at her in the bed.

The nurses came one by one and gave her the morphine with a needle. Within a couple weeks my mother was dead. In those weeks she couldn't get enough of the drug. She wanted more morphine, more often. The nurses liked to give her as little as they could. One of the nurses was a man, and I could see the shape of his penis through his tight white nurse's trousers. I wanted desperately to pull him into the small bathroom beyond the foot of my mother's bed and offer myself up to him, to do anything at all if he would help us. And also I wanted to take pleasure from him, to feel the weight of his body against me, to feel his mouth in my hair and hear him say my name to me over and over again, to force him to acknowledge me, to make this matter to him, to crush his heart with mercy for us. I held my closed book on my lap and watched him walk softly into the room in his padded white shoes. My mother asked him for more morphine. She asked for it in a way that I have never seen anyone ask for anything. A mad dog. He did not look at my mother when she asked him this, but at his wristwatch. He held the same expression on his face regardless of the answer. Sometimes he gave it to her without a word, and sometimes he told her no in a voice as soft as his shoes and his penis curled up in his pants. My mother begged and whimpered then. She cried and her tears fell in the wrong direction, not down over the lush light of her cheeks to the corners of her mouth but away from the edges of her eyes to her ears and into the nest of her hair on the bed.

I wanted it and I got it, and the more heroin we got, the stingier we became with it. Perhaps if we snorted it, we thought, we'd get higher on less. And then, of course, the needle. The hypodermic needle, I'd read, was the barrier that kept the masses from heroin. The opposite was true with me. I loved the clean smell of it, the tight clench around my arm, the stab of hurt, the dull badge of ache. It made me think of my mother. It made me think of her, and then that thought would go away into the loveliest bliss. A bliss I had not imagined.

There was a man named Santos whom we called when we wanted heroin. He would make us wait by the telephone for hours, and then he'd call and instruct us to meet him in the parking lot of a Safeway. I sat in the car while Joe took a short drive with Santos in his yellow Pinto, and then Joe would calmly get back in the car with me and we'd go home. On some occasions we went to Santos's house. Once he sat in his front window with a shotgun across his lap. Once he clutched my thigh when Joe left the room and told me that if I came to see him alone he'd give me heroin free. Another time he held his baby daughter, just a month old. I looked at her and smiled and told Santos how beautiful she was, and inside of me I felt the presence of my real life. The woman who I actually was. The kind of woman who knows the beauty of a baby, who will have a baby, who once was a baby.

The days of my mother's death, the morphine days, and those that followed, the heroin days, lasted only weeks, months — but each day was an eternity, one stacked up on the other, a cold clarity inside of a deep haze. And unoccupied as well. Just me and my mother, or the ghost of her, though others surely came and went.

Some days flowers came to my mother's hospital room, and I set them on the edges of tables and windowsills. Women came too. Women who volunteered for the hospital. Old Catholic women, with hair cut close to the scalp or woven into long braids and pinned to their heads. My mother greeted them as she did the flowers: impervious, unmoved, resolute.

The women thought it would be for the best when my mother died. They sat next to me on the vinyl furniture and told me in low tones about the deaths of their own mothers. Mothers who had died standing at kitchen sinks, in the back seats of cars, in beds lit with candles. And also about the ones who made it. The ones with the *will to live.* Of tumors vanishing and clean blood and opaque bones. People who fought it, who refused to die. The ones who went and then came back. The survivors. The heroes. It would be for the best, they whispered, when it was over. Her life, that is. My mother's.

People whom I knew came, and I did not recognize them at first. It seemed they all wore strange hats or other disguises during this time, though I am certain that is not true. They were friends of my mother's. They couldn't bear to stay in the room, so instead they left chicken pot pies and bread. Scalloped potatoes and blocks of cheddar cheese. By then my mother could not eat half a banana. Couldn't lick a lick of a popsicle without retching it back up. They said her name to her, and she said their names back to them, hoarse and confused. She said, "How nice you came." And she put a wan smile on her face. Her hair was flattened against her head, and I reached to smooth it into place.

I asked my mother if she would like for me to read to her. I had two books: *The Awakening,* by Kate Chopin, and *The Optimist's Daughter,* by Eudora Welty. These were books we'd read before, books we'd loved. So I started in, but I could not go on. Each word I said erased itself in the air. It was the same when I tried to pray. I prayed fervently, rabidly, to God, any god, to a god I could not identify or find. I prayed to the whole wide universe and thought perhaps God would be in it. I prayed and I faltered. God, I realized, had no intention of making things happen or not, of saving my mother's life. God would come later, perhaps, to help me bear it.

She taught me to knit, my mother, and I did this in the room while she slept and lived the last while. It occurred to me that she had taught me to knit for this particular occasion. So that I would have a place to put my hands and my eyes.

"What are you making?" she asked.

"A scarf."

"For who?" Her hand pinched the sheet that covered her.

"I don't know," I said. "I am simply knitting a scarf."

The best part about knitting is the tapping, tapping, tapping of the needles. A sound so silent that it is like the language of snakes or rabbits or deer.

Eventually the nurses and doctors stopped paying any mind to what my mother said or wanted. They looked to me to decide how much morphine to give her. They said I had a choice: she could be in great pain but fairly conscious, or she could be comfortable but higher than a kite, and usually passed out. Ultimately, it was not up to me.

"Promise me one thing," she said. My mother was not dramatic or concise in her dying. She hadn't offered a single directive in the past days, and I was desperate for guidance. "That you won't allow me to be in pain anymore. I've had too much pain."

"Yes," I said, "yes."

There was using heroin and also not using it. In the mornings when I woke, groggy and drained, I'd stand in front of the mirror and talk to myself. I was shocked by my own life. *This was not meant to be,* I'd think in the mornings. *Stop it,* I said. *No more.* And then I would shower and dress in my black pants and white shirt and black bow tie and take a bus downtown to serve people coffee and pancakes. At two in the afternoon I'd take the bus home again with hopefully sixty bucks in my pocket for another score of heroin. This is how it went.

Joe waited for me to get home. He cooked me macaroni and cheese and called Santos. He pulled me into his bed and jumped up when the phone rang. I made him stick the needle into me the first time, and then he taught me how to do it myself. What I loved about Joe is that he didn't love me, or himself. I loved that he would not only let me but help me destroy myself. I'd never shared that with another person. The dark glory of our united self-destruction had the force of something like love. *I get to do this,* I thought. *I get to waste my life.* I felt a terrible power within me. The power of controlling the uncontrollable. *I get to be junk,* I thought.

But this was not to be. My husband, Mark, called me. He was in town and wanted to see me. The friend I'd come to visit in Portland had told him about Joe and about my using heroin, and in response he drove from Minneapolis to talk to me. I met him within the hour at our friend's house. He sat at a table in the kitchen with the branches of a fig tree tapping on the window nearby. He said, "You look, you look . . . different. You seem so, how can I say this — you seem like you aren't here." First he put his hands on mine, and we held on to one another, locked hand to hand. I couldn't explain it to him, the why. And then we fought. He stood up and screamed at me so loudly that I put my hands over my head for cover. His arms gestured madly into the air, at nothing. He clawed at himself and ripped the shirt from his own back and threw it at me. He wanted me to go home with him in an hour. Not for a reunion but to get away, not from Joe but from heroin.

I told Mark I needed to think. I drove back to Joe's apartment and sat in the lawn chair on the sidewalk. Heroin made me dumb, or distant, rather. A thought would form and then evaporate. I couldn't get a hold of my mind. I sat in the lawn chair on the sidewalk, and a man walked up to me and said his name was Tim. He took my hand and shook it and told me I could trust him. He asked if I could give him three dollars for diapers, then if he could use my phone, and then if I had change for a five-dollar bill, and on and on in a series of twisting requests and sorry stories that confused and compelled me to stand and pull the last ten dollars I had out of my jeans pocket. He saw the money and pulled a knife out of his shirt. He held it gently up to my chest and said, "Give me that money, sweetheart."

I packed a few things and called Mark. When he pulled up to the corner where I was waiting, I got into his car. By sunset Portland was long gone. In Montana we checked into a motel to sleep. I held myself in bed, rocking with a headache, a sickness in my gut. Mark brought me water and chocolate and watched television. I sat in the car as we drove across the country, and I felt my real life present but unattainable, as if heroin had taken me entirely from myself. Mark and I fought and cried and shook the car with our fighting. We were monstrous in our cruelty. We talked kindly afterward, shocked at ourselves and each other. We decided that we would get divorced. I hated him and I loved him. He had known my mother. I felt trapped, branded, held, and beloved. Like a daughter. "I didn't ask you to come to Portland," I screamed. "You came for your own reasons," I said.

"Maybe," he said.

"You love me that much?" I asked. "You came all this way to get me? Why?"

"Because," he said, "just because."

I wanted my mother to love me, but more. I wanted her to prove it, to live. To go to battle and win. And if she was going to die, I wanted her to tell me, in the end, how I should live, without her. Until that point I had wanted just the opposite. I could not bear for her to tell me what to do or how to live. I had wanted to be unknown by her, opaque to her wondering eyes.

The last days, my mother was not so much high as down under. When she woke, she'd say, "Oh, oh." Or she'd let out a sad gulp of air. She'd look at me, and there would be a flash of love. Other times she'd roll back into sleep as if I were not there. Sometimes when my mother woke she did not know where she was. She demanded an enchilada and then some applesauce. She'd say, "That horse darn near stepped on me," and look around the room for it accusingly. During this time I wanted my mother to say to me that I had been the best daughter in the world. I did not want to want this, but I did, inexplicably, as if I had a great fever that could only be cooled by those words. I went so far as to ask her directly. "Have I been the best daughter in the world?" She said yes, I had, of course. But this was not enough. I wanted those words to knit together in my mother's mind and for them to be delivered, fresh, to me. I was ravenous for love.

One day a woman with a clipboard asked if I'd go with her to the cafeteria. She said that she wanted to talk to me about a donation my mother had made. Her name was Janet and she was dressed in a navy-colored shirt with little white fringes on each shoulder, as if she were the captain of something. Her fingernails were long and red and they clicked together when she moved her hands in certain ways.

When we sat down with two cups of coffee between us, she told me that my mother was an organ donor but that because she had cancer throughout her body they would only take her eyes.

"Her eyes?"

"Well, not the whole eye, of course, but parts of the organ." Janet took her cup up into her hands; one fingernail tapped against it. "We make it a policy to inform people close to the donor. In your mother's case, upon death, we will need to place ice on her eyes in order to preserve them." She thought about this a moment. "This way you will understand what is happening when you see that we must put the bags of ice on her face. The removal is performed within a few hours after death." Her fingernails went up to the sides of her face, hovering in midair. "Small incisions will be made at the side of each eye." Janet showed me this, pointing with her own sharp nails. "The skin will be sutured carefully to disguise signs of this procedure." She swallowed a sip of coffee and looked at me. "It does not preclude an open-casket viewing."

I dreamed of heroin. I woke in the middle of the night with a wanting so deep I was breathless. I had started seeing a therapist to talk about heroin. She told me that this wanting was normal, that indeed when you use heroin the brain responds by activating pleasure neurons that would normally remain dormant. She said it would take months for them to calm. Until then, they go on aching to be fed. Trying to trick your body into it. I could see them, spindly arms with mouths like flowers, blooming or wilting and then blooming again. "What about pain?" I asked her. "Are there neurons in the brain that come alive only with agony? And if so, how long does it take for them to die, to fold back into themselves and float away?"

I saw Joe two more times. I'd kept in touch with him; calling him late at night from Minneapolis, I could hear the heroin in his voice, making it soft and open. Within a month he was at my door. He looked weak and pale. He sat on my couch and shot up and then lurched into my kitchen and bent to vomit into my sink. He wiped his face and smiled. "It's worth it," he said, "getting sick. Because you feel so good through it all." We spent a week in my apartment using the supply of heroin he'd brought with him. I knew I had to end this, and finally I did. He left when I asked him to. The second time I saw him, a year had passed and I was moving to Portland for reasons unrelated to him. We went to the beach for the day. He was no longer the smart, sexy, simpering man I'd fallen for, but a junkie. Joe had scabs on his skin from constant scratching; his bony arms were bruised and punctured. He didn't care anymore what color his hair was. I sat on the cool sand watching the Pacific Ocean roar in while Joe locked himself in the public restroom to shoot up. I held myself stiff against the desire to join him. The ocean inched nearer and nearer to me with each passing minute. I was both sickened by Joe and compelled. I felt in the presence of a dying man, a young, dying man, and I knew that I could never see him again if I wanted to live. And I did.

My mother didn't have time to get skinny. Her death was a relentless onward march. The hero's journey is one of return, but my mother's was all forward motion. She was altered but still fleshy when she died, the body of a woman among the living. She had her hair too, brown and brittle and frayed from being in bed for weeks.

From the room where she died I could see the great Lake Superior out her window. The biggest lake in the world, and the coldest. To see it, I had to work. I pressed my face sideways, hard, against the glass, and I'd catch a slice of it going on forever into the horizon. "A room with a view!" my mother exclaimed. "All of my life I've waited for a room with a view."

I arranged the flowers closer into my mother, to the edges of the tables, so that she could see them without having to turn her head. Bouquets of pink carnations, yellow roses, daisies, and tiger lilies. Flowers that originated on other continents and were brought here to witness my mother's dying.

My mother wanted to die sitting up, so I took all the pillows I could get my hands on and made a backrest for her. I wanted to take my mother and prop her in a field of yarrow to die. I covered her with a quilt that I had brought from home, one she had sewn herself out of pieces of our old clothing. "Get that out of here," she said savagely, and then kicked her legs like a swimmer to make it go away.

I watched my mother. It was March, and outside, the sun glinted off the sidewalks and the icy edges of the snow. It was Saint Patrick's Day, and the nurses brought my mother a square block of green Jell-O that sat quivering on the table beside her. It was the last day of her life, and my mother did not sleep, she did not wake. She held her eyes still and open. They were the bluest thing in the room, perhaps in all of Duluth. Bluer than the lake. They were the color of the sky on the best day of your life.

My mother died fast but not all of a sudden. A slow-burning fire when flames disappear to smoke and then smoke to air. She never once closed her eyes. First they were bitter and then they were bewildered and they changed again to something else, to a state that I have had, finally, to see as heroic. Blue, blue eyes. Daggers of blue wanting and wanting. To stay, to stay.

ANDREW SULLIVAN

What's So Bad About Hate?

FROM THE NEW YORK TIMES MAGAZINE

I

I WONDER what was going on in John William King's head two years ago when he tied James Byrd, Jr.'s feet to the back of a pickup truck and dragged him three miles down a road in rural Texas. King and two friends had picked up Byrd, who was black, when he was walking home, half drunk, from a party. As part of a bonding ritual in their fledgling white supremacist group, the three men took Byrd to a remote part of town, beat him, and chained his legs together before attaching them to the truck. Pathologists at King's trial testified that Byrd was probably alive and conscious until his body finally hit a culvert and split in two. When King was offered a chance to say something to Byrd's family at the trial, he smirked and uttered an obscenity.

We know all these details now, many months later. We know quite a large amount about what happened before and after. But I am still drawn, again and again, to the flash of ignition, the moment when fear and loathing became hate, the instant of transformation when King became hunter and Byrd became prey.

What was that? And what was it when Buford Furrow, Jr., longtime member of the Aryan Nations, calmly walked up to a Filipino-American mailman he happened to spot, asked him to mail a letter, and then shot him at point-blank range? Or when Russell Henderson beat Matthew Shepard, a young gay man, to a pulp, removed his shoes, and then, with the help of a friend, tied him to a post, like a dead coyote, to warn off others?

For all our documentation of these crimes and others, our political and moral disgust at them, our morbid fascination with them, our sensitivity to their social meaning, we seem at times to have no better idea now than we ever had of what exactly they were about. About what that moment means when, for some reason or other, one human being asserts absolute, immutable superiority over another. About not the violence, but what the violence expresses. About what — exactly — hate is. And what our own part in it may be.

I find myself wondering what hate actually is in part because we have created an entirely new offense in American criminal law — a "hate crime" — to combat it. And barely a day goes by without someone somewhere declaring war against it. Last month President Clinton called for an expansion of hate-crime laws as "what America needs in our battle against hate." A couple of weeks later, Senator John McCain used a campaign speech to denounce the "hate" he said poisoned the land. New York's mayor, Rudolph Giuliani, recently tried to stop the Million Youth March in Harlem on the grounds that the event was organized by people "involved in hate marches and hate rhetoric."

The media concur in their emphasis. In 1985, there were eleven mentions of "hate crimes" in the national media database Nexis. By 1990, there were more than a thousand. In the first six months of 1999, there were seven thousand. "Sexy fun is one thing," wrote a *New York Times* reporter about sexual assaults in Woodstock '99's mosh pit. "But this was an orgy of lewdness tinged with hate." And when Benjamin Smith marked the Fourth of July this year by targeting blacks, Asians, and Jews for murder in Indiana and Illinois, the story wasn't merely about a twisted young man who had emerged on the scene. As the *Times* put it, "Hate arrived in the neighborhoods of Indiana University, in Bloomington, in the early-morning darkness."

But what exactly was this thing that arrived in the early-morning darkness? For all our zeal to attack hate, we still have a remarkably vague idea of what it actually is. A single word, after all, tells us less, not more. For all its emotional punch, "hate" is far less nuanced an idea than prejudice, or bigotry, or bias, or anger, or even mere aversion to others. Is it to stand in for all these varieties of human experience — and everything in between? If so, then the war against it will be so vast as to be quixotic. Or is "hate" to stand for a very specific idea or belief, or set of beliefs, with a very specific object or group of objects? Then waging war against it is almost certainly unconstitutional. Perhaps these kinds of questions are of no concern to those waging war on hate. Perhaps it is enough for them that they share a sentiment that there is too much hate and never enough vigilance in combating it. But sentiment is a poor basis for law and a dangerous tool in politics. It is better to leave some unwinnable wars unfought.

II

Hate is everywhere. Human beings generalize all the time, ahead of time, about everyone and everything. A large part of it may even be hard-wired. At some point in our evolution, being able to know beforehand who was friend or foe was not merely a matter of philosophical reflection. It was a matter of survival. And even today it seems impossible to feel a loyalty without also feeling a disloyalty, a sense of belonging without an equal sense of unbelonging. We're social beings. We associate. Therefore we disassociate. And although it would be comforting to think that the one could happen without the other, we know in reality that it doesn't. How many patriots are there who have never felt a twinge of xenophobia?

Of course, by hate we mean something graver and darker than this kind of lazy prejudice. But the closer you look at this distinction, the fuzzier it gets. Much of the time, we harbor little or no malice toward people of other backgrounds or places or ethnicities or ways of life. But then a car cuts you off at an intersection and you find yourself noticing immediately that the driver is a woman, or black, or old, or fat, or white, or male. Or you are walking down a city street at night and hear footsteps quickening behind you. You look around and see that it is a white woman and not a black man, and you are instantly relieved. These impulses are so spontaneous they are almost involuntary. But where did they come from? The mindless need to be mad at someone — anyone — or the unconscious eruption of a darker prejudice festering within?

In 1993, in San Jose, California, two neighbors, one heterosexual, one homosexual, were engaged in a protracted squabble over grass clippings. (The full case is recounted in *Hate Crimes,* by James B. Jacobs and Kimberly Potter.) The gay man regularly mowed his lawn without a grass catcher, which prompted his neighbor to complain on many occasions that grass clippings spilled over onto his driveway. Tensions grew until one day the gay man mowed his front yard, spilling clippings onto his neighbor's driveway, prompting the straight man to yell an obscene and common antigay insult. The wrangling escalated. At one point the gay man agreed to collect the clippings from his neighbor's driveway but then later found them dumped on his own porch. A fracas ensued, with the gay man spraying the straight man's son with a garden hose and the son hitting and kicking the gay man several times, yelling antigay slurs. The police were called, and the son was eventually convicted of a hate-motivated assault, a felony. But what was the nature of the hate, antigay bias or suburban property-owner madness?

Or take the Labor Day parade last year in Broad Channel, a small island in Jamaica Bay, Queens. Almost everyone there is white, and in recent years a group of local volunteer firefighters has taken to decorating a pickup truck for the parade in order to win the prize for "funniest float." Their themes have tended toward the outrageously provocative. Beginning in 1995, they won prizes for floats depicting "Hasidic Park," "Gooks of Hazzard," and "Happy Gays." Last year they called their float "Black to the Future, Broad Channel 2098." They imagined their community a century hence as a largely black enclave, with every stereotype imaginable: watermelons, basketballs, and so on. At one point during the parade, one of them mimicked the dragging death of James Byrd. It was caught on videotape, and before long the entire community was depicted as a caldron of hate.

It's an interesting case, because the float was indisputably in bad taste and the improvisation on the Byrd killing was grotesque. But was it hate? The men on the float were local heroes for their volunteer work; they had no record of bigoted activity and were not members of any racist organizations. In previous years they had made fun of many other groups, and they saw themselves more as provocateurs than bigots. When they were described as racists, it came as a shock to them. They apologized for poor taste but refused to confess to bigotry. "The people involved aren't horrible people," protested a local woman. "Was it a racist act? I don't know. Are they racists? I don't think so."

If hate is a self-conscious activity, she has a point. The men were primarily motivated by the desire to shock and to reflect what they thought was their community's culture. Their display was not aimed at any particular black people or at any blacks who lived in Broad Channel — almost none do. But if hate is primarily an unconscious activity, then the matter is obviously murkier. And by taking the horrific lynching of a black man as a spontaneous object of humor, the men were clearly advocating indifference to it. Was this an aberrant excess? Or the real truth about the men's feelings toward African-Americans? Hate or tastelessness? And how on earth is anyone, even perhaps the firefighters themselves, going to know for sure?

Or recall H. L. Mencken. He shared in the anti-Semitism of his time with more alacrity than most and was an indefatigable racist. "It is impossible," he wrote in his diary, "to talk anything resembling discretion or judgment into a colored woman. They are all essentially childlike, and even hard experience does not teach them anything." He wrote at another time of the "psychological stigmata" of the "Afro-American race." But it is also true that during much of his life, day to day, Mencken conducted himself with no regard to race and supported a politics that was clearly integrationist. As the editor of his diary has pointed out, Mencken published many black authors in his magazine, *The Mercury,* and lobbied on their behalf with his publisher, Alfred A. Knopf. The last thing Mencken ever wrote was a diatribe against racial segregation in Baltimore's public parks. He was good friends with leading black writers and journalists, including James Weldon Johnson, Walter White, and George S. Schuyler, and played an underappreciated role in promoting the Harlem Renaissance.

What would our modern view of hate do with Mencken? Probably ignore him, or change the subject. But with regard to hate, I know lots of people like Mencken. He reminds me of conservative friends who oppose almost every measure for homosexual equality yet genuinely delight in the company of their gay friends. It would be easier for me to think of them as haters, and on paper, perhaps, there is a good case that they are. But in real life, I know they are not. Some of them clearly harbor no real malice toward me or other homosexuals whatsoever.

They are as hard to figure out as those liberal friends who support every gay rights measure they have ever heard of but do anything to avoid going into a gay bar with me. I have to ask myself in the same frustrating kind of way, are they liberal bigots or bigoted liberals? Or are they neither bigots nor liberals, but merely people?

III

Hate used to be easier to understand. When Sartre described anti-Semitism in his 1946 essay "Anti-Semite and Jew," he meant a very specific array of firmly held prejudices, with a history, an ideology, and even a pseudoscience to back them up. He meant a systematic attempt to demonize and eradicate an entire race. If you go to the Web site of the World Church of the Creator, the organization that inspired young Benjamin Smith to murder in Illinois earlier this year, you will find a similarly bizarre, pseudo-rational ideology. The kind of literature read by Buford Furrow before he rained terror on a Jewish kindergarten last month and then killed a mailman because of his color is full of the same paranoid loopiness. And when we talk about hate, we often mean this kind of phenomenon.

But this brand of hatred is mercifully rare in the United States. These professional maniacs are to hate what serial killers are to murder. They should certainly not be ignored, but they represent what Harold Meyerson, writing in *Salon,* called "niche haters": cold-blooded, somewhat deranged, often poorly socialized psychopaths. In a free society with relatively easy access to guns, they will always pose a menace.

But their menace is a limited one, and their hatred is hardly typical of anything very widespread. Take Buford Furrow. He famously issued a "wake-up call" to "kill Jews" in Los Angeles before he peppered a Jewish community center with gunfire. He did this in a state with two Jewish female senators, in a city with a large, prosperous Jewish population, in a country where out of several million Jewish Americans, a total of sixty-six were reported by the FBI as the targets of hate-crime assaults in 1997. However despicable Furrow's actions were, it would require a very large stretch to describe them as representative of anything but the deranged fringe of an American subculture.

Most hate is more common and more complicated, with as many varieties as there are varieties of love. Just as there are possessive love and needy love, family love and friendship, romantic love and unrequited love, passion and respect, affection and obsession, so hatred has its shadings. There is hate that fears, and hate that merely feels contempt; there is hate that expresses power, and hate that comes from powerlessness; there is revenge, and there is hate that comes from envy. There is hate that was love, and hate that is a curious expression of love. There is hate of the other, and hate of something that reminds us too much of ourselves. There is the oppressor's hate and the victim's hate. There is hate that burns slowly and hate that fades. And there is hate that explodes and hate that never catches fire.

The modern words that we have created to describe the varieties of hate — "sexism," "racism," "anti-Semitism," "homophobia" — tell us very little about any of this. They tell us merely the identities of the victims; they don't reveal the identities of the perpetrators, or what they think, or how they feel. They don't even tell us how the victims feel. And this simplicity is no accident. Coming from the theories of Marxist and post-Marxist academics, these isms are far better at alleging structures of power than at delineating the workings of the individual heart or mind. In fact, these isms can exist without mentioning individuals at all.

We speak of institutional racism, for example, as if an institution can feel anything. We talk of "hate" as an impersonal noun, with no hater specified. But when these abstractions are actually incarnated, when someone feels something as a result of them, when a hater actually interacts with a victim, the picture changes. We find that hates are often very different phenomena one from another, that they have very different psychological dynamics, that they might even be better understood by not seeing them as varieties of the same thing at all.

There is, for example, the now unfashionable distinction between reasonable hate and unreasonable hate. In recent years we have become accustomed to talking about hates as if they were all equally indefensible, as if it could never be the case that some hates might be legitimate, even necessary. But when some 800,000 Tutsis are murdered under the auspices of a Hutu regime in Rwanda, and when a few thousand Hutus are killed in revenge, the hates are not commensurate. Genocide is not an event like a hurricane, in which damage is random and universal; it is a planned and often merciless attack of one group upon another. The hate of the perpetrators is a monstrosity. The hate of the victims, and their survivors, is justified. What else, one wonders, were surviving Jews supposed to feel toward Germans after the Holocaust? Or, to a different degree, South African blacks after apartheid? If the victims overcome this hate, it is a supreme moral achievement. But if they don't, the victims are not as culpable as the perpetrators. So the hatred of Serbs for Kosovars today can never be equated with the hatred of Kosovars for Serbs.

Hate, like much of human feeling, is not rational, but it usually has its reasons. And it cannot be understood, let alone condemned, without knowing them. Similarly, the hate that comes from knowledge is always different from the hate that comes from ignorance. It is one of the most foolish clichés of our time that prejudice is always rooted in ignorance and can usually be overcome by familiarity with the objects of our loathing. The racism of many Southern whites under segregation was not appeased by familiarity with Southern blacks; the virulent loathing of Tutsis by many Hutus was not undermined by living next door to them for centuries. Theirs was a hatred that sprang, for whatever reasons, from experience. It cannot easily be compared with, for example, the resilience of anti-Semitism in Japan, or hostility to immigration in areas where immigrants are unknown, or fear of homosexuals by people who have never knowingly met one.

The same familiarity is an integral part of what has become known as "sexism." Sexism isn't, properly speaking, a prejudice at all. Few men live without knowledge or constant awareness of women. Every single sexist man was born of a woman and is likely to be sexually attracted to women. His hostility is going to be very different from that of, say, a reclusive member of the Aryan Nations toward Jews he has never met.

In her book *The Anatomy of Prejudices,* the psychotherapist Elisabeth Young-Bruehl proposes a typology of three distinct kinds of hate: obsessive, hysterical, and narcissistic. It's not an exhaustive analysis, but it's a beginning in any serious attempt to understand hate rather than merely declaring war on it. The obsessives, for Young-Bruehl, are those, like the Nazis or Hutus, who fantasize a threat from a minority and obsessively try to rid themselves of it. For them, the very existence of the hated group is threatening. They often describe their loathing in almost physical terms: they experience what Patrick Buchanan, in reference to homosexuals, once described as a "visceral recoil" from the objects of their detestation. They often describe those they hate as diseased or sick, in need of a cure. Or they talk of "cleansing" them, as the Hutus talked of the Tutsis, or call them "cockroaches," as Yitzhak Shamir called the Palestinians. If you read material from the Family Research Council, it is clear that the group regards homosexuals as similar contaminants. A recent posting on its Web site about syphilis among gay men was headlined "Unclean."

Hysterical haters have a more complicated relationship with the objects of their aversion. In Young-Bruehl's words, hysterical prejudice is a prejudice that "a person uses unconsciously to appoint a group to act out in the world forbidden sexual and sexually aggressive desires that the person has repressed." Certain kinds of racists fit this pattern. White loathing of blacks is for some people at least partly about sexual and physical envy. A certain kind of white racist sees in black America all those impulses he wishes most to express himself but cannot. He idealizes in "blackness" a sexual freedom, a physical power, a Dionysian release that he detests but also longs for. His fantasy may not have any basis in reality, but it is powerful nonetheless. It is a form of love-hate, and it is impossible to understand the nuances of racism in, say, the American South, or in British imperial India, without it.

Unlike the obsessives, the hysterical haters do not want to eradicate the objects of their loathing; rather, they want to keep them in some kind of permanent and safe subjugation in order to indulge the attraction of their repulsion. A recent study, for example, found that the men most likely to be opposed to equal rights for homosexuals were those most likely to be aroused by homoerotic imagery. This makes little rational sense, but it has a certain psychological plausibility. If homosexuals were granted equality, then the hysterical gay-hater might panic that his repressed passions would run out of control, overwhelming him and the world he inhabits.

A narcissistic hate, according to Young-Bruehl's definition, is sexism. In its most common form, it is rooted in many men's inability even to imagine what it is to be a woman, a failing rarely challenged by men's control of our most powerful public social institutions. Women are not so much hated by most men as simply ignored in nonsexual contexts, or never conceived of as true equals. The implicit condescension is mixed, in many cases, with repressed and sublimated erotic desire. So the unawareness of women is sometimes commingled with a deep longing or contempt for them.

Each hate, of course, is more complicated than this, and in any one person hate can assume a uniquely configured combination of these types. So there are hysterical sexists who hate women because they need them so much, and narcissistic sexists who hardly notice that women exist, and sexists who oscillate between one of these positions and another. And there are gay-bashers who are threatened by masculine gay men and gay-haters who feel repulsed by effeminate ones. The soldier who beat his fellow soldier Barry Winchell to death with a baseball bat in July had earlier lost a fight to him. It was the image of a macho gay man — and the shame of being bested by him — that the vengeful soldier had to obliterate, even if he needed a gang of accomplices and a weapon to do so. But the murderers of Matthew Shepard seem to have had a different impulse: a visceral disgust at the thought of any sexual contact with an effeminate homosexual. Their anger was mixed with mockery, as the cruel spectacle at the side of the road suggested.

In the same way, the pathological anti-Semitism of Nazi Germany was obsessive, inasmuch as it tried to cleanse the world of Jews, but also, as Daniel Jonah Goldhagen shows in his book, *Hitler's Willing Executioners,* hysterical. The Germans were mysteriously compelled as well as repelled by Jews, devising elaborate ways, like death camps and death marches, to keep them alive even as they killed them. And the early Nazi phobia of interracial sex suggests as well a lingering erotic quality to the relationship, partaking of exactly the kind of sexual panic that persists among some homosexual-haters and antimiscegenation racists. So the concept of "homophobia," like that of "sexism" and "racism," is often a crude one. All three are essentially cookie-cutter formulas that try to understand human impulses merely through the one-dimensional identity of the victims, rather than through the thoughts and feelings of the haters and hated.

This is deliberate. The theorists behind these isms want to ascribe all blame to one group in society — the "oppressors" — and render specific others — the "victims" — completely blameless. And they want to do this in order in part to side unequivocally with the underdog. But it doesn't take a genius to see how this approach too can generate its own form of bias. It can justify blanket condemnations of whole groups of people — white straight males, for example — purely because of the color of their skin or the nature of their sexual orientation. And it can condescendingly ascribe innocence to whole groups of others. It does exactly what hate does: it hammers the uniqueness of each individual into the anvil of group identity. And it postures morally over the result.

In reality, human beings and human acts are far more complex, which is why these isms and the laws they have fomented are continually coming under strain and challenge. Once again, hate wriggles free of its definers. It knows no monolithic groups of haters and hated. Like a river, it has many eddies, backwaters, and rapids. So there are anti-Semites who actually admire what they think of as Jewish power, and there are gay-haters who look up to homosexuals and some who want to sleep with them. And there are black racists, racist Jews, sexist women, and anti-Semitic homosexuals. Of course there are.

IV

Once you start thinking of these phenomena less as the isms of sexism, racism, and homophobia, once you think of them as independent psychological responses, it's also possible to see how they can work in a bewildering variety of ways in a bewildering number of people. To take one obvious and sad oddity: people who are demeaned and objectified in society may develop an aversion to their tormentors that is more hateful in its expression than the prejudice they have been subjected to. The FBI statistics on hate crimes throw up an interesting point. In America in the 1990s, blacks were up to three times as likely as whites to commit a hate crime, to express their hate by physically attacking their targets or their property. Just as sexual abusers have often been victims of sexual abuse and wife-beaters often grew up in violent households, so hate criminals may often be members of hated groups.

Even the Columbine murderers were in some sense victims of hate before they were purveyors of it. Their classmates later admitted that Dylan Klebold and Eric Harris were regularly called "faggots" in the corridors and classrooms of Columbine High and that nothing was done to prevent or stop the harassment. This climate of hostility doesn't excuse the actions of Klebold and Harris, but it does provide a more plausible context. If they had been black, had routinely been called "nigger" in the school, and had then exploded into a shooting spree against white students, the response to the matter might well have been different. But the hate would have been the same. In other words, hate victims are often hate victimizers as well. This doesn't mean that all hates are equivalent, or that some are not more justified than others. It means merely that hate goes both ways; and if you try to regulate it among some, you will find yourself forced to regulate it among others.

It is no secret, for example, that some of the most vicious anti-Semites in America are black, and that some of the most virulent anti-Catholic bigots in America are gay. At what point, we are increasingly forced to ask, do these phenomena become as indefensible as white racism or religious toleration of antigay bigotry? That question becomes all the more difficult when we notice that it is often minorities who commit some of the most hate-filled offenses against what they see as their oppressors. It was the mainly gay AIDS activist group Act Up that perpetrated the hateful act of desecrating communion hosts at a mass at St. Patrick's Cathedral in New York. And here is the playwright Tony Kushner, who is gay, responding to the Matthew Shepard beating in *The Nation* magazine: "Pope John Paul II endorses murder. He, too, knows the price of discrimination, having declared anti-Semitism a sin. . . . He knows that discrimination kills. But when the Pope heard the news about Matthew Shepard, he, too, worried about spin. And so, on the subject of gay-bashing, the Pope and his cardinals and his bishops and priests maintain their cynical political silence. . . . To remain silent is to endorse murder." Kushner went on to describe the pope as a "homicidal liar."

Maybe the passion behind these words is justified. But it seems clear enough to me that Kushner is expressing hate toward the institution of the Catholic Church and all those who perpetuate its doctrines. How else to interpret the way in which he accuses the pope of cynicism, lying, and murder? And how else either to understand the brutal parody of religious vocations expressed by the Sisters of Perpetual Indulgence, a group of gay men who dress in drag as nuns and engage in sexually explicit performances in public? Or T-shirts with the words "Recovering Catholic" on them, hot items among some gay and lesbian activists? The implication that someone's religious faith is a mental illness is clearly an expression of contempt. If that isn't covered under the definition of hate speech, what is?

Or take the following sentences: "The act male homosexuals commit is ugly and repugnant and afterwards they are disgusted with themselves. They drink and take drugs to palliate this, but they are disgusted with the act and they are always changing partners and cannot be really happy." The thoughts of Pat Robertson or Patrick Buchanan? Actually, that sentence was written by Gertrude Stein, one of the century's most notable lesbians. Or take the following, about how beating up "black boys like that made us feel *good* inside. . . . Every time I drove my foot into his [expletive], I felt better." It was written to describe the brutal assault on an innocent bystander for the sole reason of his race. By the end of the attack, the victim had blood gushing from his mouth as his attackers stomped on his genitals. Are we less appalled when we learn that the actual sentence was how beating up "white boys like that made us feel *good* inside. . . . Every time I drove my foot into his [expletive], I felt better"? It was written by Nathan McCall, an African-American who later in life became a successful journalist at the *Washington Post* and published his memoir of this "hate crime" to much acclaim.

In fact, one of the stranger aspects of hate is that the prejudice expressed by a group in power may often be milder in expression than the prejudice felt by the marginalized. After all, if you already enjoy privilege, you may not feel the anger that turns bias into hate. You may not need to. For this reason, most white racism may be more influential in society than most black racism — but also more calmly expressed.

So may other forms of minority loathing — especially hatred within minorities. I'm sure that black conservatives like Clarence Thomas and Thomas Sowell have experienced their fair share of white racism. But I wonder whether it has ever reached the level of intensity of the hatred directed toward them by other blacks? In several years of being an openly gay writer and editor, I have experienced the gamut of responses to my sexual orientation. But I have only directly experienced articulated, passionate hate from other homosexuals. I have been accused over the years by other homosexuals of being a sellout, a hypocrite, a traitor, a sexist, a racist, a narcissist, a snob. I've been called selfish, callous, hateful, self-hating, and malevolent. At a reading, a group of lesbian activists portrayed my face on a poster within the crosshairs of a gun. Nothing from the religious right has come close to such vehemence.

I am not complaining. No harm has ever come to me or my property, and much of the criticism is rooted in the legitimate expression of political differences. But the visceral tone and style of the gay criticism can only be described as hateful. It is designed to wound personally, and it often does. But its intensity comes in part, one senses, from the pain of being excluded for so long, of anger long restrained bubbling up and directing itself more aggressively toward an alleged traitor than an alleged enemy. It is the hate of the hated. And it can be the most hateful hate of all. For this reason, hate-crime laws may themselves be an oddly biased category — biased against the victims of hate. Racism is everywhere, but the already victimized might be more desperate, more willing to express it violently. And so more prone to come under the suspicious eye of the law.

V

And why is hate for a group worse than hate for a person? In Laramie, Wyoming, the now-famous "epicenter of homophobia," where Matthew Shepard was brutally beaten to death, vicious murders are not unknown. In the previous twelve months, a fifteen-year-old pregnant girl was found east of the town with seventeen stab wounds. Her thirty-eight-year-old boyfriend was apparently angry that she had refused an abortion and left her in the Wyoming foothills to bleed to death. In the summer of 1998, an eight-year-old Laramie girl was abducted, raped, and murdered by a pedophile, who disposed of her young body in a garbage dump. Neither of these killings was deemed a hate crime, and neither would be designated as such under any existing hate-crime law. Perhaps because of this, one crime is an international legend; the other two are virtually unheard of.

But which crime was more filled with hate? Once you ask the

question, you realize how difficult it is to answer. Is it more hateful to kill a stranger or a lover? Is it more hateful to kill a child than an adult? Is it more hateful to kill your own child than another's? Under the law before the invention of hate crimes, these decisions didn't have to be taken. But under the law after hate crimes, a decision is essential. A decade ago, a murder was a murder. Now, in the era when group hate has emerged as our cardinal social sin, it all depends.

The supporters of laws against hate crimes argue that such crimes should be disproportionately punished because they victimize more than the victim. Such crimes, these advocates argue, spread fear, hatred, and panic among whole populations and therefore merit more concern. But of course all crimes victimize more than the victim and spread alarm in the society at large. Just think of the terrifying church shooting in Texas only two weeks ago. In fact, a purely random murder may be even more terrifying than a targeted one, since the entire community and not just a part of it feels threatened. High rates of murder, robbery, assault, and burglary victimize everyone, by spreading fear, suspicion, and distress everywhere. Which crime was more frightening to more people this summer: the mentally ill Buford Furrow's crazed attacks in Los Angeles, killing one, or Mark Barton's murder of his own family and several random day-traders in Atlanta, killing twelve? Almost certainly the latter. But only Furrow was guilty of "hate."

One response to this objection is that certain groups feel fear more intensely than others because of a history of persecution or intimidation. But doesn't this smack of a certain condescension toward minorities? Why, after all, should it be assumed that gay men or black women or Jews, for example, are as a group more easily intimidated than others? Surely in any of these communities there will be a vast range of responses, from panic to concern to complete indifference. The assumption otherwise is the kind of crude generalization the law is supposed to uproot in the first place. And among these groups, there are also likely to be vast differences. To equate a population once subjected to slavery with a population of Mexican immigrants or third-generation Holocaust survivors is to equate the unequatable. In fact, it is to set up a contest of vulnerability in which one group vies with another to establish its particular variety of suffering, a contest that can have no dignified solution.

Rape, for example, is not classified as a hate crime under most existing laws, pitting feminists against ethnic groups in a battle for recognition. If, as a solution to this problem, everyone except the white straight able-bodied male is regarded as a possible victim of a hate crime, then we have simply created a two-tier system of justice in which racial profiling is reversed, and white straight men are presumed guilty before being proved innocent, and members of minorities are free to hate them as gleefully as they like. But if we include the white straight male in the litany of potential victims, then we have effectively abolished the notion of a hate crime altogether, for if every crime is possibly a hate crime, then it is simply another name for crime. All we will have done is widened the search for possible bigotry, ratcheted up the sentences for everyone, and filled the jails up even further.

Hate-crime law advocates counter that extra penalties should be imposed on hate crimes because our society is experiencing an "epidemic" of such crimes. Mercifully, there is no hard evidence to support this notion. The federal government has only been recording the incidence of hate crimes in this decade, and the statistics tell a simple story. In 1992, there were 6,623 hate-crime incidents reported to the FBI by a total of 6,181 agencies, covering 51 percent of the population. In 1996, there were 8,734 incidents reported by 11,355 agencies, covering 84 percent of the population. That number dropped to 8,049 in 1997. These numbers are of course hazardous. They probably underreport the incidence of such crimes, but they are the only reliable figures we have. Yet even if they are faulty as an absolute number, they do not show an epidemic of hate crimes in the 1990s.

Is there evidence that the crimes themselves are becoming more vicious? None. More than 60 percent of recorded hate crimes in America involve no violent physical assault against another human being at all, and again, according to the FBI, that proportion has not budged much in the 1990s. These impersonal attacks are crimes against property or crimes of intimidation. Murder, which dominates media coverage of hate crimes, is a tiny proportion of the total. Of the 8,049 hate crimes reported to the FBI in 1997, a total of 8 were murders. Eight. The number of hate crimes that were aggravated assaults (generally involving a weapon) in 1997 is less than 15 percent of the total. That's 1,237 assaults too many, of course, but to put it in perspective, compare it with a reported

1,022,492 "equal opportunity" aggravated assaults in America in the same year. The number of hate crimes that were physical assaults is half the total. That's 4,000 assaults too many, of course, but to put it in perspective, it compares with around 3.8 million "equal opportunity" assaults in America annually.

The truth is, the distinction between a crime filled with personal hate and a crime filled with group hate is an essentially arbitrary one. It tells us nothing interesting about the psychological contours of the specific actor or his specific victim. It is a function primarily of politics, of special-interest groups carving out particular protections for themselves, rather than a serious response to a serious criminal concern. In such an endeavor, hate-crime law advocates cram an entire world of human motivations into an immutable, tiny box called hate and hope to have solved a problem. But nothing has been solved, and some harm may even have been done.

In an attempt to repudiate a past that treated people differently because of the color of their skin or their sex or religion or sexual orientation, we may merely create a future that permanently treats people differently because of the color of their skin or their sex, religion, or sexual orientation. This notion of a hate crime, and the concept of hate that lies behind it, takes a psychological mystery and turns it into a facile political artifact. Rather than compounding this error and extending it even further, we should seriously consider repealing the concept altogether.

To put it another way: violence can and should be stopped by the government. In a free society, hate can't and shouldn't be. The boundaries between hate and prejudice and between prejudice and opinion and between opinion and truth are so complicated and blurred that any attempt to construct legal and political fire walls is a doomed and illiberal venture. We know by now that hate will never disappear from human consciousness; in fact, it is probably, at some level, definitive of it. We know after decades of education measures that hate is not caused merely by ignorance and, after decades of legislation, that it isn't cured entirely by law.

To be sure, we have made much progress. Anyone who argues that America is as inhospitable to minorities and to women today as it has been in the past has not read much history. And we should of course be vigilant that our most powerful institutions, most notably the government, do not actively or formally propagate hatred, and insure that the violent expression of hate is curtailed by the same rules that punish all violent expression.

But after that, in an increasingly diverse culture, it is crazy to expect that hate, in all its variety, can be eradicated. A free country will always mean a hateful country. This may not be fair, or perfect, or admirable, but it is reality, and while we need not endorse it, we should not delude ourselves into thinking we can prevent it. That is surely the distinction between toleration and tolerance. Tolerance is the eradication of hate; toleration is coexistence despite it. We might do better as a culture and as a polity if we concentrated more on achieving the latter than the former. We would certainly be less frustrated.

And by aiming lower, we might actually reach higher. In some ways, some expression of prejudice serves a useful social purpose. It lets off steam; it allows natural tensions to express themselves incrementally; it can siphon off conflict through words rather than actions. Anyone who has lived in the ethnic shouting match that is New York City knows exactly what I mean. If New Yorkers disliked each other less, they wouldn't be able to get on so well. We may not all be able to pull off a Mencken — bigoted in words, egalitarian in action — but we might achieve a lesser form of virtue: a human acceptance of our need for differentiation without a total capitulation to it.

Do we not owe something more to the victims of hate? Perhaps we do. But it is also true that there is nothing that government can do for the hated that the hated cannot better do for themselves. After all, most bigots are not foiled when they are punished specifically for their beliefs. In fact, many of the worst haters crave such attention and find vindication in such rebukes. Indeed, our media's obsession with "hate," our elevation of it above other social misdemeanors and crimes, may even play into the hands of the pathetic and the evil, may breathe air into the smoldering embers of their paranoid loathing. Sure, we can help create a climate in which such hate is disapproved of — and we should. But there is a danger that if we go too far, if we punish it too much, if we try to abolish it altogether, we may merely increase its mystique, and entrench the very categories of human difference that we are trying to erase.

For hate is only foiled not when the haters are punished but when the hated are immune to the bigot's power. A hater cannot psychologically wound if a victim cannot psychologically be wounded. And that immunity to hurt can never be given; it can merely be achieved. The racial epithet only strikes at someone's core if he lets it, if he allows the bigot's definition of him to be the final description of his life and his person — if somewhere in his heart of hearts, he believes the hateful slur to be true. The only final answer to this form of racism, then, is not majority persecution of it but minority indifference to it. The only permanent rebuke to homophobia is not the enforcement of tolerance but gay equanimity in the face of prejudice. The only effective answer to sexism is not a morass of legal proscriptions but the simple fact of female success. In this, as in so many other things, there is no solution to the problem. There is only a transcendence of it. For all our rhetoric, hate will never be destroyed. Hate, as our predecessors knew better, can merely be overcome.

STEVEN WEINBERG

A Designer Universe?

FROM THE NEW YORK REVIEW OF BOOKS

I HAVE BEEN ASKED to comment on whether the universe shows signs of having been designed.* I don't see how it's possible to talk about this without having at least some vague idea of what a designer would be like. Any possible universe could be explained as the work of some sort of designer. Even a universe that is completely chaotic, without any laws or regularities at all, could be supposed to have been designed by an idiot.

The question that seems to me to be worth answering, and perhaps not impossible to answer, is whether the universe shows signs of having been designed by a deity more or less like those of traditional monotheistic religions — not necessarily a figure from the ceiling of the Sistine Chapel, but at least some sort of personality, some intelligence, who created the universe and has some special concern with life, in particular with human life. I expect that this is not the idea of a designer held by many here. You may tell me that you are thinking of something much more abstract, some cosmic spirit of order and harmony, as Einstein did. You are certainly free to think that way, but then I don't know why you use words like "designer" and "God," except perhaps as a form of protective coloration.

It used to be obvious that the world was designed by some sort of intelligence. What else could account for fire and rain and light-

*This article is based on a talk given in April 1999 at the Conference on Cosmic Design of the American Association for the Advancement of Science in Washington, D.C.

ning and earthquakes? Above all, the wonderful abilities of living things seemed to point to a creator who had a special interest in life. Today we understand most of these things in terms of physical forces acting under impersonal laws. We don't yet know the most fundamental laws, and we can't work out all the consequences of the laws we do know. The human mind remains extraordinarily difficult to understand, but so is the weather. We can't predict whether it will rain one month from today, but we do know the rules that govern the rain, even though we can't always calculate their consequences. I see nothing about the human mind any more than about the weather that stands out as beyond the hope of understanding as a consequence of impersonal laws acting over billions of years.

There do not seem to be any exceptions to this natural order, any miracles. I have the impression that these days most theologians are embarrassed by talk of miracles, but the great monotheistic faiths are founded on miracle stories — the burning bush, the empty tomb, an angel dictating the Koran to Mohammed — and some of these faiths teach that miracles continue at the present day. The evidence for all these miracles seems to me to be considerably weaker than the evidence for cold fusion, and I don't believe in cold fusion. Above all, today we understand that even human beings are the result of natural selection acting over millions of years of breeding and eating.

I'd guess that if we were to see the hand of the designer anywhere, it would be in the fundamental principles, the final laws of nature, the book of rules that govern all natural phenomena. We don't know the final laws yet, but as far as we have been able to see, they are utterly impersonal and quite without any special role for life. There is no life force. As Richard Feynman has said, when you look at the universe and understand its laws, "the theory that it is all arranged as a stage for God to watch man's struggle for good and evil seems inadequate."

True, when quantum mechanics was new, some physicists thought that it put humans back into the picture, because the principles of quantum mechanics tell us how to calculate the probabilities of various results that might be found by a human observer. But starting with the work of Hugh Everett forty years ago, the tendency of physicists who think deeply about these things has been to reformulate quantum mechanics in an entirely objective way, with observers treated just like everything else. I don't know if this program has been completely successful yet, but I think it will be.

I have to admit that even when physicists have gone as far as they can go, when we have a final theory, we will not have a completely satisfying picture of the world, because we will still be left with the question "Why?" Why this theory rather than some other theory? For example, why is the world described by quantum mechanics? Quantum mechanics is the one part of our present physics that is likely to survive intact in any future theory, but there is nothing logically inevitable about quantum mechanics; I can imagine a universe governed by Newtonian mechanics instead. So there seems to be an irreducible mystery that science will not eliminate.

But religious theories of design have the same problem. Either you mean something definite by a God, a designer, or you don't. If you don't, then what are we talking about? If you do mean something definite by "God" or "design" — if, for instance, you believe in a God who is jealous, or loving, or intelligent, or whimsical — then you still must confront the question "Why?" A religion may assert that the universe is governed by that sort of God rather than some other sort of God, and it may offer evidence for this belief, but it cannot explain why this should be so.

In this respect, it seems to me that physics is in a better position to give us a partly satisfying explanation of the world than religion can ever be, because although physicists won't be able to explain why the laws of nature are what they are and not something completely different, at least we may be able to explain why they are not *slightly* different. For instance, no one has been able to think of a logically consistent alternative to quantum mechanics that is only slightly different. Once you start trying to make small changes in quantum mechanics, you get into theories with negative probabilities or other logical absurdities. When you combine quantum mechanics with relativity, you increase its logical fragility. You find that unless you arrange the theory in just the right way, you get nonsense, like effects preceding causes or infinite probabilities. Religious theories, on the other hand, seem to be infinitely flexible, with nothing to prevent the invention of deities of any conceivable sort.

Now, it doesn't settle the matter for me to say that we cannot see the hand of a designer in what we know about the fundamental principles of science. It might be that although these principles do not refer explicitly to life, much less human life, they are nevertheless craftily designed to bring it about.

Some physicists have argued that certain constants of nature have values that seem to have been mysteriously fine-tuned to just the values that allow for the possibility of life, in a way that could only be explained by the intervention of a designer with some special concern for life. I am not impressed with these supposed instances of fine-tuning. For instance, one of the most frequently quoted examples of fine-tuning has to do with a property of the nucleus of the carbon atom. The matter left over from the first few minutes of the universe was almost entirely hydrogen and helium, with virtually none of the heavier elements like carbon, nitrogen, and oxygen that seem to be necessary for life. The heavy elements that we find on earth were built up hundreds of millions of years later in a first generation of stars, and then spewed out into the interstellar gas out of which our solar system eventually formed.

The first step in the sequence of nuclear reactions that created the heavy elements in early stars is usually the formation of a carbon nucleus out of three helium nuclei. There is a negligible chance of producing a carbon nucleus in its normal state (the state of lowest energy) in collisions of three helium nuclei, but it would be possible to produce appreciable amounts of carbon in stars if the carbon nucleus could exist in a radioactive state with an energy roughly 7 million electron volts (MeV) above the energy of the normal state, matching the energy of three helium nuclei, but (for reasons I'll come to presently) not more than 7.7 MeV above the normal state.

This radioactive state of a carbon nucleus could be easily formed in stars from three helium nuclei. After that, there would be no problem in producing ordinary carbon; the carbon nucleus in its radioactive state would spontaneously emit light and turn into carbon in its normal nonradioactive state, the state found on earth. The critical point in producing carbon is the existence of a radioactive state that can be produced in collisions of three helium nuclei.

In fact, the carbon nucleus is known experimentally to have just such a radioactive state, with an energy 7.65 MeV above the normal state. At first sight this may seem like a pretty close call; the energy of this radioactive state of carbon misses being too high to allow the formation of carbon (and hence of us) by only 0.05 MeV, which is less than one percent of 7.65 MeV. It may appear that the constants of nature on which the properties of all nuclei depend have been carefully fine-tuned to make life possible.

Looked at more closely, the fine-tuning of the constants of nature here does not seem so fine. We have to consider the reason why the formation of carbon in stars requires the existence of a radioactive state of carbon with an energy not more than 7.7 MeV above the energy of the normal state. The reason is that the carbon nuclei in this state are actually formed in a two-step process: first, two helium nuclei combine to form the unstable nucleus of a beryllium isotope, beryllium 8, which occasionally, before it falls apart, captures another helium nucleus, forming a carbon nucleus in its radioactive state, which then decays into normal carbon. The total energy of the beryllium 8 nucleus and a helium nucleus at rest is 7.4 MeV above the energy of the normal state of the carbon nucleus, so if the energy of the radioactive state of carbon were more than 7.7 MeV, it could only be formed in a collision of a helium nucleus and a beryllium 8 nucleus if the energy of motion of these two nuclei were at least 0.3 MeV — an energy that is extremely unlikely at the temperatures found in stars.

Thus the crucial thing that affects the production of carbon in stars is not the 7.65 MeV energy of the radioactive state of carbon above its normal state, but the 0.25 MeV energy of the radioactive state, an unstable composite of a beryllium 8 nucleus and a helium nucleus, above the energy of those nuclei at rest.* This energy misses being too high for the production of carbon by a fractional amount of 0.05 MeV/0.25 MeV, or 20 percent, which is not such a close call after all.

This conclusion about the lessons to be learned from carbon synthesis is somewhat controversial. In any case, there *is* one constant whose value does seem remarkably well adjusted in our favor. It is the energy density of empty space, also known as the cosmological

*This was pointed out in a 1989 paper by M. Livio, D. Hollowell, A. Weiss, and J. W. Truran, "The anthropic significance of the existence of an excited state of ^{12}C," *Nature* 340, no. 6231 (July 27, 1989). They did the calculation quoted here of the 7.7 MeV maximum energy of the radioactive state of carbon, above which little carbon is formed in stars.

constant. It could have any value, but from first principles one would guess that this constant should be very large, and could be positive or negative. If large and positive, the cosmological constant would act as a repulsive force that increases with distance, a force that would prevent matter from clumping together in the early universe, the process that was the first step in forming galaxies and stars and planets and people. If large and negative, the cosmological constant would act as an attractive force increasing with distance, a force that would almost immediately reverse the expansion of the universe and cause it to recollapse, leaving no time for the evolution of life. In fact, astronomical observations show that the cosmological constant is quite small, very much smaller than would have been guessed from first principles.

It is still too early to tell whether there is some fundamental principle that can explain why the cosmological constant must be this small. But even if there is no such principle, recent developments in cosmology offer the possibility of an explanation of why the measured values of the cosmological constant and other physical constants are favorable for the appearance of intelligent life. According to the "chaotic inflation" theories of André Linde and others, the expanding cloud of billions of galaxies that we call the big bang may be just one fragment of a much larger universe in which big bangs go off all the time, each one with different values for the fundamental constants.

In any such picture, in which the universe contains many parts with different values for what we call the constants of nature, there would be no difficulty in understanding why these constants take values favorable to intelligent life. There would be a vast number of big bangs in which the constants of nature take values unfavorable for life, and many fewer where life is possible. You don't have to invoke a benevolent designer to explain why we are in one of the parts of the universe where life is possible: in all the other parts of the universe there is no one to raise the question.* If any theory

*The same conclusion may be reached in a subtler way when quantum mechanics is applied to the whole universe. Through a reinterpretation of earlier work by Stephen Hawking, Sidney Coleman has shown how quantum mechanical effects can lead to a split of the history of the universe (more precisely, in what is called the wave function of the universe) into a huge number of separate possibilities, each one corresponding to a different set of fundamental constants. See Sidney Coleman, "Black holes as red herrings: Topological fluctuations and the loss of quantum coherence," *Nuclear Physics* B307 (1988): 867.

of this general type turns out to be correct, then to conclude that the constants of nature have been fine-tuned by a benevolent designer would be like saying, "Isn't it wonderful that God put us here on earth, where there's water and air and the surface gravity and temperature are so comfortable, rather than some horrid place like Mercury or Pluto?" Where else in the solar system other than on earth could we have evolved?

Reasoning like this is called "anthropic." Sometimes it just amounts to an assertion that the laws of nature are what they are so that we can exist, without further explanation. This seems to me to be little more than mystical mumbo-jumbo. On the other hand, if there really is a large number of worlds in which some constants take different values, then the anthropic explanation of why in our world they take values favorable for life is just common sense, like explaining why we live on the earth rather than Mercury or Pluto. The actual value of the cosmological constant, recently measured by observations of the motion of distant supernovas, is about what you would expect from this sort of argument: it is just about small enough so that it does not interfere much with the formation of galaxies. But we don't yet know enough about physics to tell whether there are different parts of the universe in which what are usually called the constants of physics really do take different values. This is not a hopeless question; we will be able to answer it when we know more about the quantum theory of gravitation than we do now.

It would be evidence for a benevolent designer if life were better than could be expected on other grounds. To judge this, we should keep in mind that a certain capacity for pleasure would readily have evolved through natural selection, as an incentive to animals who need to eat and breed in order to pass on their genes. It may not be likely that natural selection on any one planet would produce animals who are fortunate enough to have the leisure and the ability to do science and think abstractly, but our sample of what is produced by evolution is very biased, by the fact that it is only in these fortunate cases that there is anyone thinking about cosmic design. Astronomers call this a selection effect.

The universe is very large, and perhaps infinite, so it should be no surprise that among the enormous number of planets that may support only unintelligent life and the still vaster number that cannot support life at all, there is some tiny fraction on which there are living beings who are capable of thinking about the universe, as we are doing here. A journalist who has been assigned to interview lottery winners may come to feel that some special providence has been at work on their behalf, but he should keep in mind the much larger number of lottery players whom he is not interviewing because they haven't won anything. Thus, to judge whether our lives show evidence for a benevolent designer, we not only have to ask whether life is better than would be expected in any case from what we know about natural selection, but we need also to take into account the bias introduced by the fact that it is we who are thinking about the problem.

This is a question that you all will have to answer for yourselves. Being a physicist is no help with questions like this, so I have to speak from my own experience. My life has been remarkably happy, perhaps in the upper 99.99 percentile of human happiness, but even so, I have seen a mother die painfully of cancer, a father's personality destroyed by Alzheimer's disease, and scores of second and third cousins murdered in the Holocaust. Signs of a benevolent designer are pretty well hidden.

The prevalence of evil and misery has always bothered those who believe in a benevolent and omnipotent God. Sometimes God is excused by pointing to the need for free will. Milton gives God this argument in *Paradise Lost:*

> I formed them free, and free they must remain
> Till they enthrall themselves: I else must change
> Their nature, and revoke the high decree
> Unchangeable, eternal, which ordained
> Their freedom; they themselves ordained their fall.

It seems a bit unfair to my relatives to be murdered in order to provide an opportunity for free will for Germans, but even putting that aside, how does free will account for cancer? Is it an opportunity of free will for tumors?

I don't need to argue here that the evil in the world proves that the universe is not designed, but only that there are no signs of benevolence that might have shown the hand of a designer. But in fact the perception that God cannot be benevolent is very old. Plays by Aeschylus and Euripides make a quite explicit statement that the gods are selfish and cruel, though they expect better behavior from humans. God in the Old Testament tells us to bash the heads of infidels and demands of us that we be willing to sacrifice our children's lives at his orders, and the God of traditional Christianity and Islam damns us for eternity if we do not worship him in the right manner. Is this a nice way to behave? I know, I know, we are not supposed to judge God according to human standards, but you see the problem here: if we are not yet convinced of his existence and are looking for signs of his benevolence, then what other standards *can* we use?

The issues that I have been asked to address here will seem to many to be terribly old-fashioned. The "argument from design" made by the English theologian William Paley is not on most people's minds these days. The prestige of religion seems today to derive from what people take to be its moral influence, rather than from what they may think has been its success in accounting for what we see in nature. Conversely, I have to admit that although I really don't believe in a cosmic designer, the reason I am taking the trouble to argue about it is that I think on balance the moral influence of religion has been awful.

This is much too big a question to be settled here. On one side, I could point out endless examples of the harm done by religious enthusiasm, through a long history of pogroms, crusades, and jihads. In our own century it was a Muslim zealot who killed Sadat, a Jewish zealot who killed Rabin, and a Hindu zealot who killed Gandhi. No one would say that Hitler was a Christian zealot, but it is hard to imagine Nazism taking the form it did without the foundation provided by centuries of Christian anti-Semitism. On the other side, many admirers of religion would set countless examples of the good done by religion. For instance, in his recent book *Imagined Worlds,* the distinguished physicist Freeman Dyson has emphasized the role of religious belief in the suppression of slavery. I'd like to comment briefly on this point, not to try to prove anything with one example but just to illustrate what I think about the moral influence of religion.

It is certainly true that the campaign against slavery and the slave trade was greatly strengthened by devout Christians, including the Evangelical layman William Wilberforce in England and the Unitarian minister William Ellery Channing in America. But Christianity, like other great world religions, lived comfortably with slavery for many centuries, and slavery was endorsed in the New Testament. So what was different for antislavery Christians like Wilberforce and Channing? There had been no discovery of new sacred scriptures, and neither Wilberforce nor Channing claimed to have received any supernatural revelations. Rather, the eighteenth century had seen a widespread increase in rationality and humanitarianism, which led others — for instance, Adam Smith, Jeremy Bentham, and Richard Brinsley Sheridan — also to oppose slavery, on grounds having nothing to do with religion. Lord Mansfield, the author of the decision in Somersett's Case, which ended slavery in England (though not its colonies), was no more than conventionally religious, and his decision did not mention religious arguments. Although Wilberforce was the instigator of the campaign against the slave trade in the 1790s, this movement had essential support from many in Parliament like Fox and Pitt, who were not known for their piety. As far as I can tell, the moral tone of religion benefited more from the spirit of the times than the spirit of the times benefited from religion.

Where religion did make a difference, it was more in support of slavery than in opposition to it. Arguments from scripture were used in Parliament to defend the slave trade. Frederick Douglass told in his *Narrative* how his condition as a slave became worse when his master underwent a religious conversion that allowed him to justify slavery as the punishment of the children of Ham. Mark Twain described his mother as a genuinely good person whose soft heart pitied even Satan but who had no doubt about the legitimacy of slavery, because in years of living in antebellum Missouri, she had never heard any sermon opposing slavery but only countless sermons preaching that slavery was God's will. With or without religion, good people can behave well and bad people can do evil; but for good people to do evil — that takes religion.

In an e-mail message from the American Association for the Advancement of Science, I learned that the aim of this conference is to have a constructive dialogue between science and religion. I am all in favor of a dialogue between science and religion, but not a constructive dialogue. One of the great achievements of science has been, if not to make it impossible for intelligent people to be religious, then at least to make it possible for them not to be religious. We should not retreat from this accomplishment.

TERRY TEMPEST WILLIAMS

A Shark in the Mind of One Contemplating Wilderness

FROM THE NATION

A SHARK SWIMS past me in a kelp forest that sways back and forth with the current. It is deliberate and focused. I watch the shark's sleek body dart left and right as its caudal fin propels it forward. Its eyes seem to slice through the water in a blood gaze as the gills open and close, open and close. Around and around, I watch the shark maneuver through schools of fish. It must not be hungry. The only thing separating me from the shark is a tall glass pane at the Monterey Sea Aquarium. Everything is in motion. I press my hands on the glass, waiting for the shark to pass by again, and when it does I feel my own heart beating against the mind of this creature that kills.

In the enormous blue room of the American Museum of Natural History, I stare at the tiger shark mounted on the wall of the second floor. Its surface shines with the light of taxidermy, creating the illusion of having just left the sea, now our own natural-history trophy. I see how out of proportion its mouth is to the rest of its body and wonder how many teeth hung from its gums during its lifetime, the rows of teeth, five to twenty of them, biting and tearing, thrashing and chomping on flesh, the teeth constantly being replaced by something akin to a conveyor-belt system. Somewhere in my mind I hold the fact that a shark may go through 20,000 teeth in a life span of ten years. I imagine the shark sensing the electrical field of a seal, swimming toward the diving black body now rising to the surface, delivering with great speed its deadly blow, the jaws that dislocate and protrude out of its mouth, the strong muscles that open, then close, the razor teeth that clamp down on the prey with such force that skin, cartilage, and bone are reduced to one clean round bite, sustained over and over again. The blue water now bloody screams to the surface. Even in death, I see this shark in motion.

Sensation. I enter the Brooklyn Museum of Art to confront another tiger shark, this the most harrowing of all the requiem sharks I have encountered in a week-long period. Requiem sharks. They say the name is derived from the observation that once these large sharks of the family Carcharhinidae attack a victim, the only task remaining is to hold a requiem, a mass for the dead. *Galeocerdo cuvieri.* It is neither dead nor alive, but rather a body floating in space, a shark suspended in solution. Formaldehyde. To preserve. What do we choose to preserve? I note the worn, used sense of its mouth, shriveled and receding, looking more manly than fish. The side view creates a triptych of head, dorsal fin, and tail through the three panels of glass in the frame of white painted steel. I walk around the shark and feel the charge of the front view, a turquoise nightmare of terror that spills into daylight. Sensation. Damien Hirst is the creator of *The Physical Impossibility of Death in the Mind of Someone Living* (1991).

I do not think about the shark.

I like the idea of a thing to describe a feeling. A shark is frightening, bigger than you are, in an environment unknown to you. It looks alive when it's dead and dead when it's alive. . . . I like ideas of trying to understand the world by taking things out of the world. . . . You expect [the shark] to look back at you. — Damien Hirst

As a naturalist who has worked in a museum of natural history for more than fifteen years, how am I to think about a shark in the context of art, not science? How is my imagination so quickly rearranged to see the suspension of a shark, pickled in formaldehyde, as the stopped power of motion in the jaws of death, an image of my own mortality?

My mind becomes wild in the presence of creation, the artist's creation. I learn that the box in which the shark floats was built by the same company that constructs the aquariums of Brighton Sea World. I think about the killer whales kept in tanks for the amusement of humans, the killer whales that jump through hoops, carry humans on their backs as they circle and circle and circle the tank, day after day after week after month, how they go mad, the sea of insanity churning inside them, inside me as I feel my own captivity within a culture — any culture — that would thwart creativity: we are stopped cold, our spirits suspended, controlled, controlled sensation.

Tiger shark, glass, steel, 5 percent formaldehyde solution.

Damien Hirst calls the shark suspended in formaldehyde a sculpture. If it were in a museum of natural history, it would be called an exhibit, an exhibit in which the organism is featured as the animal it is. Call it art or call it biology, what is the true essence of shark?

How is the focus of our perceptions decided?

Art. Artifact. Art by designation.

Thomas McEvilley, art critic and author of *Art & Otherness,* states,

> The fact that we designate something as art means that it is art for us, but says nothing about what it is in itself or for other people. Once we realize that the quest for essences is an archaic religious quest, there is no reason why something should not be art for one person or culture and non-art for another.

Wild. Wilderness. Wilderness by designation. What is the solution to preserving that which is wild?

I remember standing next to an old rancher in Escalante, Utah, during a contentious political debate over wilderness in the canyon country of southern Utah. He kicked the front tire of his pickup truck with his cowboy boot.

"What's this?" he asked me.

"A Chevy truck," I responded.

"Right, and everybody knows it."

He then took his hand and swept the horizon. "And what's all that?" he asked with the same matter-of-fact tone.

"Wilderness," he answered before I could speak. "And everybody knows it, so why the hell do you have to go have Congress tell us what it is?"

Damien Hirst's conceptual art, be it his shark or his installation called *A Thousand Years* (1990) — where the eye of a severed cow's head looks upward as black flies crawl over it and lay eggs in the flesh that metamorphose into maggots that mature into flies that gather in the pool of blood to drink, leaving tiny red footprints on the glass installation, while some flies are destined to die as a life-stopping buzz in the electric fly-killing machine — all his conceptual pieces of art, his installations, make me think about the concept and designation of wilderness.

Why not designate wilderness as an installation of art? Conceptual art? A true sensation that moves and breathes and changes over time with a myriad of creatures that formulate an instinctual framework of interspecies dialogues; call them predator-prey relations or symbiotic relations, niches and ecotones, never before seen as art, as dance, as a painting in motion, but imagined only through the calculations of biologists, their facts now metamorphosed into designs, spontaneously choreographed moment to moment among the living. Can we not watch the habits of animals, the adaptations of plants, and call them performance art within the conceptual framework of wilderness?

To those who offer the critique that wilderness is merely a received idea, one that might be "conceptually incoherent" and entranced by "the myth of the pristine," why not answer with a resounding yes, yes, wilderness is our received idea as artists, as human beings, a grand piece of performance art that can embody and inspire *The Physical Impossibility of Death in the Mind of Someone Living* or *Isolated Elements Swimming in the Same Direction for the Purpose of Understanding* (1991).

Call it a cabinet of fish preserved in salt solution to honor the diversity of species, where nothing is random. Or call it a piece of art to celebrate color and form found in the bodies of fishes. Squint your eyes: *imagine a world of spots.* Colored dots in the wilderness. *They're all connected.* Damien Hirst paints spots.

"Art's about life and it can't really be about anything else. There isn't anything else." Tell us again, Damien Hirst, with your cabinet of wonders; we are addicted to wonders, bottles of drugs lined up, shelf after shelf, waiting to be opened, minds opened, veins opened, nerves opened. Wilderness is a cabinet of pharmaceuticals waiting to be discovered.

Just as we designate art, we designate wilderness, large and small, as much as we can, hoping it begins a dialogue with our highest and basest selves. We are animals, in search of a home, in relationship to Other, an expanding community with a mosaic of habitats, domestic and wild; there is nothing precious or nostalgic about it. We designate wilderness as an installation of essences, open for individual interpretation, full of controversy and conversation.

"I always believe in contradiction, compromise . . . it's unavoidable. In life it can be positive or negative, like saying, 'I can't live without you.'" Damien Hirst speaks again.

I cannot live without art. I cannot live without wilderness. Call it *Brilliant Love* (1994–95). Thank the imagination that some people are brave enough, sanely crazy enough, to designate both.

"Art is dangerous because it doesn't have a definable function. I think that is what people are afraid of."

Yes, Damien, exactly, you bad boy of British art who dares to slice up the bodies of cows, from the head to the anus, and mix them all up to where nothing makes sense and who allows us to walk through with no order in mind, twelve cross-sections of cow, so we have to take note of the meat that we eat without thinking about the topography of the body, the cow's body, our body; we confront the wonder of the organism as is, not as a continuum but as a design, the sheer beauty and texture of functional design. We see the black-and-white hide; there is no place to hide inside the guts of a cow sliced and stretched through space like an accordion between your very large hands. You ask us to find *Some Comfort Gained from the Acceptance of the Inherent Lies in Everything* (1996).

We have been trying to explain, justify, codify, give biological and ecological credence as to why we want to preserve what is wild, like art, much more than a specimen behind glass. But what if we were to say, Sorry, you are right, wilderness has no definable function. Can we let it be, designate it as art, *art of the wild,* just in case one such definition should arise in the mind of one standing in the tallgrass prairies of middle America or the sliding slope of sandstone in the erosional landscape of Utah?

Wilderness as an aesthetic.

Freeze. Damien Hirst brought together a community of artists and displayed their work in a warehouse in England, these neo-conceptualists who set out to explore the big things like death and sex and the meaning of life. Wilderness designation is not so dissimilar. In your tracks, *freeze,* and watch the performance art of a grizzly walking through the gold meadows of the Hayden Valley in Yellowstone. In your tracks, *freeze,* a constellation of monarch butterflies has gathered in the mountains of Mexico. No definable function except to say, wilderness exists like art, look for an idea with four legs, with six legs and wings that resemble fire, and recognize this feeling called survival, in this received idea of wilderness, our twentieth-century installation as neo-conservationists.

A shark in a box.

Wilderness as a box.

Wilderness as *A Thousand Years* with flies and maggots celebrating inside the corpse of things.

Q: What is in the boxes?

A: Maggots.

Q: So you're going to put maggots in the white boxes, and then they hatch and then they fly around . . .

A: And then they get killed by the fly-killer, and maybe lay eggs in the cow heads.

Q: It's a bit disgusting.

A: A bit. I don't think it is. I like it.

Q: Do you think anyone will buy it?

A: I hope so.

— Damien Hirst interview with Liam Gillick, *Modern Medicine,* 1990

Do I think anyone will buy the concept of wilderness as conceptual art? It is easier to create a sensation over art than a sensation over the bald, greed-faced sale and development of open lands, wild lands, in the United States of America.

I would like to bring Damien Hirst out to the American West, let him bring along his chain saw, *Cutting Ahead* (1994), only to find out somebody has beat him to it, creating clear-cut sculptures out of negative space, eroding space, topsoil running like blood down the mountainsides as mud. Mud as material. He would have plenty of material.

The art of the wild is flourishing.

How are we to see through the lens of our own creative destruction?

A shark in a box.
Wilderness as an installation.
A human being suspended in formaldehyde.

My body floats between contrary equilibriums. — Federico García Lorca

When I leaned over the balcony of the great blue room in the American Museum of Natural History, I looked up at the body of the blue whale, the largest living mammal on earth, suspended from the ceiling. I recalled being a docent, how we brought the schoolchildren to this room to lie on their backs, thrilled beyond words as they looked up at this magnificent leviathan, who, if alive, with one quick swoosh of its tail would be halfway across Central Park.

I only then noticed that the open space below where the children used to lie on their backs in awe was now a food court filled with plastic tables and chairs. The tables were crowded with visitors chatting away, eating, drinking, oblivious to the creatures surrounding them. How had I missed the theater lights, newly installed on the balcony, pointing down to illuminate the refrigerators humming inside the showcases with a loud display of fast foods advertising yogurt, roast beef sandwiches, apples and oranges?

The blue whale, the tiger shark, sunfish, tunas, eels and manta rays, the walrus, the elephant seals, the orca with its head poking through the diorama of ice in Antarctica, are no longer the natural histories of creatures associated with the sea but simply decoration.

Everything feels upside-down these days, created for our entertainment. Requiem days. The natural world is becoming invisible, appearing only as a backdrop for our own human dramas and catastrophes: hurricanes, tornadoes, earthquakes, and floods. Perhaps if we bring art to the discussion of the wild we can create a sensation where people will pay attention to the shock of what has always been here *Away from the Flock* (1994).

Wild Beauty in the Minds of the Living.

Biographical Notes

Notable Essays of 1999

Biographical Notes

André Aciman is the author of *Out of Egypt: A Memoir* (Farrar, Straus & Giroux/Riverhead) and the coauthor and editor of *Letters of Transit* (New Press). He was born in Alexandria and lived in Egypt, Italy, and France. Educated at Harvard, he has taught at Princeton and now teaches at Bard College. He is the recipient of a Whiting Writers' Award and a Guggenheim fellowship. A contributor to the *New York Times, The New Yorker,* the *New Republic,* the *New York Review of Books,* and *Commentary,* he is currently working on a novel entitled *Over the Footbridge. False Papers* (Farrar, Straus & Giroux), his collected essays on exile and memory, was published this summer.

Wendell Berry's nonfiction books include *What Are People For?; Standing on Earth; Sex, Economy, Freedom, and Community;* and *Another Turn of the Crank.* Counterpoint Press will publish two books in 2000: a long essay, *Life Is a Miracle,* and a novel, *The Life Story of Jayber Crow.* An earlier version of "In Distrust of Movements" was written as a speech for the Northeast Organic Farmers Association and originally appeared in that group's newsletter, *The Natural Farmer.*

Ian Buruma is the author of a novel, *Playing the Game,* and several books of nonfiction that cover Asian culture and politics, such as *God's Dust, The Wages of Guilt, Behind the Mask, A Japanese Mirror,* and *The Missionary and the Libertine.* His most recent book is *Anglomania.* The culture editor of the *Far Eastern Economic Review* (in Hong Kong), he is currently an Alistair Horne Fellow at St. Anthony's College, Oxford.

Fred D'Aguiar is the author of three books of poetry, *Mama Dot, Airy Hall,* and *British Subjects;* a play, *A Jamaican Airman Foresees His Death;* and three novels, *The Longest Memory* (winner of Great Britain's Whitbread and David Higham First Novel Awards), *Dear Future*, and *Feeding the Ghosts*. He has also won the Guyanese National Poetry Award. He teaches in the English department at the University of Miami in Florida and also directs its MFA program. A verse-novel, *Bloodlines*, will be published in 2000.

EDWIDGE DANTICAT is the author of two novels, *Breath, Eyes, Memory* and *The Farming of Bones*, and a collection of stories, *Krik? Krak!* She is also the editor of *The Beacon Best of 2000: Creative Writing by Women and Men of All Colors*, as well as of *The Butterfly's Way: Voices from the Haitian Diaspora in the United States*.

WILLIAM H. GASS is the author of ten books of fiction and nonfiction, including *Omensetter's Luck, In the Heart of the Heart of the Country, On Being Blue, The World Within the Word*, and *Habitations of the Word*, which won the 1986 National Book Critics Circle Award for criticism. He is the David May Distinguished University Professor in the Humanities and director of the International Writers Center at Washington University in St. Louis. He has been the recipient of grants from both the Rockefeller Foundation and the Guggenheim Foundation and has also received the American Academy and Institute of Arts and Letters Award for fiction. His most recent books include a novel, *The Tunnel;* an essay collection, *Finding a Form*, which won the 1996 National Book Critics Circle Award for criticism; *Cartesian Sonata*, a collection of novellas; and *Reading Rilke*, a commentary on and translation of the Duino Elegies.

MARY GORDON's novels — *Final Payments, The Company of Women, Men and Angels, The Other Side*, and *Spending* — have been bestsellers. She has also published a memoir, *The Shadow Man;* a book of novellas, *The Rest of Life;* a collection of stories, *Temporary Shelter;* and two books of essays, *Good Boys and Dead Girls* and *Seeing Through Places*. Her most recent work is a biography of Joan of Arc. She has received the Lila Acheson Wallace Reader's Digest Award and a Guggenheim fellowship. She is a professor of English at Barnard College.

EDWARD HOAGLAND has published eight collections of essays, most recently *Balancing Acts* and *Tigers & Ice;* five books of fiction, including *Seven Rivers West;* and two travel books, *Notes from the Century Before: A Journal from British Columbia* and *African Calliope: A Journey to the Sudan*, both of which were reissued in 1995. He also writes criticism and is the editor of the Penguin Nature Classics Series. He is a member of the American Academy of Arts and Letters and has taught at ten colleges; he is currently at Bennington.

JAMAICA KINCAID is the author of *Annie John, A Small Place*, and *Lucy*. Her first book, *At the Bottom of the River*, received the Morton Dauwen

Zabel Award of the American Academy and Institute of Arts and Letters. She was guest editor of *The Best American Essays 1995*, and her most recent books include *An Autobiography of My Mother, My Brother,* and (with Marianna Cook) *Generations of Women.*

GEETA KOTHARI's writing has appeared in various journals and anthologies. She is currently completing her first novel and working on a collection of essays, *Transit Passengers Only.* She lives in Pittsburgh, Pennsylvania.

RICHARD MCCANN is the author of *Ghost Letters,* which won the 1994 Beatrice Hawley Award and the 1993 Capricorn Poetry Award, and the editor (with Michael Klein) of *Things Shaped in Passing: More 'Poets for Life' Writing from the AIDS Pandemic.* His prose and poetry appear in such magazines as the *Atlantic Monthly, Esquire, Ploughshares, Poz,* and *The Nation* and in numerous anthologies, including *The Penguin Book of Gay Short Stories; I Know Some Things: Writing on Childhood; Body; Survival Stories: Memoirs of Crisis;* and *Men on Men 2000: Best New Gay Fiction.* For his work he has received awards and fellowships from the National Endowment for the Arts, the District of Columbia Commission on the Arts, Yaddo, the MacDowell Colony, and the Fine Arts Work Center in Provincetown, where he now serves on the writing committee and the board of advisers. He is currently working on a collection of stories and on a series of personal essays exploring the experience and meanings of liver transplantation. He lives in Washington, D.C, where he teaches in the graduate program in creative writing at American University. "The Resurrectionist" is dedicated to Carole Horn, M.D., Vinod Rustgi, M.D., Timothy Shaver, M.D., and Sarah Priestman.

CYNTHIA OZICK is the author of three collections of essays — *Art & Ardor, Metaphor & Memory,* and *Fame & Folly* — three collections of short stories, and five novels, the most recent being *The Puttermesser Papers.* She is the recipient of numerous awards, including four O. Henry first prizes, a Guggenheim fellowship, and the Rea Award for the Short Story. She was the 1998 guest editor of this series and is a member of the American Academy of Arts and Letters. A fourth collection of essays is in preparation.

SCOTT RUSSELL SANDERS is the author of fifteen books, including *Secrets of the Universe, Writing from the Center, Staying Put, Hunting for Hope,* and *The Country of Language.* He has won Guggenheim and National Endowment for the Arts fellowships in support of his writing, and for his work in nonfiction he has received the Lannan Literary Award. "The Force of Spirit" is the title essay in a book that appears from Beacon Press this fall. Another of the pieces in that book won the 1999 John

Burroughs Award for outstanding natural history essay. Sanders teaches literature and writing at Indiana University, in Bloomington, where he lives with his wife and where his two grown children currently study.

LYNNE SHARON SCHWARTZ's most recent books are a comic novel of manners, *In the Family Way: An Urban Comedy;* a collection of essays, *Face to Face;* and *Ruined by Reading: A Life in Books.* Her earlier books include the novels *The Fatigue Artist, Disturbances in the Field, Rough Strife* (nominated for a National Book Award and the PEN/Hemingway Award), *Leaving Brooklyn* (nominated for a PEN/Faulkner Award), and *Balancing Acts,* as well as two story collections, *The Melting Pot and Other Subversive Stories* and *Acquainted with the Night.* Her work has been widely anthologized and is collected in *A Lynne Sharon Schwartz Reader: Selected Prose and Poetry.* Though eschewing the academic life, she has nomadically taught fiction writing in many graduate programs, most recently at Washington University in St. Louis.

PETER SINGER was born in Melbourne, Australia, and studied philosophy there and at Oxford University. His books include *Animal Liberation, Practical Ethics, How Are We to Live?, Rethinking Life and Death,* and *Ethics into Action.* He is currently DeCamp Professor of Bioethics in the Center for Human Values at Princeton University.

FLOYD SKLOOT is the author of three novels, two books of poetry, and a collection of essays. His work has been included in *The Best American Essays 1993, The Art of the Essay 1999,* and *The Best American Science Writing 2000.* "Gray Area: Thinking with a Damaged Brain" won *Creative Nonfiction*'s award for best essay on the brain and will be included in Skloot's newly completed book of essays, *In the Shadow of Memory.* He lives in Amity, Oregon.

MARK SLOUKA is the author of a collection of stories, *Lost Lake,* and *War of the Worlds,* a cultural critique of the digital revolution. His essays and fiction have appeared in *Harper's Magazine, Story, Epoch,* the *Georgia Review,* and *The Best American Essays 1999,* and his fiction has won a National Magazine Award. A contributing editor at *Harper's Magazine,* he is the recipient of a fellowship from the National Endowment for the Arts for the year 2000. He divides his time between a cabin with an outhouse and a cave in New York City, where he teaches at Columbia University.

CHERYL STRAYED is a graduate student in the Creative Writing Program at Syracuse University, where she is completing her first novel, *Linger.* She is the recipient of numerous awards, including a grant from the Barbara Deming Memorial Fund. In 1999 she designed and led "Three Truths and a Lie," a poetry project for teenage girls living in the poorest neighborhood in Portland, Oregon. The essay in this volume also appears in *Sorrow's Company: Writers on Grief and Loss,* published by Beacon Press.

ANDREW SULLIVAN writes for the *New York Times Magazine,* the *New Republic,* and the *Sunday Times* (London). Born in England, he was educated at Oxford University, where he studied modern history and modern languages, and Harvard University, from which he holds a master's degree in public administration and a Ph.D. in political science. His dissertation on the English philosopher Michael Oakeshott won the departmental prize for best dissertation in political theory in 1990. Sullivan was the editor of the *New Republic* from 1991 to 1996, in which period the magazine won three National Magazine Awards. He is the author of two books, *Virtually Normal: An Argument About Homosexuality* and *Love Undetectable: Notes on Friendship, Sex, and Survival,* and the editor of a collection, *Same-Sex Marriage: Pro and Con.* He is at work on a new book about the politics of genetics, and lives with his beagle in Washington, D.C., and Provincetown, Massachusetts.

Among the books that STEVEN WEINBERG has written for the general reader are *The First Three Minutes, The Discovery of Subatomic Particles,* and *Dreams of a Final Theory.* He is also the author of the scientific treatises *Gravitation and Cosmology* and *The Quantum Theory of Fields.* He has written more than two hundred scientific articles on elementary particle physics, cosmology, and other topics and is an occasional contributor to such periodicals as the *New York Review of Books, Time, Newsweek,* the *Times Literary Supplement,* the *New Republic, Daedalus, Forbes,* and others. His writing for general readers has been honored with the U.S. Steel–American Institute of Physics Science Writing Prize, the Gemant Prize of the American Physical Society, and the Lewis Thomas Award for the Scientist as Poet. For his research in physics he has received numerous prizes and awards, including the 1979 Nobel Prize in physics, the 1991 National Medal of Science, and a dozen honorary doctoral degrees from universities in the United States and abroad. He has been elected to the U.S. National Academy of Science, the Royal Society of London, the American Philosophical Society, and the American Academy of Arts and Sciences. He taught at Columbia, Berkeley, MIT, and Harvard before coming to Austin in 1982 to found the Theory Group of the University of Texas.

TERRY TEMPEST WILLIAMS has written about her experiences as a naturalist, a woman, a Mormon, an environmentalist, and a westerner in such books as *Refuge: An Unnatural History of Family and Place; Pieces of a White Shell: A Journey to Navajoland; Coyote's Canyon; An Unspoken Hunger: Stories from the Field;* and *Desert Quartet.* Her most recent book is *Leap: A Traveler in the Garden of Delights* (Pantheon, 2000).

Notable Essays of 1999

Selected by Robert Atwan

Laurie Abraham
The Landscape of Desire. *Mirabella,* September.

Marcia Aldrich
Purse. *Northwest Review,* vol. 37, no. 3.

Hilton Als
The Dope Show. *The New Yorker,* February 22/March 1.

Nancy Anderson
Hoop Scenes. *Under the Sun,* Summer.

Gene Armao
Pas de Deux. *Northeast Corridor,* no. 7.

Don Asher
Lab Notes. *Harper's Magazine,* May.

Will Baker
Tony and the Cows. *The Georgia Review,* Winter.

Helen Barolini
A Fish Tale. *The Missouri Review,* vol. 22, no. 2.

Lionel Basney
Immanuel's Ground. *The American Scholar,* Summer.

Rick Bass
Valley of the Dogs. *Five Points,* Spring/Summer.

Adria Bernardi
Hep-Lock. *The Missouri Review,* vol. 22, no. 1.

Jane Bernstein
Rachel Flies Alone. *The Massachusetts Review,* Summer.

Michael Berube
You're an Egg. *The American Scholar,* Summer.

Buzz Bissinger
My Son Zachary. *Philadelphia,* December.

Jonathan Blum
May Be Habit-Forming. *Black Warrior Review,* Fall/Winter.

Barrie Jean Borich
What Kind of King. *The Gettysburg Review,* Spring.

Catharine Savage Brosman
After the Flood. *The American Scholar,* Spring.

Jane Brox
Twilight of the Apple Growers. *The Georgia Review,* Spring.

BILL BUFORD
Lions and Tigers and Bears. *The New Yorker,* August 23/30.
FREDERICK BUSCH
My Father's War. *Five Points,* Winter.

DAVID CARKEET
Titanic Blunders. *St. Louis Magazine,* May.
DOUGLAS CARLSON
Just Imagine. *Ascent,* Spring.
TOM CHIARELLA
Vicodin, My Vicodin. *Esquire,* January.
PHIL CHOI
Choosing Burden. *Manoa,* vol. 11, no. 1.
PAUL CHRISTENSEN
In Praise of Bluffing. *The Antioch Review,* Spring.
NORMA V. L. CLARKE
Post Mortem. *Creative Nonfiction,* no. 12.
JONATHAN CREWE
Jargon. *The Yale Journal of Criticism,* Spring.

JIM DAMERON
How to Tie a Dry Fly. *Ascent,* Winter.
GUY DAVENPORT
Right! *The Threepenny Review,* Winter.
LYDIA DAVIS
"Remember the Van Wagenens." *Southern Humanities Review,* Winter.
JODI DAYNARD
Lost Pictures. *New England Review,* Fall.
NICHOLAS DELBANCO
Scribble, Scribble, Scribble. *Harper's Magazine,* January.
MARK DOTY
Visits to Babylon. *Provincetown Arts,* vol. 14.
BRIAN DOYLE
Filled with Grace. *Notre Dame Magazine,* Autumn.
STUART DYBEK
Ralston. *Fourth Genre,* Fall.

DAVE EGGERS
The Orphans Are Coming! *The New Yorker,* October 18/25.
GRETEL EHRLICH
On the Road with God's Fool. *The New York Times Magazine,* June 6.
JOSEPH EPSTEIN
Taking the Bypass. *The New Yorker,* April 12.
LEAH ESKIN
Requiem for a Silver Maple. *Chicago Tribune Magazine,* May 9.

CHARLES FERGUS
Stones. *The Yale Review,* October.
ROBERT FINCH
Wilderness Ride. *New Age,* May/June.
GARY FINCKE
The Canals of Mars. *Shenandoah,* Fall.
PATRICIA FOSTER
The New Royalists. *Southern Humanities Review,* Summer.
TOM FRANKLIN
Hunting Years. *Quarterly West,* Spring/Summer.
RUSSELL FRASER
Paree Bis. *Iowa Review,* Spring.
IAN FRAZIER
Pick Your Part. *The Atlantic Monthly,* March.
KIMBERLY FRENCH
Meat Eater. *Tikkun,* March/April.

PHILIP GARRISON
Love Stories, Exile, and the Greek-Chorus Effect. *Northwest Review,* vol. 37, no. 1.

HENRY LOUIS GATES, JR.
Rope Burn. *The New Yorker,* August 23 and 30.

AMY GERSTLER
A Eulogy of Sorts. *The Seneca Review,* Fall.

DAVID GESSNER
Going Outward. *Puerto del Sol,* Summer.

REBECCA KAISER GIBSON
Of Paradise. *The Harvard Review,* Fall.

DAGOBERTO GILB
010100. *The Texas Observer,* December 24.

OWEN GINGERICH
The Return of the Seagoing Cowboy. *The American Scholar,* Autumn.

MALCOLM GLADWELL
The Physical Genius. *The New Yorker,* August 2.

TERENCE GLASS
Just Act Natural. *The Gettysburg Review,* Autumn.

CECILE GODING
Six Degrees of Fluency. *The Georgia Review,* Fall.

RIGOBERTO GONZALEZ
Our Secret Other Worlds. *Crab Orchard Review,* Fall/Winter.

ADAM GOPNIK
The Rookie. *The New Yorker,* October 4.

EMILY FOX GORDON
Kafka and Me. *Boulevard,* Spring.

TYLER C. GORE
A Day at the Beach. *Literal Latte,* Summer.

VIVIAN GORNICK
Loren Eiseley. *The American Scholar,* Winter.

STEPHEN JAY GOULD
Bacon, Brought Home. *Natural History,* June.

GORDON GRICE
After the Stillbirth. *The Sun,* October.

ALLAN GURGANUS
The Invention of Suburbia. *Preservation,* September/October.

JOHN HALES
Hiking In, and Hiking Out. *The Hudson Review,* Spring.

DAVID HAMILTON
Lavender Whippets. *The Connecticut Review,* Fall.

JEFFREY HAMMOND
The ABC of It: A Meditation on the Alphabet. *Southern Humanities Review,* Spring.

ELIZABETH HARDWICK
Head over Heels. *The New York Review of Books,* April 22.

DANIEL HARRIS
Coolness. *The American Scholar,* Autumn.
Deliciousness. *Salmagundi,* Winter/Spring.

BARBARA GRIZZUTI HARRISON
The Incubator of Dreams. *The New York Times Magazine,* October 17.

STEVE HARVEY
Bluing. *Five Points,* Fall.

LINDA HASSELSTROM
Looking for the Dark: Buffalo Winter. *Big Sky Journal,* Winter.

MICHAEL HEHER
Words to Match. *Image,* Summer.

MARK HELPRIN
The Lesson of the Century. *American Heritage,* March.

DEWITT HENRY
My Own Private Cambridge. *The Nebraska Review,* Winter.

WILLIAM HEYEN
The Boulder: A Journal. *The Ohio Review,* no. 59.

CHRISTOPHER HITCHENS
Imagining Hitler. *Vanity Fair,* February.

KATHRYN HOFFMAN
Hughes, Dreamland. *Creative Nonfiction,* no. 12.

PAT C. HOY II
Homage to Vietnam. *The Virginia Quarterly Review,* Autumn.

ANDREW HUDGINS
Half-Answered Prayers. *The American Scholar,* Spring.
The Secret Sister. *The Hudson Review,* Autumn.

GABRIEL HUDSON
The Sky Hermit. *The Denver Quarterly,* Spring.

CYNTHIA HUNTINGTON
Days at the Beach. *The Boston Globe Magazine,* July 18.

BETTE LYNCH HUSTED
Following the Deer. *Northwest Review,* vol. 37, no. 3.

PICO IYER
The End of Empire. *Harper's Magazine,* December.

AKASH KAPUR
The Street. *Transition,* no. 79.

STEVEN KELLMAN
Swan Songs. *The American Scholar,* Autumn.

HEATHER KING
Smiles. *Northwest Review,* vol. 37, no. 3.

JUDITH KITCHEN
Three Landscapes. *The Ohio Review,* no. 59.

GEORGINA KLEEGE
On the Borders of the Wild. *Raritan,* Spring.

HAROLD H. KOLB, JR.
Border Collie. *The Virginia Quarterly Review,* Autumn.

KEN LAMBERTON
Queen. *The Gettysburg Review,* Autumn.

DENISE LARRABEE
If a Thought Is a Prayer. *Northeast Corridor,* no. 7.

DANIEL LAZARE
Your Constitution Is Killing You. *Harper's Magazine,* October.

BARBARA F. LEFCOWITZ
The Shapes of Fire. *The Cream City Review,* Spring.
Horns, Knobs, Branches. *Southwest Review,* Summer.

NATON LESLIE
Hungry Hill. *High Plains Literary Review,* Spring.

DAN LEVIN
Ava Gardner's Smile. *Boston Magazine,* November.

MARK LEWANDOWSKI
Tourist Season at Auschwitz. *The Gettysburg Review,* Summer.

NANCY MAIRS
Sex and the Gimpy Girl. *River Teeth,* Fall.

GERALD MAJER
Lower Farm: A Memoir. *Western Humanities Review,* Summer.

PETER MAKUCK
The Trouble with Smitty. *The Hudson Review,* Summer.

DEBRA MARQUART
On Lost & Crazy Sisters. *New Letters,* vol. 65, no. 2.

LEE MARTIN
Bad Boy. *The Georgia Review,* Fall.

MICHAEL MARTONE
What I Want to Tell: A Sequence of Rooms. *Michigan Quarterly Review,* Winter.

ANITA MATHIAS
I Was a Teenage Atheist. *Commonweal,* October 8.

ISABELLE MAYNARD
Hot Property. *ZYZZYVA,* Fall.

NANCY MCCABE
The End of the Tunnel. *Prairie Schooner,* Summer.

ERIN MCGRAW
My Parents' Religion. *Image,* Winter/Spring.

Jay McInerney
Naked on the Grass. *The New Yorker,* January 18.

Bill McKibben
The End of Growth. *Mother Jones,* November/December.

John McPhee
Farewell to the Nineteenth Century. *The New Yorker,* September 27.

Daphne Merkin
Our Money, Ourselves. *The New Yorker,* April 26/May 3.

Arthur Miller
On Broadway. *Harper's Magazine,* March.

Stephen Miller
Why Read Samuel Johnson? *The Sewanee Review,* Winter.

William Ian Miller
Near Misses. *Michigan Quarterly Review,* Winter.

Donna Minkowitz
Love and Hate in Laramie. *The Nation,* July 12.

David Mook
Fishing. *Northeast Corridor,* no. 7.

Donald Morrill
Getting Close to Her Cats. *Connecticut Review,* Spring.

James Morrison
Practice. *The Massachusetts Review,* Autumn.

Thylias Moss
An Apology for Forgiveness' Close Association with Cowardice. *Fourth Genre,* Fall.

Cullen Murphy
The Mirror of Dorian Gray. *The Atlantic Monthly,* June.

Michael Nelson
Frank Sinatra: The Loneliness of the Long-Distance Singer. *The Virginia Quarterly Review,* Autumn.

Herman Nibbelink
Of Flour Sacks and War. *The Briar Cliff Review,* Spring.

Michelle Nickol
Ackerman's k. *Black Warrior Review,* Spring/Summer.

Lewis Nordan
"Welcome to Itta Bena, Little Lady!" *The Oxford American,* November/December.

Howard Norman
The Insult. *TriQuarterly,* no. 106, Fall.

Josip Novakovich
A Sip of Music. *Boulevard,* no. 1/2, Fall.

Joyce Carol Oates
Where Is an Author? *The Gettysburg Review,* Spring.

Michael O'Rourke
Pocket Wilderness, and The Good Dr. Pepper Defiled. *North American Review,* March/April.

Cynthia Ozick
The Rights of History and the Rights of Imagination. *Commentary,* March.

Thomas Palakeel
A Boy's Death. *North Dakota Quarterly,* vol. 66, no. 1.

Orlando Patterson
The Liberal Millennium. *The New Republic,* November 8.

John Plotz
Out of Circulation. *Southwest Review,* Autumn.

Charles Portis
Combinations of Jacksons. *The Atlantic Monthly,* May.

Lukie Chapman Reilly
Mother. *The Florida Review,* Winter.

SUZANNE RHODENBAUGH
The One Story. *Northeast Corridor,* no. 6.
JAMES RICHARDSON
Vectors: 56 Aphorisms and Ten-Second Essays. *Michigan Quarterly Review,* Spring.
TIM ROBINSON
A Crystallography. *The Recorder,* Spring.
BILL ROORBACH
Scioto Blues. *The Missouri Review,* vol. 22, no. 3.
CHARLES ROSEN
On Playing the Piano. *The New York Review of Books,* October 21.
EDGAR ROSENBERG
Hitler over My Head. *Judaism,* Summer.
TACEY A. ROSOLOWSKI
Monsters. *Southwest Review,* vol. 84, no. 2.
PAUL RUFFIN
Norther. *Michigan Quarterly Review,* Spring.

OLIVER SACKS
Brilliant Light. *The New Yorker,* December 20.
DAVID F. SALLY
Genderator 1.1: A Modish Proposal. *The Georgia Review,* Summer.
ARTHUR M. SALTZMAN
Incipience and Other Alibis. *The Gettysburg Review,* Autumn.
SCOTT RUSSELL SANDERS
Through the Eyes of a Hawk. *Audubon,* July/August.
MARJORIE SANDOR
On Leaving Florida. *The Georgia Review,* Spring.
REG SANER
Desert River, Different River. *The Georgia Review,* Spring.
LUC SANTE
Triumph of the Image. *The New York Times Magazine,* September 19.
STEVEN BOYD SAUM
Blessings. *The Literary Review,* Winter.
SARAH D. SCALET
The Cosmpolitan Cockroach. *Audubon,* September/October.
MIMI SCHWARTZ
My Father Always Said. *Fourth Genre,* Spring.
JOHN SEABROOK
Nobrow Culture. *The New Yorker,* September 20.
RICHARD SELZER
Four Deceptions: A Writing Lesson. *Ohio Review,* no. 60.
LISA JENNIFER SELZMAN
Sabbatical Houses. *House Beautiful,* February.
ALICIA SHANK
Last Summer's Song. *Michigan Quarterly Review,* Summer.
ROGER SHATTUCK
When Evil Is "Cool." *The Atlantic Monthly,* January.
REGINALD SHEPHERD
Coloring Outside the Lines: An Essay at Definition. *Callaloo,* Winter.
JOHN SHEPLEY
Sonata. *Salmagundi,* Winter/Spring.
Three-Part Invention. *Southern Humanities Review,* Spring.
CHARLES SIMIC
The Bandit Charuga. *Boulevard,* Spring.
LAUREN SLATER
Prozac Mother and Child. *The New York Times Magazine,* October 17.
MARY SLOWIK
Lessons in Fire. *Iowa Review,* Spring.
JANE SMILEY
900 Pages of Homework. *The Washington Post Magazine,* July 18.
PATRICIA SMITH
Journey Back from Shame. *Essence,* September.

Kristine A. Somerville
Katie Suber. *Black Dirt,* Spring/Summer.

Laurie Stieber
Her Private Devil. *New York,* January 4.

Adrienne Su
My Middle Kingdom. *Prairie Schooner,* Winter.

Ron Tanner
My Small Murders. *Ascent,* Spring.

Donna Tartt
The Belle and the Lady. *The Oxford American,* March/May.

Calvin Trillin
The Chicken Vanishes. *The New Yorker,* February 8.

James Trilling
My Father and the Weak-Eyed Devils. *The American Scholar,* Spring.

Scott Turow
Something's Up. *Vanity Fair,* September.

John Updike
The Future of Faith. *The New Yorker,* November 29.

Jeffrey Utzinger
Chemical Reactions. *Chattahoochee Review,* Winter.

Jonathan Veitch
Jay Gatsby, Shane, Nevada Smith: A "Memoir." *Southwest Review,* vol. 84, no. 2.

Michael Ventura
In the Eye of the Millennium. *Family Networker,* November/December.

Abraham Verghese
Death and Desire. *Mirabella,* April.

Robert Vivian
The Taxonomy of Garbage. *Sycamore Review,* Summer/Fall.

Chuck Wachtel
On Truth. *Western Humanities Review,* Summer.

Anneliese Wagner
In Praise of Walking. *Boulevard,* no. 1/2, Fall.

Garry Wallace
Making Hay. *High Plains Register,* vol. 11.

Peter Walpole
Mayou. *Southern Humanities Review,* Fall.

Michael Walzer
Rescuing Civil Society. *Dissent,* Winter.

George Watson
Call Me Mister. *The Wilson Quarterly,* Autumn.

Jess Wegman
Six Days. *The Atlantic Monthly,* May.

Alec Wilkinson
Notes Left Behind. *The New Yorker,* February 15.

Joy Williams
Cabin Cabin. *Joe,* vol. 1., no. 1.

Garry Wills
Lincoln's Greatest Speech? *The Atlantic Monthly,* September.

Anthony Winner
Reaching Out to Memoir. *Southwest Review,* Summer.

Adam Zagajewski
The Shabby and the Sublime. *The New Republic,* April 5.

Paul Zimmer
The Catcher. *The Gettysburg Review,* Summer.

Special Issues

Chattahoochee Review, Summer, nonfiction issue, ed. Lawrence Hetrick

Fourth Genre, Spring, essays and memoirs, ed. Michael Steinberg

Creative Nonfiction, no. 13, "The Brain: A Nonfiction Mystery," ed. Lee Gutkind

ZYZZYVA, "Lucky Break: How I Became a Writer," ed. Howard Junker

Note: Mary Swander's fine essay "The Fifth Chair" (*Image,* Fall 1998) was accidentally omitted from last year's list.